NEW LAMPS FOR OLD?

NEW LAMPS FOR OLD?

Gender Paradoxes of Political Decentralization in Kerala

J Devika
Binitha V Thampi

zubaan

ZUBAAN
an imprint of Kali for Women
128 B Shahpur Jat, 1st floor
NEW DELHI 110 049
Email: contact@zubaanbooks.com
Website: www.zubaanbooks.com

First published by Zubaan 2012

10 9 8 7 6 5 4 3 2 1

ISBN 978 93 81017 18 0

Zubaan is an independent feminist publishing house based in New Delhi with a strong academic and general list. It was set up as an imprint of India's first feminist publishing house, Kali for Women, and carries forward Kali's tradition of publishing world quality books to high editorial and production standards. *Zubaan* means tongue, voice, language, speech in Hindustani. Zubaan is a non-profit publisher, working in the areas of the humanities, social sciences, as well as in fiction, general non-fiction, and books for children and young adults under its Young Zubaan imprint.

Typeset by Recto Graphics, Delhi - 100 096
Printed at Raj Press, R-3 Inderpuri, New Delhi - 110 012

Contents

Acknowledgements

Yoga teachers often advise their students to stretch 'a bit more' every day; stretching more can be painful, they tell us, but one always grows the stronger for it, and the pain ultimately metamorphoses into pleasure. This book was born out of a project, 'Gendering Governance or Governing Women: Politics, Patriarchy, and Democratic Decentralization in Kerala', carried out with the support of IDRC, Canada. Each of us in this project – and we were a large group of women researchers – has gone through stretching 'a bit more' intellectually. There were many well-wishers who felt that this project was too ambitious. The fact that we pulled it off together was a wonderful dream come true.

This book partially builds upon the insights gained from our project, but has been fortified by more fieldwork. There are many who we remember at this moment – starting with all those who generously gave their time and energy to our interviews. We have learned so much from all our interviewees that the debt we owe them can never be fully repaid. Many of them are fulltime public workers, and indeed, we cannot thank them enough. We do hope that this book will document and celebrate their struggles even when we voice our differences and disagreements with them. More generally, we hope this book will bring to light the struggles of Malayalee women of many generations to enter the political public and thus connect us critically to a generation completely forgotten now – the 'first generation feminists' of Malayalee society.

The Centre for Development Studies was, in many ways, an ideal nesting place for this project. The Registrar of CDS, Soman Nair, and Chandra in the Accounts Section were patient and generous with advice and time – they are remembered with much warmth. The IDRC project brought us many new friends – especially Navsharan Singh, Maitrayee Mukhopadhyay, Seema Kulkarni, and Alice, who are warmly thanked. We would also like to thank Reshma Radhakrishnan who ably supported us in the interviewing process in the early phase and Ranjith P M, who helped us with a number of crucial interviews towards the end.

Friends have guided us through this work. The team members who worked on other parts of this project, and other friends who were keenly interested in it are remembered with much affection and infinite gratitude: Usha Zacharias, A K Rajasree, Ranjini Krishnan, Santhy S, Anitha S, Rekha Raj, Reshma Bharadwaj, Gouridasan Nair, and N C Narayanan. Our early discussions on fieldwork were enriched by Vineetha Menon. Special thanks are due to Janaki Abraham, Mary John, G Arunima and the audiences at seminars at Delhi and Thiruvananthapuram, and Shamshad Hussain in Kerala who responded with critical enthusiasm to our ideas. Urvashi Butalia of Zubaan has been enthusiastic about this work right from the beginning. We thank her for her patience and friendship. There are many who helped us in other ways – those who attended our inception workshop and offered useful suggestions, those who helped us reach out to women leaders of the panchayats, or find accommodation in remote places – their contribution to this work is gratefully acknowledged.

As usual, our families have sacrificed much. Seethalakshmy Amma, Shibu, Anitha, Ajayan, Meenu, and many others kept us going through thick and thin. We lovingly thank them. This book is dedicated to our daughters who were amazingly patient with their mothers' three-hour-long telephone conversations: we hope that Janaki, Sreeranjini and Rajashree, will grow older in a world in which women-intellectuals and women-politicians will not be regarded as rare or strange species.

We don't know if it is done to thank ourselves – maybe we should. For it is not often that many of us take the risk of coming out of the narrow little cells that a rapidly individualizing society assigns us, of allowing ourselves to be transformed through each other's insights. Time flew and we negotiated ill-health, personal losses, and other disappointments, but the interviewing and the writing went on. We do hope that the book communicates at least a share of the excitement that spurred us to write it.

J Devika and Binitha V Thampi

Introduction

Fear of Flying

Let me tell you the truth. I didn't get into this out of the desire to be zooming about the panchayat sitting in the front seat of this Jeep. I have never thought that there's anything more in this, than an opportunity to serve the people. Because I was not very familiar with public work, I did fear whether this is within my ability. I contested only on the insistence of my husband and the local folk. Well, I contested, won, and learned all the rules with a lot of effort. I have also managed to do many things here.

... I think the panchayat is not a place for politics at all... we women presidents have to hold everyone together and take all of us forward. Politics should end soon after the elections, and then we must all work together. So there was never any question of me playing 'politics', as the rumor-mongers claim.

.... But it is people who are nearest to you who feel disturbed when they see you hanging on and not falling off. They say, 'she is zooming about in the Jeep and playing politics—the same lowly woman who used to walk up and down our road in rubber slippers...!' I have never flown about like that ... nor have I ever even desired to fly...

Pre-empting questions from us on the rumors floating about the panchayat about her 'over-ambitious' nature, a woman-president of a village panchayat in coastal Kerala presented this spirited self-defense. We were not taken by surprise. In the course of our fieldwork in Kerala's panchayats studying gender, governance and politics, we had indeed noticed how the 'Jeep'—or the official vehicle of the panchayat—often proved to be the instance in which the faultlines of gender power struggles, sometimes well-concealed in politically correct responses to our questions, were revealed. The question of who controls the 'Jeep' often stood for who held 'real power'—and most often the woman leader of the panchayat was engaged in a tussle over this with the male local politician or male panchayat official. However, we also noticed that very few of the women who told us 'Jeep stories' explicitly recognized their acts as resistance; they were more inclined to project themselves as hapless and innocent victims of assaults by powerful local male politicians or officials. Equally intriguing was the intense reluctance among women leaders of local self-government, who have entered the domain of local governance through the reservation of thirty-three per cent seats in the panchayati raj institutions as a result of the 73rd and 74th Amendments to the Indian Constitution, even the most successful and popular of them, to admit to political ambition in the more familiar sense of upward mobility in party politics. That is, as ambition for public-political power, understood as 'power from within' and 'power to' but also involving a certain degree of 'power over' (Rowlands 1997). Many women we interviewed openly declared that their ambitions were not around political power but development. This is in sharp contrast to their male counterparts who pursue both agendas with equal fervour.

Indeed, their words did not appear to contradict reality: after three whole terms of local self-government in Kerala since the mid 1990s through which a large number of capable women have been identified in all political parties, very few of them are visible in the top leadership of any party. And while capable women running the village panchayats have been widely feted by their parties, these women's achievements do not seem to be accorded merit in candidate-selection for state or central legislatures. Many women politicians, for example, the women legislators of the Communist Party of India (Marxist) (CPM from now) in the present Kerala State

Assembly, have been presidents of panchayats; however, this was not their entry-point into politics. Most of them earned their political credentials through political work especially in mass organizations of the party. This may not, of course, mean that the women who have entered through the panchayats do not desire political power. It could be argued that responses like the one quoted above are socially correct ones and perhaps resorted to as a strategic move to bypass explicit misogyny or present oneself as less of a threat to entrenched but defensive masculine interests. However, there are questions, still. It is apparent by now that this adherence to social correctness has not broken down male defensiveness within the parties (as evident in women's poor presence in the higher levels of party hierarchies and from their own responses to other questions). If so, why do many women village panchayat leaders in Kerala, even those who have far greater experience and recognition than the one quoted above, continue to respond thus?

At a superficial level, the reluctance of women to be identified with political ambition is a familiar story. As Sonali Sathaye's interview with Usha Badhe, the sarpanch of Nimbagaon village in Maharasthra in *And Who Shall Make the Chapatis?* (Datta 1998) showed, the political ambition of women leaders is often regarded as inimical to the welfare functions of local government and destructive to the interests of the village. Also, there are many studies from across India which observe that women tend to identify their public roles within the ambit of (feminized and politically passive) 'social service' (for instance, Ghosh and Lama-Rewal 2005; Strulik 2008). Nevertheless, the question still looked like an intriguing one to us in the specific context of Kerala, where many women leaders do possess several key advantages that would have us expect a different response.

First, women in Kerala did not lack powerful role models. For example, the figure of K R Gouri, the legendary communist leader, famed for her skill at both militant struggle and administration, still circulates actively in the Malayalee public and commands much respect at all levels of Kerala's political field. Given women's high literacy and the all-pervasiveness of public discourse in this society, it is still available to women even in the remotest and marginalized communities. Perhaps one could surmise that K R Gouri's bitter experiences in politics (Jeffrey 2003: 214–6)—her failure to get past masculine dominance within the party—are a deterrent to new entrants. However, what is striking about the above quote is not really the fear of failure to access political power, but fear of moral censure by the community against a woman seeking it.

Secondly, compared to many other regions, women-members and leaders of panchayats here are much better-educated with considerable experience of heading institutions such as schools and government offices.[1] Many of the women leaders we interviewed were supremely confident of their command over 'the rules': that their in-depth knowledge of the 'government-order regime' was weapon enough to ward off the insidious efforts of hostile local male politicians of the opposition and within their own parties, and of corrupt or inefficient officials. We heard several inspiring stories of how they had held their own through calculated attempts to defame them or disregard their status, all on the strength of their superior knowledge of the rules and regulations. Certainly, many of these women did cite the putative 'feminine' ability for public caregiving as a key reason for their successes—but this was not all. What struck us was the extent to which a *form of expertise*—knowledge of the huge body of rules and regulations that constitute the everyday working of local governance—was cited as an *equally* important reason for success by these women. To quote another woman leader, particularly known for her development successes, from central Kerala:

Study, yes, study hard. That's what I'd like to tell women who wish to enter the panchayats. If you know the rules and regulations, no one can reduce you to a non-entity. I started studying after bitter experiences when I was still inexperienced in office. I became determined, and that's what's given me the strength to carry on fighting till today. If we have the knowledge, we can argue with those who try to put pressure on us and indeed thwart them. I always tell younger women this: never be a rubber stamp. Never sign any paper without first asking a question about it. If some mistake does indeed happen, never hesitate to raise a question openly.

Yet even this fighter—and many others like her—preferred to describe her work as essentially 'service' and 'keeping the rules'—something she felt duty-bound to carry forward, separate from, and through ignoring or fending off, what she called the "constant badgering of petty politicians". In other words, to her, the very process of struggle she described did not seem to involve the exercise of power despite obvious references to power and hierarchy. To exercise the legitimately exercisable power of the panchayat president was not 'politics', it was simply 'following the rules'.

Thirdly, this response also came from women who were nominated by political parties and indeed were often party members and office-bearers. The local level is highly politicized in Kerala and major political parties field most of the candidates in elections to the local governments.[2] Most of our women interviewees were by no means complete novices to their ways; many were members and minor functionaries of political parties. This was true especially of many women leaders belonging to Kerala's dominant left party, the CPM. The CPM itself has been ardent champion of reservations for women in the panchayati raj institutions and in legislative bodies; in the 2010 elections to the former, reservations for women have been increased to 50 per cent by the ruling Left Democratic Front (LDF from now) government in Kerala. Also, recently, the CPM has also emphasized the need to actively integrate more women into party cadre, promote them in committees and as full-timers.[3] Nevertheless, a very large number of women presidents who were CPM members insisted that there should be no 'politics' in the panchayat and the role of the president should be to minimize 'power-politics' and carefully maintain the boundaries between the roles of party functionary and panchayat president.

Lastly, and perhaps most intriguingly, many of the same women also expressed concern that their work was not being adequately recognized and rewarded in the party. Here they blamed not just male dominance but also the hierarchy of political activisms in which the work of a panchayat president was granted less importance than that of a member of the state or central legislature. Yet they claimed to be free of aspiration to these higher bodies, even as they argued that candidature to the latter was a form of recognition granted by parties to their best and trusted workers.

In sum, many women leaders of the panchayats (especially women belonging to the more powerful communities in Kerala) (a) expressed disinterest in and claimed distance from possessing power like 'politicians', (b) did not feel that their association with political parties as members or functionaries necessarily implicated them in struggles around conflicting interests: 'power games that politicians play'. In other words, to be 'in politics' was not to always to be a 'politician', (c) felt aggrieved that their particular model of disinterested public work was neither fully acknowledged nor rewarded within their parties. These views were bolstered by the view they held about politics, that ideal, 'true' politics did not involve group interests or power but the neutral aspiration to distribute welfare equally and impartially to poor people. This troubled relation of women leaders to power and by implication, to politics, quickly became the focus of our research, for it raised crucial questions about gender, citizenship, empowerment, and politics in the local context. Clearly, these were 'empowered' women speaking. In that case, what were the implications of such 'empowerment' that distanced itself from a dominant form of power in Kerala, public-political power?

The Importance of Public-Political Power

This book, we hope, will contribute towards constructing a richer and more complex account of women's entry into the political-public in Kerala facilitated by political decentralization since the mid-1990s. We attempt to capture the understandings and assessments of politics, governance, and gender held by women leaders in the PRIs in Kerala, of the possibilities opened up to them, and the hurdles that slow down their ascent to leadership and full presence in the political realm. In much of the laudatory literature that straddles academics and journalism, which celebrates the successes of political decentralization in Kerala, the presence of large numbers of women within these spaces is taken as evidence for the greater autonomy for women, which is then interpreted as the beginning of a decisive break with the earlier non-inclusion of women in the political-public (Parameswaran 2005; Isaac 2005; Heller et all 2007; Biju 2007). Nevertheless, there is much evidence from research that indicates otherwise. It appears to us, however, that researchers need to move beyond documenting the hurdles that women face or their powerlessness. Rather, they must analyse the specific political conjuncture at which a certain form of 'empowerment' of women has been rendered possible, and its consequences for their agency and chances of greater presence in the public-political realm. There is little doubt that the participation of women in public institutions of governing has been heightened through reservations. However, there are good reasons—which we discuss later in this section—to think that women's failure to gain greater presence in the public-political realm is a serious failing in the specific context of contemporary Kerala. Our focus in this book is mostly on the gender politics of Kerala's dominant left parties—the CPM and the CPI (Communist Party of India)—because it is they who have had a firm and explicitly-stated policy favouring women's entry into the public and women's reservations in legislative bodies. But it also pays attention to the ways in which women of other parties, with no such firm committments, have seen this opportunity.

Many studies on elected women leaders and members of the local bodies in India have sought to probe the extent to which such participation has empowered them. They have often focused on the question whether reservations have improved their active participation in the business of government, and thus pay attention to such quantifiable aspects as attendance in various bodies, interventions in council debates, number of project initiatives introduced, as also to empowerment indicators to probe their mobility, access to economic resources and information, networking, changes in self-image and self-esteem, changes in their bargaining power within the household and so on. Such studies have also examined the capabilities of elected women before and after their entry into local bodies—their education, health, cultural and economic capabilities (Nanivadekar 1997; Santha 1999; PRIA 1999; Mohanty 1999; Datta 1998; Nussbaum 2003; Baviskar 2003; Sharma 2003; Kudwa 2003; Sinha 2004; Duflo 2005; Hust 2004; Ghosh and Tama-Rawal 2005; Vissandjee et al 2006; Singla 2007).

Such studies have been attempted in Kerala also (Chathukulam and John 2000 George 2006; Georgekutty 2003; Sharma 2009: 116;152; Isaac 2005; Vijayan 2007), which reveal many challenges that women members and leaders encounter while trying to create space for themselves in the hitherto-exclusively male domain of government. Almost all these studies agree that the substantial reservation for women was definitely a major step towards inducting women as participants in local governance. They also agree to a greater or lesser extent that there was effort by the top architects of the People's Planning Campaign (henceforth, PPC) which ushered in decentralized planning in Kerala to introduce gender-sensitivity in the guidelines, documents, and training for members and leaders of local bodies. More energetic effort was made in the second round of planning, after it was observed that the low participation of women in the PPC was one of the three major weaknesses of the first round of planning (Isaac 1998).

However, contrary to the laudatory accounts cited earlier, almost all these studies do identify women's lack of experience and access to politics as a major handicap in their 'empowerment'.[4] They point out that little cognisance was taken of the fact that women's members' near-total inexperience in politics called for special measures to help them learn the ropes of political activity. The study by Vijayan and Sandhya (2004), based on field work in 2000, points out that the rotation of wards reserved for women every five years is detrimental to building the political capacities of women; that political parties are not keen to utilize the mandatory Women's Component Plan imaginatively; that they pay little attention to providing favourable conditions and developing women's skills in the political domain (Vijayan and Sandhya 2004: 77). Also, women's reservation does not automatically ensure the politicization of women as a group. Several reports therefore have recommended continuous capacity building and sensitization programmes for elected women representatives (Mukherjee and Seema 2000: 42–44; Radha and Roy Chowdhury 2002: 33–35; Vijayan and Sandhya 2004: 76–77). They also mention that women representatives who refused assigned roles have often been made to suffer (Chathukulam and John 2000; Mukherjee and Seema 2000: 30; Muralidharan 2003: 6; Radha and Roy Chowdhury 2002: 28–31 ; Sukumar and Thomas 2003: 9–10; Vijayan and Sandhya 2004).

It may be argued that this observed lacuna may be serious enough to jeopardize, in the specific context of Kerala, the very claim that the women inducted into the local bodies have been 'empowered'. As Kabeer (1999: 437) puts it succinctly, empowerment is "the expansion in people's ability to make strategic life-choices in a context *where this ability was denied to them*" (our emphasis). The empowering act must challenge historical exclusions, strengthen the bargaining power of the oppressed (thus widen the possibility of strategic choices), contribute in the long term to the dismantling of the structures and cultures of oppression, and enable the full membership of the oppressed in the public. Its specific content, however, will emerge only in reference to local configurations of power and the imperatives of local struggles. If this is so, then it is indeed difficult to imagine women's 'empowerment' in the specific context of Kerala without their heightened public-political presence. It is very important, however, to avoid collapsing the question of women's access to the public-political realm, with that of their access to masculinist 'power-over' (Peterson and Runyan 1999).

It is important also to note that historically, the project of 'women's liberation' in early twentieth century Kerala which sought to release women from pre-modern family and community structures, was premised on a strongly gendered vision of the world in which public-political power was identified as masculine privilege (Devika 2007). As we may see in Chapter 2, women did contest this idea but were repeatedly rebuffed through the twentieth century. The first wave of 'empowerment' in the early twentieth century, however, identified women closely with the 'social'. The 'social' was eminently associated with issues of conserving life and furthering it: with health, nutrition, education, household management, reform of family life and so on, all of which appeared to be distanced to a certain extent from the 'political' (Riley 1995). In late-19th century Malayalee society, for missionaries and 'progressive princely states', especially those of Travancore and Cochin, the extension of such 'social' space was a major element in emergent modernizing agendas. In the early 20th century, the first-generation of Malayalee feminists would claim it as 'women's space' and even seek actively to extend it further, but they could make little headway as far as the emergent public-political realm was concerned (Devika 2007). It is by now well-noticed that a pattern of exclusion from the political continues to characterize women's unequal citizenship in Kerala (Jeffrey 2003; Erwer 2003). Therefore, any serious efforts towards women's 'empowerment' in

Kerala, cannot but call for their full presence in the realm of public-politics (and not just formal presence in the institutions of governance) and without the expectation that women be 'better and less corrupt' politicians or, indeed, they be gender justice warriors. Moreover, the enthusiasm for public life and knowledge of public affairs that women members have generally displayed all over India, even in the most deprived communities (see for instance, Hust 2004) certainly serve the important feminist political goal of breaking down misogynist stereotypes through positive symbolic presence.

Secondly, such presence may help to crystallize 'women' as a distinct group with the capacity for collective action, which, it is hoped, will further struggles for gender justice especially around welfare here. Given that the government in Kerala does devote a large share of welfare resources to women of the poorer sections, efforts to reclaim women's agency in defining needs and demanding resources which would combat the state's effort to reduce 'women' into a passive governmental category, the passive recipient of welfare benefits, are certainly very relevant here. Historically, the empowerment of disadvantaged caste-groups in Kerala occurred through their entry into the modern public-political as re-formed communities which then actively bargained with the state and with and within political parties for access to rights and resources. While a women's 'community' may not be called for, certainly, newer forms of collective public power by 'women' are indeed necessary in the present for actualizing gender justice. Also, since the power to make major decisions regarding welfare entitlements resides in the public-political realm—in the higher institutional tiers of legislatures and in political parties—women's presence in these levels may be essential to strengthen the collective power of women as a group. In the late 1990s, Kerala's feminist movement fought long, hard battles with powerful politicians over cases of sexual violence (Devika and Kodoth 2001). The disadvantages to the women's movement from women's poor presence in public politics were apparent then. Activists had few political figures to appeal to. Those women politicians who did fight for gender justice found themselves quite isolated precisely because they were so few among the top decision-makers of their parties and further, these few were heavily dependent on male largesse.

Thirdly, women's access to public-political power may also be crucial to the feminist agenda of altering the masculinist content of citizenship and the male-centred norms that presently structure the political field. Feminist political theorists have pointed out that the content of citizenship has been traditionally shaped in the mould of the property-owning, householder-male (Pateman 1988; Mendus 1992). Feminist re-inscriptions of citizenship have therefore striven to challenge the inbuilt masculinism of citizenship that poses as gender neutrality (Phillips 1995). There is also the argument that as women gain political power, the nature of citizenship rights also changes, for example, and comes to include such elements as redefined inheritance and childcare needs (Siim 2004).[5] Given the fact that more and more women have been inducted into the public through governmental initiatives in Kerala in the past two decades—for instance through the very extensive network of self-help groups of women from below-poverty-line (BPL) families facilitated by the state, known as the Kudumbashree, which now takes up more and more public activities and responsibilities—there is indeed the urgent need to challenge the privileging of the masculine in the structures and everyday conduct of public life.

Quotas for women in formal bodies have been recommended to ensure women's representation in the political field on the grounds mentioned above—that of justice and of symbolic value—in feminist political theory (Dahlerup 1998; Sawer 2000). Feminists have also advanced the 'substantive argument' for women's representation (and women's quotas as means of furthering it), which claims that female politicians' experience of being women will incline them to identify with women and act for women's interests (Dahlerup 1998; Childs 2004). However, feminist researchers have tended not to overemphasize the efficacy of quotas in remedying women's exclusion from public-political power. Shirin Rai, for instance, argues that quotas may be regarded only as "one part of a multi-faceted strategy for empowering women, which must, together with increased political participation, also involve a redistribution of socio-economic resources within societies." (Rai 2008: 92). Comparative studies of the empowering effects of quotas across countries have stressed the importance of the specificities of local contexts. Comparing reservations in India and South Africa, Shireen Hashim (2010) remarks that the empowering effects of quotas for women are dependent "on the overall political context in which women's organizations operate." (p. 22) Feminist researchers have also pointed out that the outcomes of quotas and other measures like gender mainstreaming may well be ambiguous (Waylen 2009; Manicom 2001). Indeed, observers even point out that reservations for women may be easier in non-democratic, rather than democratic, regimes, since they provide a convenient way to legitimize the non-democratic regimes' determination to be 'inclusive' (Krook 2009: 106). And as has been observed for the communist regimes of Eastern Europe, the large presence of women in formal bodies may not be empowering without democratic space to organize in and make demands from (Jezerska 2003). We partake of such caution in the framing of our research problem and therefore desist from assuming that quotas will automatically ensure women public-political power, choosing to focus carefully on the local context.

Observers have expressed scepticism on whether the 33 per cent reservation of seats in the panchayati raj institutions for women in India can lead to their political advancement. Reservations for women in India were justified on the grounds that women had "a special capacity to represent the needs of women (or of children)". The argument justifying reservations for the Other Backward Classes (OBCs), in contrast, identified these groups as people "who have been 'disadvantaged by prejudice' in the past" (Singer 2007: 122). In this formulation 'women' do not figure as a political category, unlike the OBCs. While the depoliticized advocacy for women's reservation is unmistakable in Kerala as well, feminists need to continue demanding them on political grounds. The significance of these reservations can be scarcely belittled in Kerala. It is for the first time since the 1940s—since the pre-Independence legislatures in the Princely States of Travancore and Cochin[6]— that 'women' seem to have been recognized as a political category in their own right. Women have also achieved adequate formal representation in the local bodies; indeed, their numbers now exceed the stipulated quota.[7] These growing numbers make a contrast with the observed reluctance of women leaders of local governance regarding political power. Senior women politicians on the left in Kerala, however, did see reservations in local government as a training ground for women politicians, in fact, identifying this possibility as the primary merit of reservations in local bodies.[8] If such a goal has not been realized—it appears obvious that it has not—the failure is one that needs to be investigated.[9]

Theoretical and Methodological Considerations

Five critical trends that have emerged in recent debates within feminism are of particular significance to this research: one, the insistence on treating seriously the internal heterogeneity of 'women' as a social group; two, the cautiousness with which the project of 'retrieving women's voices' is now taken; three, the debate around women's agency; four, the need to complicate the private-public dichotomy but without collapsing one into the other; and five, the rejection of the idea that all forms of state power are necessarily and equally harmful to women.

Feminist social science research takes care to avoid simplistic and homogenizing notions of 'women's interests' (Crenshaw 1994). The challenge of advancing women's collective interests premised on recognition of difference has also been much debated between feminist political theorists recently (Dean 1996; Young 2000; Mouffe 1992; Fraser 1995). We draw from these insights and analyse the women leaders' narratives as intersectionally constructed—indeed, the challenge is precisely to trace out the mutual mediations of the different axes of power relations with sufficient clarity so as to illuminate the specific ways in which women of different groups relate to politics.

Secondly, though we do hope the voices of our interviewees will emerge as the most vital part of this book, our research is not a simple retrieval of 'women's voice' in the sense of recovering 'authentic' feminine voice. It is, rather, to see how both long-standing socio-political and cultural structures and recent developments have gone into shaping the plurality of such voices. Thus, we not only listened to 'women's voices', but also sought to record and interpret these rich narratives within emergent and historical contexts. We however do not claim to have resolved the tension between listening to women's voices and placing them within discursive and non-discursive contexts. Indeed, it may be necessary to retain the tension rather than offer unsatisfactory resolutions one way or the other. Such resolutions would only affirm our own location within the dominant as privileged researchers. Further, not allowing the tension to dissipate also lets us reflect on critical political agency in these troubled times.

Thirdly, we wish to address the question of women's agency and its relation to their empowerment in a complex sense, without emphasizing in it either the question of individual autonomy (say, as in Jejeebhoy 1995) or internal transformation (say, as in Rowlands 1997)—self-confidence or a 'sense of agency'. While we would not certainly devalue either of these, it seems important to emphasize that the absence of full autonomy need not necessarily imply passivity; also, the presence of self-confidence and a 'sense of agency' need not imply any loosening of patriarchal structures. Thus, following Kabeer (2000), we would argue for an expansion of the notion of agency as not necessarily requiring full individual autonomy and inclusive of a wide range of purposive action including bargaining, negotiation, deception, subversion and so on; however, the patriarchal structures within which these become necessary must be certainly highlighted (Ramazanoglu, 1993; Parpart et. al 2001). We also need to be sensitive to the fact that at times, certain sorts of agency secured by women do give them power over other women—and that the former would function then as agents of patriarchy. For instance, Ester Gallo's research on women working migrants from Kerala to Italy does show how the marriage strategies of such women endow them with a sense of agency, and how they come to gain considerable (patriarchal) control over their other, especially younger, female kin (Gallo 2004). While collective action is impossible without a drive towards individual autonomy and an individual sense of agency and self-worth, these are necessary but not sufficient conditions for collective action.

Fourthly, we take seriously the observation made by Mary Dietz that while the democratization of the private sphere and making demands for civic rights and inclusion are equally vital for women's citizenship, they must be clearly distinguished from each other (Dietz 1992). Taking a cue from this, we feel that the extension of full public presence to women should not be instrumentalized to the purpose of democratizing domestic relations. In other words, we are in agreement with theorists who believe that both active citizenship and the public sphere in which collective deliberation takes place may be restructured to be inclusive of multiple gender interests. Therefore, the focus of this research is not really on the kinds of bargaining power within the domestic domain that these women may have secured through their public roles.

Last, we also draw upon recent feminist thinking which critiques an earlier tendency to reject all manifestations of state power as essentially harmful. While feminists continue to recommend critical distance from the state, they now often agree that the state is a site of power that one can bargain with, that need not be rejected fully, and may be conceived as one of the actors in a complex political field (Ray 1999; Phillips 1998; Randall 1998).

Our methodology has been crafted out of specific elements, to gather more than quantifiable outcomes. Our methods have been mostly those of qualitative fieldwork—semi-structured and in-depth interviews, focus group discussions, memo-writing, and participant observation in the panchayat office and other public spaces—and textual analysis. Statistical analysis of a very basic kind in this work uses state election commission data for 2005, and also data which we collected as part of fieldwork. Our fieldwork covered the whole of Kerala and covered all regions evenly. Seventy women presidents of village panchayats were interviewed between 2007 and 2010, which was nearly one-fifth of the total number of women presidents in that tier in 2007. Besides, twelve out of a total of fifty-five women presidents at the Block-level, and two out of a total of five women presidents and the sole female vice-president at the District-level in 2007 were also interviewed. In addition we spoke to ten randomly-chosen women members of panchayats and some male members and panchayat presidents as well. In order to avoid homogenizing women's experiences, we differentiated between women who contested in the General Category, Dalit women, and Muslim women in our selection of interviewees, ensuring that at least one-third of the total numbers of women village panchayat presidents of latter groups were present in our sample. Since urban governance involves an entirely different set of issues, we decided to study it separately. Eight out of eighteen women leaders of municipalities and one out of the two women Mayors were interviewed.

Besides these women most of who had entered the political public recently, we also interviewed women politicians of the earlier generations and state- and district-level women leaders of political parties who have positioned themselves outside the field of local governance. We have also relied upon contemporary writings in the press and interviews with leading women politicians in Malayalam journalism. In all, 58 interviews were conducted with women politicians from the major political parties, most of them office-bearers and committee members from the highest to the lowest levels of the party hierarchy. The larger share of this comprised 29 interviews that were conducted with women activists of the CPM and its women's front. Eleven interviews were conducted with state and district-level women leaders of the Indian National Congress. Besides, two of the leading women politicians in the Muslim League's women's front, the Vanita League, ten leading women activists of the Kerala Sastra Sahitya Parishat (KSSP from now), a civil social organization close to the CPM and highly involved in the PPC, two women leaders each of the BJP and the Janata Dal, and two independent feminist activists with experience in party politics were also interviewed. Since the semi-structured interview allows precedence to the interviewee's narrative, the possibility of producing a richer text that captures the specificity of the interviewee's experience and views is much higher. This is particularly important as the data was to be closely analysed for its complexity, and not treated as simple information on choices or opinions. Also, given that the issues we seek to focus on are at the centre of highly charged debate in Kerala, we needed tools that would help us avoid eliciting stock answers.

Since our allegiances are more towards that strand of qualitative research which focuses on the cultural/structural analysis of everyday meanings and perceptions and highlights the institutional settings and the socio-cultural matrices that shape these meanings, a historical perspective serves an important purpose here. It helps us construct a holistic account of contemporary processes of women's politicization; it also serves in assessing the singular effects of the recent political experiments, and the extent to which they are so. Particularly, the possibility of 'conjunctural analysis'

(Grossberg 2006) interests us as a method to make sense of the events of the 1990s which opened up several possibilities of women's induction into the public in Kerala. Conjunctures are particular formations in time and space in which multiple tendencies and forces converge; the analysis of conjunctures allows us to question assumptions of linear history that the laudatory accounts rely upon. Conjunctural analysis helps us to trace out the ways in which particular political projects construct a certain direction out of multiple emergent possibilities, adapting or appropriating some, rejecting others, and accommodating yet others through reworking them into subordinate positions vis-à-vis the dominant (Hall 2003). The latter appears particularly useful: Stuart Hall refers to this through his concept of 'articulation' as a practice of 'transformism'—processes of reworking alternate political discourses into subordinate positions. He also remarks that 'articulation' also implies 'disarticulation': the denial of certain other alternatives or their demobilization (Hall 2003).

The last section of this chapter lays out the larger context of political decentralization in the mid-1990s in Kerala. The dominant left—mainly the CPM, the most powerful of Kerala's communist parties—attempted to construct out of a conjuncture of global, national, and regional forces that emerged in that decade, a certain direction of socio-political change that was projected as 'necessary' and 'inevitable'. This process gave shape to the routes by which many of our interviewees entered local governance. The spaces opened up in this process were undoubtedly 'glocal' (Dirilik 1998). As Mohan and Stokke have noted, this was part of a world-wide scalar reconfiguration of politics, the ongoing localization of politics mediated by institutional reform towards decentralization, and good governance. This calls for " ... concrete and critical political analyses of the relations of power and political practices among actors involved in making, using and changing local political spaces and practices." (Mohan and Stokke, nd: 27)

Political Decentralization and the Refurbishment of Left Hegemony

The PPC,[10] announced as a significant effort at democratiz-ing development and mainstreaming gender through the emergent institutions of local governance in Kerala, was launched in August 1996 and has been much celebrated since in the literature on 'deepening democracy' in the South (Harris 2001; Isaac 2005; Heller et al 2007; Sandbrook et al 2006; Saito and Kato 2008). In this work, we wish to reframe it as a political project specifically of the dominant left in Kerala, represented by the CPM. There is no doubt that the PPC as a developmental project has produced some gains in local level development in some areas; here, however, our primary concern is with its political consequences. (And though this is not the place to embark on such an inquiry, the developmental gains from the PPC may indeed be profitably analysed through the lens of politics.) There have been other efforts to view it as a political project. Appearing as it did at a crucial conjuncture of many forces, it is only natural that it appeared to be many things to many people. Even within the CPM in Kerala, it appeared to be different things. As Tornquist and Tharakan (1995) noted, there were huge differences between the 'state-developmentalists' to whom it looked like the consecration of the neoliberal economic and political agenda, and the 'popular-developmentalists' for whom it represented the replacement of unworkable welfarist and statist development with genuine participatory development. The latter were mainly activists of the popular science movement, the KSSP (Zacharia and Sooryamoorthy 1994). Tornquist and Tharakan characterize it as an attempt by the left to renew itself under the hostile conditions of the late 20th century (1995). Recently, it has been re-examined as a manifestation of 'late socialism' in Kerala (Mannathukaren 2010). Despite their differences, both these accounts argue that the PPC was indeed a political project, and one connected to refurbishing the hegemony of the left, which has been under threat from a variety of forces.[11]

Indeed, many of the forces that shaped the 1990s did pose serious threats to the hegemony of the dominant left in Kerala. The decades following independence were the heyday of leftist political society in Kerala, during which political parties successfully steered popular demands for health, land, housing, education and higher wages, towards the developmental state (Jeffrey 2003: 150–211). In these decades, the dominant left parties managed to integrate into their mass organizations, elements of 'political society' (Chatterjee 2003)—many groups located outside civil society and at the fringes of politics. The consolidation of the Malayalee leftist 'national popular' between the late 1930s and the 1960s, a process which accompanied such militant redistributionist politics, did allow several 'political societies'—ranging from such groups as squatters to headload workers—and their 'unconstitutional' struggles to proliferate in Kerala in those decades. For many of these groups which were subsequently absorbed into the organized left, a certain citizenship that claimed state welfare as 'peoples' rights' became available. Such absorption was mediated by members of civil communities such as school teachers (Jeffrey 2003) or lower level civil servants, besides party activists. As has been pointed out for Bengal, the mediation of such (stratified) social capital was "instrumental in resisting the disciplinary mechanism of the liberal institutions, locating their loopholes, subverting their precepts, and turning them into more inclusive, just and representative structures of power." (Bhattacharya 2001: 605). The gains made by the poor have been indisputable, as the 'Kerala Model' literature shows (Parayil 2001; Jeffrey 2003).

However, this by no means ended social stratification—access to citizenship was not even for all included groups, and there is reference in the literature on the Kerala Model to the 'outliers' of social development and politics—the Dalits, the tribal peoples, the coastal people (Kurien 2000).

Of the included groups, women remained marginal to leftist political society, and the woman question was posed as a developmental, not political, question (Devika 2008). Thus women's citizenship has remained unequal, and in fact citizenship has been, and remains largely inaccessible to women of the most deprived communities. Secondly, left politics in Kerala remained wedded to Nehruvian developmentalism that emphasized large-scale industries and centralized systems of government, even though leaders like EMS Nambutiripad often espoused decentralized government.[12] (And despite the fact that the vision of panchayati raj espoused by the Communist Party in the late 50s differed radically from that of the Congress government at the centre in that it was clearly directed against "overcentralized bureaucracy" (Sharma 2009: 85)—quite in keeping, one could say, with the communists' militant self-distancing from bureaucratic authority in those times.) Thirdly, by the 1970s, with the successful implementation of land reforms, the radical thrust of left politics seems to have dissipated, and new forces were emergent, shaped mainly by the migration to the Gulf, which began to create pockets of affluence. By early 1990s, this had grown into full-blown consumerism, the seeds of which were already present in the leftist 'national-popular' (Devika 2007a), but which now grew to threatening proportions.

The same period—between the 1970s and 1990s— saw a shift in civil society—which looked increasingly less Gramscian, and more like an oppositional space from which to challenge the exclusions of organized politics and the developmentalist state. While its interlocutors were clearly educated middle-class people who had benefited from the expansion of welfare in the 1950s and 60s, it provided a space for diverse movements challenging developmentalism and its other concomitants (such as modern patriarchy and casteism). Sceptical voices raised against the dominant left from civil society began to be heard more frequently from the 1970s, ranging from the manifestations of Naxalite politics, to public pleas on behalf of incarcerated psychiatric patients. The well-known instance, of course, is the struggle around protecting the ecologically rich rainforests of the Silent Valley in the early 1980s. All three cultural pillars of political society in Kerala—faith in the desirability of large-scale development, the notion of social justice rooted in the rhetoric of class struggle, and the consecration of the ideal of the consumption-oriented bourgeois domesticity as the best arrangement for the shaping of productive subjects—came to be questioned. The first came under attack with increasing reflexivity regarding industrial development, a sharper perception of risk. The second was destabilized when, from the early 1980s into the 1990s, groups that were marginal to Kerala's social development—women, tribal people, fisherfolk, Dalits—began to emerge into public view as political identities. The feminist groups that sprouted in the late 1980s challenged the fundamental understanding of the political that animated entrenched public politics. In the 1990s, they brought up issues that demonstrated the extent to which the entrenched notion of politics completely bypassed non-sovereign forms of power, and indeed rested on them. None of these really added up to 'reflexive modernity' (Giddens 1994); nor were they numerically large or well-organized enough to upset electoral calculations. Nevertheless, they did become forces to reckon with in and through Kerala's vibrant public sphere, and did shake the very foundations of leftist hegemony in the state. In sum, in the 1990s, the dominant left faced serious political challenge from three locally emergent forces: feminism and environmentalism, which advanced other notions of politics, and consumerism, which unleashed processes of depoliticization.

Adding to this were shifts in the national scene: the politics of public finance in India which led to the steady decline of the financial status of Kerala after the 1980s, began to accelerate in the post-reform period, after the mid-1990s (Raman 2010: 138–9) and successive Finance Commissions have encouraged structural adjustment reforms. In Kerala, by the early 1990s, there was a growing consensus that the Kerala Model of development was in crisis. In this debate, the concern was about the continuing stagnation in Kerala's economic growth (EPW 1990; George 1993). These discussions percolated into the Malayalam public sphere and the International Congress on Kerala Studies organized by the CPM's AKG Centre for Research and Studies in 1994 highlighted the 'crisis of the Kerala Model' as a key theme. In his inaugural speech at the Congress, EMS Namboodiripad emphasized this aspect: "I have a request. Let it not be the case that our attention wavers from the severe economic crisis that we face, distracted by praise that scholars shower upon us on account of our achievements. We are far behind other states in economic growth. We must resolve this crisis without delay" (Namboodiripad 1994: 8). And even as these concerns were being articulated, the gains in social development seemed to be under threat as well. Expenditure on education and healthcare, already declining in the 1980s, continued to fall in the early 1990s as well (Oommen 2010: 75). In this context, decentralized development appeared to be a promising means of accelerating economic growth without compromising on social development.[13] Besides, anxieties generated by the fall of the Soviet Union led to reflection among intellectuals in the dominant left about alternatives to face the onslaught of the neoliberal order. Writing about the failure of really-existing socialism and India's imminent liberalization in 1991, T M Thomas Isaac and K N Harilal recommended an alternate path that would not compromise "national pride" (Isaac and Harilal 1991: 162). Decentralization was highlighted as the "basic political structure" of this alternate path (ibid., p. 176). Besides, it appeared crucial for triggering growth as well. Decentralization was identified as a crucial pre-condition for an agricultural growth strategy rooted in regional planning; it was also seen as the effective way of mobilizing human power in rural areas for a fresh thrust in agriculture (ibid., p. 177). Decentralization continued to be projected as a shield against the neoliberal global order even after the CPM began to deal with the Asian Development Bank (Isaac 1998).

A third pull came from concern over the stagnation of left politics and welfare policy itself. The impact of globalization ('globalization' in a broader sense, as Malayalees had begun to slowly turn away from the nation state and towards the international job market for employment since the 1970s) was also becoming apparent by the early 1990s, with very complex social repercussions. More and more educated Malayalees seemed to have lesser and lesser stake in reshaping socio-economic life in Kerala (Tornquist 2000). These were essentially problems that the earlier sorts of democratic mobilizations could not solve, and indeed, seemed to undermine such mobilizations themselves. In short, contradictory pulls were at work upon the dominant left in Kerala as it geared up to shape the emergent conjuncture into a project of refurbishing hegemony. The PPC sought to begin by projecting the 'people' as the major historical agent of social transformation and economic growth, in a much broader sense than ever before.

It is important to stress these different pulls that the left was trying to negotiate—and not dismiss the internal differences or the terminological and conceptual confusion within the discourse of the PPC as 'mere rhetoric' that conceals 'true neoliberal intentions'. It is true that the PPC did not actively draw on alternate models of participatory democracy in India that were more explicitly ranged against globalized capitalism such as that of the National Alliance of Peoples' Movements (Keating 2003) and this was probably to be expected, as will be argued below. But to flatly project it as 'neo-liberal' would be to ignore the local concerns that informed the PPC which were carried over from public discussions about the ills of the Kerala Model: the poverty of 'outliers', the need to further social development, to enhance food production. It would also ignore the fact that the dominant left is primarily a political force, a political agent, and not merely a governmental one. True, in the wake of the deepening of the fiscal crisis, the left in power had to indeed consider a new regime of government. But it could not simply capitulate to the seductions of predatory capital. Being a political agent that attempts to rule by renewing its moral standing with trad-itional supporters and new groups, it could not slip into that role too easily. Therefore what it attempted through decentralized governance and people's planning in the PPC and after was not some direct form of marketization or direct concession to global capital. [14]

We argue that in Kerala, these heterogeneous imperatives came to be managed very soon through a division of leftist political space into two specific domains, 'high politics' and 'local governance'.[15] The former represents state-wide politics with direct links to the national scene where competition between parties and ideologies is fierce and often acrimonious. It is the domain in which the key transformative processes must be played out. It is also the seat of the power over all major decisions affecting the whole population of the state, both legislative and executive. In contrast, the domain of local governance consists of a number of interconnected governable units—the different tiers of the panchayats—and of which the most basic unit is the 'neighbourhood group'. These are 'hypermoralized communities' of neoliberal governance, as Nikolas Rose (Rose 2007: 182) calls them.[16] In the words of M P Parameswaran, one of the chief architects of the PPC and a leading intellectual of the KSSP, the neighbourhood group is "a unit that lies in between a joint family and a commune, in size and mutual relationship …a true extended family in which every house is a home for all." (Parameswaran 2005: 157–8)

'High politics' and 'local governance' in political space in present-day Kerala differ from each other in crucial ways, three of which are of particular importance here. The first is in the degree of activity and autonomy. The former is characterized by hyperactivity especially in political decisions and policy innovation. This is demonstrated by the many dramatic instances of state action undertaken by leaders, including the dramatic ushering of the PPC itself (called the 'big-bang approach') and the more recent 'Munnar demolitions' by the present (at the time of writing) LDF Chief Minister, V S Achuthanandan (Mannathukaren 2010). In contrast, 'local governance' is subordinate to 'high politics' and is marked by governing-by-rule-and-procedure, and squarely under the supervision and guardianship of several agencies such as the Department of Local Self-Government, the Planning Board, and the Ombudsman.[117] Secondly, the modes of rule prominent in each also seem to differ. In 'high politics', the dominant left's political and moral authoritarianism and use of force, if not violence, to silence critics, is amply evident, whereas in 'local governance', there is great concession to consensus-building, and panchayat members of the left, while controlled by the party local committees, are still expected to function together with their political opponents. Thirdly, the relation of each domain to capital is different: while in high politics leaders struggle to smoothly translate the earlier agenda of state-led, large-scale industrialized development into approval for neoliberal growth, the domain of local governance tries out 'sustainable and small-scale development programmes' and even tries to fight predatory global capital, such as in Plachimada, where the panchayat took on Coca-Cola (Wrammer 2004). It must not be assumed, however, that these are watertight compartments. There are instances in which features of the former are shared by the latter, especially in panchayats where earlier left militancy is somewhat more prominent—and in panchayats in northern Kerala, where the CPM forms a strong 'moral community' bound together by ties of affect (Chaturvedi 2008).

PPC, as a bid for hegemony, was housed in the emergent space of local governance, and essentially involved four key moves:

First, through the construction of the discourse of local governance that drew eclectically on several political and ideological agendas that emerged in the 1980s and through 'Third Wave Democratization' after the fall of the Soviet Union, the dominant left sought to gain flexibility in rhetoric. While the untangling of the various strands of thinking on development and democracy that went into the discourse of the PPC and people's planning in general is an important task, it is beyond the scope of the present work. Nevertheless, a whole host of keywords from a variety of paradigms such as participatory development/citizenship, 'pro-poor growth', Putnamite exhortations towards 'social capital', the new public management discourse, along with vestiges of the earlier discourse of social justice such as the rhetoric of class struggle, that of Gandhian village self-rule, and newer forms of demotic populism, were all thrown in. This, indeed, was noticed by observers (Chathukulam and John 2002; Tornquist and Tharakan 1995: 74). There is reason to think that the ambiguity of this complex construction did initially provide the flexibility required for the left struggling to resolve multiple dilemmas and contradictory pulls. Notice, for instance, how M P Parameswaran's description of the experimental beneficiary-built-and-controlled drinking water project implemented by the KSSP at Olavanna may be interpreted both as 'participatory development' and as 'self-financed' water supply (Parameswaran uses the latter term) (2005: 37). Observers have remarked that it is this project that became the model for the World Bank's Jalanidhi rural water supply scheme later (Narayanan and Irshad 2009: footnote 23, p. 22). Nevertheless, the utility of this move diminished rapidly, since it left the advocates of the PPC open to charges of bad faith and ultimately eroded the fragile consensus that had been achieved about decentralization within the CPM, leading to one of the most acrimonious public debates in the history of Kerala, in which leading figures in the CPM and intellectuals close to it publicly traded charges against each other (Devika 2007a).

Secondly, the dominant left sought to deal with the challenges it faced—from feminism and environmentalism on the one hand and consumerism on the other—through incorporating them in ways similar to New Labour's 'transformism' described by Stuart Hall (2003). Here the dominant strand was the CPM's effort to meet neoliberalism halfway, and the subaltern strands were the issues raised by feminists and environmentalists in their critiques of the ideology of egalitarian developmentalism (which supplied the 'three pillars' of cultural hegemony mentioned earlier). This worked by blunting the political edge of these critiques while addressing a few selected issues they raised, in ways that would not affect these 'pillars'. Oppositional civil society was itself often reduced in the PPC discourse to a depoliticized 'social-capital'-oriented version. This stands in conspicuous contrast to the ways in which the new social movements were understood as elements of civil society in Latin America. Far from being liberal interest groups, these movements were regarded as the agents of counter-hegemonic projects. The difference in the PPC's conception of 'civil society' is evident in the manner in which leading PPC intellectuals conceived of the participation of women in it. In his controversial volume on the 'Fourth World' (2004) that lay in a participatory future, Parameswaran's major recommendations revolved around ensuring equal representation for women in public institutions and fostering the conditions that would enable women to pursue an active public life around 'development'. However, women's groups in Kerala in the late 1980s and 90s had refused to accept distinctions between politics and development or public and private; their critique included an intense questioning of sexual norms, unequal family structures, and the question of the woman's control over her own body. These were ignored even as the question of women's access to the public was partially adapted, instrumentalized to community well-being and local development. Indeed, there is reason to believe that the 'empowerment' envisaged by the PPC stayed well within the bounds of the 'social', a domain historically conceded to the 'feminine' in Kerala and identified as women's space, and did not open up the political to women (Devika 2008). It is also interesting to note that it was the cause of environmental activism that he stressed the most, something that also seems more amenable to become a 'general' cause. (Muralikrishnan 2003; Parameswaran 2004). But environmentalism too was adapted with its political edge blunted. Parameswaran writes: "KSSP conceived that only participatory democracy and decentralized development can bring the world back to stability. Both demand a modification of Schumacher's dictum 'Small is Beautiful'. Smallness and beauty are not enough. 'Small has to become powerful also'. This is possible only at a much higher level of science and technology, on the one hand, and change in the understanding of human development and progress, on the other." (Parameswaran 2005: 159). [18] Such blunting of the political edge of new social movements is what uncritical admirers of Kerala's CPM, such as Patrick Heller, who claims that the CPM has embraced "the "new social movement project of grassroots empowerment," (2000: 511), fail to notice.

Consumerism, however, was never critiqued in a fundamental sense. It was rather perceived as an 'external intruder': Parameswaran viewed it as the major cultural instrument of global capitalism that the anti-capitalist new world ought to actively battle. Isaac, however claimed that this was mistaken, as the need is to "control the ostentatious consumption of the rich minority" of the developing countries, and that there is no general spread of greed. (Isaac 2005: 170). However, that the consuming-bourgeois householder-norm of respectability was well-entrenched in Kerala as one of the 'pillars' of left developmentalism indicates that the enabling conditions for consumerism were well-entrenched in Kerala much earlier (Osella and Osella 2000). Both accounts ignored this. This probably reveals their (minimal) critique to be moralistic and apolitical, resting on the perception of a sharp and belligerent distinction between inside (leftist Kerala) and outside (global capitalism). Instead, consumerism among the poor was 'articulated' through the welfare entitlements distributed through the panchayats. Welfare is now highly individualized, targeting poor households perceived as a consumer-category, the 'below poverty line' rather than oriented towards the welfare of groups, and focused on the state's handouts

(Williams et al, 2010). As Williams et al. note, this has engendered a shift from "the politics of claiming state support from
union-based demands articulated collectively (and often con-
frontationally) in relation to the Government of Kerala, to far
more diffuse strategies to influence *local* government and its
representatives." (p. 14). Studies in Kerala's decentralization
have shown that the successes of the experiment are largely
in the provision of basic needs to the poor—in housing and
drinking water—though there is apprehension regarding the
sustainability of such provision (Santhakumar et al 2008).
It has also been noted that rising consumption aspirations
in housing erode sustainability (Gopikuttan 2002). The basic
unit of welfare, more often than not, is the individual bene-
ficiary/household; individual beneficiary programmes tend to
form the larger share of welfare projects in the panchayats
(Nair 2000; Nair and Krishnakumar 2004; Heller et al 2007;
Sharma 2009; Babu 2009). In contrast, productive investment
by panchayats has been low, and the returns from such investment poor. This continues to be the situation, as a recent
report commissioned by the Government of Kerala reveals
(Go K 2009), which also makes the pertinent observation
that in the case of welfare handouts, the boundaries between
welfare entitlements that promote social development and
those which feed consumerist impulses are not clear (Go K
2009: 147). More seriously, it has been observed that the
funds spent for SC/ST welfare are not being spent on building
marketable skills among them, or generating durable assets
(p. 124). Clearly, the indication is that such welfare essentially 'manages' poorer consumers through handouts, but
rarely helps them to enter either the labour market or the
productive sector on superior terms, which would have put
them in an entirely different relation to consumption.

'Transformative' articulation of this sort may contain
the threat perceived by the dominant left, but it promises
ultimately to backfire on the political itself. On the one
hand, the sapping of the political charge of feminism and
environmentalism weakens the possibility of alternate ways

of imagining politics; on the other, consumerism is not curtailed but appeased in this move, and it continues to erode
the wider support for the leftist agenda. Consumerism is
hardly about social positions alone; it is far more about
the significance of the difference between social positions.
Increased welfare allotments do not disturb the latter and
so social inequality remains sanctioned silently. The worst
consequence of this falls precisely on Kerala's dominant left.
Consumerism leads people away from public services even
when they are of reasonable quality towards 'high-status'
private sector alternatives, a process very visible in education
in contemporary Kerala. This destroys the wider 'moral
constituency' of the dominant left, which was rooted in the
shared experience of public education and health care across
social class.[19]

A third move was to mobilize a pool of expertise outside the
bureaucracy to deal with the business of local government and
planning. The PPC involved a great many activists who were
drafted in as 'resource persons'; retired government officials
were invited to form 'voluntary technical corps' to help project
formulation. M P Parameswaran cites the presence of "active
and informed citizens who strengthen civil society" as a major
achievement of the PPC (Parameswaran 2005: 214–5); 'local-
level experts' were to be brought together in working groups
to plan projects. Politically, the gains from this were obvious:
it would bring a large number of educated middle-class people
with broad left sympathies closer to the dominant left and
directly involved in governmental processes. Yet this proved
be one of the weakest links. The KSSP, which had been the
major architect of the PPC, withdrew once the LDF lost the
elections in 2000. But more crucially, as Chathukulam and
John note, the reverence of bureaucracy was often shared
even by KSSP activists, many of whom were bureaucrats and
technocrats themselves—in other words, they express the
doubt whether the KSSP activists were themselves sufficiently
'de-bureaucratized' (2002: 4919–20; also see, Das 2000;
Mukundan and Bray 2004). Over time, the Technical Support

Groups and the working groups, which were responsible for converting the suggestions raised in the village assemblies—the Grama Sabhas—into technically viable, socially beneficial, and economically feasible projects, have been found to be greatly lacking. Indeed, recent observers find that the working groups have been "stuffed with favourites"; that they possess little expert knowledge; and that their failing contributes to the continuing power of the bureaucracy in the planning process (Go K 2009: 75–9). The weakness in technical support has also been identified as a major reason for the failure of the PPC to deliver concrete gains in development (Sharma 2009). It has been also noted that women were a minor presence among the resource persons trained for the PPC, even at the height of its enthusiasm (Isaac and Franke 2000; Chathukulam and John 2000: 85; Sharma 2009: 143).

Fourthly, there was also the move towards the 'disarticulation' of some ideas and goals associated with the early left. Marked among these was the CPM's commitment to redistribution of land to the Dalits and Adivasis, who were not full beneficiaries of land redistribution during the land reforms of the 1970s. Rashmi Sharma notes about the village panchayats of tribal areas in Kerala that they could not address severe and immediate issues, such as that of land alienation and loss of employment; however, they were "expected to address the manifestations of these problems, i.e., unemployment and poverty" (Sharma 2009: 161). Contrary to expectations that welfare disbursement targeting the Scheduled Castes and Tribes, streamlined and strengthened through local bodies would be effective as a substitute for earlier demands for land as a productive resource, militant struggles broke out in the post-millennium years in Kerala for precisely this resource from among the Dalits and Adivasis (Bijoy and Raman 2003; Steur 2010; Rammohan 2008). The divide between high politics and local governance became blatantly clear in the course of these struggles. During the recent Dalit-led land struggle at Chengara, the Chief Minister of Kerala and veteran communist V S Achuthanandan told the protestors to return to their native villages and put in applications for three cents of (housing) land in their panchayats (Devika 2008). In defiance, these struggles located themselves in high politics, addressing not the domain of local governance, but that of high politics, refusing to be disciplined into the former (Bhaskar 2008a). And as the idea of land redistribution to Dalits was being disarticulated, advocates of the PPC tried to project EMS Namboodiripad's interest in decentralization as a fundamental aspect of the dominant left's political legacy since the mid-20th century.[20] Besides, the prolonged battle fought by the women's movement in Kerala against politicians from across almost the entire political spectrum over cases of sexual violence did reveal that the question of patriarchy could not be encompassed by the limited and markedly economistic liberal-feminist solutions that were being advanced in People's Planning. Indeed, the difficulties of trying to contain social difference and conflict within such domains as 'community' or 'partnership' evident in other situations, in the first and third-worlds, are more apparent now (Craig and Porter 2005).

Thus, the present in Kerala is one in which this bid by the left to refurbish its hegemony has been severely damaged.[21] In the recent years, the CPM has tried other strategies, like building alliances with emergent forces among the Muslim community—a strategy that they now interpret to have backfired badly in the last Lok Sabha elections (Devika 2009). Recent incidents give one a sense of the acute crisis of the dominant left in the present, for example, in the increasing use of violence in the face of criticism, even against leading intellectuals sympathetic to the left (Devika 2010), and in the polling violence in the 2010 elections to the local bodies, very rarely heard of in Kerala hitherto. Meanwhile, new forces have emerged in the politico-economic field. The threat from predatory neoliberal capital, especially around key resources like land, is well-perceived now (Mannathukaren 2010). If decentralization in Kerala has been compared with the municipal socialism of Porto Alegre (Parameswaran 2005), there are other aspects of its present that place it closer to the post-communist East European economies, marked by "mafia gangs, the consolidation of property relations and widespread corruption," a situation in which the political elite has become fully part of the power bloc of the state, as Ravi Raman observes (Raman 2010: 1470). Inequalities have risen in the post-reform period post-1996 with the Gini Coefficient soaring for both urban and rural areas; social development continues to be under severe threat (Oommen 2010).

However, it may be argued that the CPM continues to grow in Kerala. The All-India Democratic Women's Association (AIDWA, henceforth) has contributed in no small measure to this growth: membership grew from 21, 97,070 in 2004 to 30, 79,360 in 2007 (CPM 2008: 134). However, female membership in the CPM has been low—a mere 12 per cent in Kerala in 2008 (CPM 2008: 114). It may be noted, however, that the increasing presence of women is also true for non-left organizations. The post-millennium Dalit and Adivasi struggles have also produced a few eminent women leaders, for instance, the leader of the Adivasi Gotra Sabha, C K Janu, who left the CPM to struggle for tribal land rights outside (Bhaskaran 2004). As these conflicts continue to surface in high politics and local governance, women leaders often speak of the need to 'set aside' politicians so that development in the panchayat may not be interrupted. Before we discuss these views, it may be necessary to take a quick look at the views of the women who articulate various shades of gender politics within the fold of the dominant left. This we attempt to do in the next chapter.

Notes

1. Bhaskar (1997) who studied 84 women panchayat members in Kerala in the first term noted that 53.2 per cent had high school education and 24 per cent had studied up to the higher secondary levels. Out of the rest, 19 per cent were graduates (p. W15). Chathukulam and John (2000) remark that in their

sample, the average educational levels of women members were higher than those of male members. In our own sample, out of the 62 women leaders of village panchayats who gave clear responses on their education, 20 were postgraduates, and this was the single biggest group. The second biggest group was of the 15 diploma-holders, mostly in teaching. Many of the latter had actually retired as Headmistresses in government schools. Also see, Isaac 2005.

2. The total number of women in the last term (2005–2010) was 6026. It has gone up considerably in the present term starting in 2010, with the hike in reserved posts for women to 50 per cent. This time, there are 11,135 women members, counting the urban bodies as well.

3. The CPM's document titled 'Party's Perspective of Women's Issues and Tasks' (2005) spelt this out: it regretted that "there is no policy to encourage women whole-timers even in states were the Party is strong." It also notes that there is a male preference in deciding the full-timers and recommends that this should be avoided. Further, it noted with satisfaction that in Kerala, the "decision that there should be one woman whole-timer under each area committee is being implemented" (p. 23).

4. 'Empowerment' is not defined or measured in the same way in these studies; nevertheless the definitions used converge broadly on a few indicators like self-confidence, motivation, freedom to act, and mobility.

5. This is somewhat different from the argument that women politicians will bring a different 'style' of functioning and even gradually rid politics of its intense masculinism (Gill 1999; McMillan 2001), introducing into political judgment the ethic of care (Mackay 2001).

6. Kerala State was formed only in 1956 uniting the three Malayalam-speaking areas on the south-west coast of the Indian peninsula, Travancore, Cochin, and Malabar, which had been part of the Madras Presidency of British India.

7. There was a modest increase in all three tiers from the stipulated numbers in the last term (2005–2010), with women constituting about 37 per cent of the total. This, however, is no recent achievement. George Mathew (1991) noted that in the District Councils of 1991, some 35 per cent of all members had been women, which exceeded the quota of 30 per cent for women.

8. In an interview with Abhilasha Kumari and Sabina Kidwai, Susheela Gopalan, a leading communist politician in Kerala of the 20th century, remarked about the 33 per cent quota for women in the panchayats thus: "Initially I was against reservations but today there is no option...when women become Panchayat members they acquire earning capacity and become independent. ... They develop confidence and can be trained as potential candidates for Assembly and Parliamentary elections in the future." (Kumari and Kidwai 1999: 163–4). Scholars too, have nurtured such hopes about decentralization, as holding the possibility of nurturing leaders with local experience—for example, Jean Dreze and Amartya Sen (cited in Kumar 2006: 209). A Ghosh and S Tawa Lama-Rewal (2005) mention the possibility of local government becoming a training ground for women politicians as one the three major arguments advanced in favour of women's reservations in the debate on women's reservations at the national level (p. 7). Mary John (2007) points out that urban governance probably serves the purpose better—this seems to be confirmed by our own fieldwork as well.

9. Many point out that there is no firm empirical evidence that backs up the effectiveness of a 'critical mass'—the proportion of members of a marginalized group in a formal body being large enough to ignite the chain reaction of change; Yoder (1991) even warns of a backlash. Drude Dahlerup (1988) has argued that more than 'critical mass' it is 'critical acts' that may be decisive. However, it is also pointed out that the significance of numbers should not be underplayed. Lister (2003) reminds us that the larger the numbers of women, the greater the scope for critical acts; also the impact of numbers is not necessarily best assessed in the short-run, but in the long-run and therefore, while 'critical mass' may not be a useful concept, but that does not devalue the strength of numbers (Stokes 2005).

10. The PPC was launched in August 1996 by the LDF government and was hailed as a unique effort to draw in people as participants in planning for development and implementation of projects. Local bodies were promoted as powerful institutions of governance, and considerable financial devolution was made available to them, of some 35–40 per cent of the resources of the Ninth Plan. Efforts were also made to institutionalize local-level planning and implementation by setting up the

Administrative Reforms Committee. The PPC was to unfold in six stages: (1) (September–October 1997): the convening of the local village assemblies, the Grama Sabhas, with maximum popular participation, (special attention was to be paid to ensure participation of women) in which people were to voice their needs and demands through group discussions aided by trained facilitators. An estimated two million people took part in the assemblies, of which some 26.22 per cent were women. (2) (October–December 1997): assessments of local resources were made through participatory studies, presented as the Panchayat Development Report at Development Seminars to be attended by delegates from the Grama Sabhas. The report was to have a mandatory chapter on women and development. (3) (November 1997–March 1998): the election of 'task forces' for various sectors, consisting of elected representatives, experts and activists, who were to formulate projects. Gender impact statements were made mandatory for all projects and a separate task force was set up for women's development projects. (4) (March–June 1998): involved plan finalization at the local level in meetings of elected representatives, and the plan document was to have a separate chapter on women's development projects, with 10 per cent of the resources set apart of the Women's Component Plan. (5) (April–July 1998): consisted of the integration of local plans at the block and district levels. (6) (May–October 1998): formulation of a State Plan from the District Plans, in which the local-level plans were to be evaluated by the District Planning Committees. In this phase the Voluntary Technical Corps was raised, consisting of retired government officials with various technical skills to help the local bodies to assess the feasibility of the plans. For a detailed account, see Isaac and Franke 2000.

11. It may be noted that Rashmi Sharma's account of the new thrust towards decentralization in the national scene as a "balancing act in favour of rural producers" as state policy tilted more and more in favour of the urban elites in the wake of liberalization does not seem to be directly applicable to Kerala (2009: 44). She argues that here, decentralization has been viewed by the dominant left in Kerala as a positive initiative for long, but appeared relevant suddenly in the mid-1990s as a panacea for various developmental ills and to rejuvenate the flagging left morale in the wake of the collapse of the Soviet Union (p. 93).

12. Dwaipayan Bhattacharya notes that though EMS wrote a dissent note to the Asoka Mehta Committee's report on decentralization, he did not differ very fundamentally from the Committee's central views. While he criticized the Committee's alleged failure to acknowledge the value of 'political will' in making decentralization successful and also added an economic dimension to its perception of 'weaker sections', he continued to see it as a project of 'democratic development management'. His input was the insight that this would not work well unless construed as a political, not administrative, problem. Bhattacharya 2006: 102.

13. As Go K (2009) notes, a comparison between pre-Amendment and post-Amendment growth rates in various sectors shows that the new dispensation has been unable to make a serious dent in the growth trends identified as unhealthy. Overall growth rates have been positive but agriculture is still declining alarmingly, showing a negative growth rate of -0.29 per cent for 1994–2007. Construction sector growth continued to rise, from 3.69 in 1991–93 to 6.57 per cent; the tertiary sector grew from 4.47 per cent to 9.39. (p. 63). The authors of the report comment that it may be unfair to blame decentralization alone—indeed, the depressed rate of growth in agriculture does reveal the powerlessness of the panchayats to contain the effects of external change that affected agricultural growth negatively, as Harilal (2005) remarks. The report also notes that there is a "land mafia", which is "making inroads into paddy lands for reclaiming them into tourist spots and urban habitats", which, it seems, the panchayat is unable to confront effectively (p. 68).

14. Though its middle-class bias seems unmistakable. Here it may be worth noting that according to the CPM's official statistics, the Party members in Kerala hail largely from the 'working classes' and 'agricultural labour', constituting 53. 48 per cent and 24.90 per cent of the total membership respectively. The 'middle-class' accounts for a miniscule 2.56 per cent, and even counting other better-off groups like the 'landlord' (.06 per cent), 'bourgeois' (.01 per cent), 'middle peasant' (10.65 per cent) and 'rich peasant' (.30 per cent), the better-off do not add up to much (CPM 2008: 130). In that case, the PPC agenda, which has been noticed to be a largely middle-class agenda within the CPM by sympathetic observers, (Tornquist and Tharakan 1995) was surely the work of a miniscule minority

who were, however, endowed with considerable stocks of intellectual capital and influence in the Party far beyond their numbers.

15. It may also be mentioned that this division may not be entirely the outcome of the specific circumstances obtained in Kerala. As Bandhopadhyay et al (2003) remark, panchayats are still heavily dependent on superior government institutions, and this is a legacy of their colonial roots. Even the 73rd Amendment has not remedied this dependence. Also see Vyasulu 2004.

16. However, the process of building such groups was itself heavily mediated by the presence of the CPM, as accounts of the famous 'Kalliassery experiment' in local development initiated by the KSSP reveal. This panchayat is entirely dominated by the CPM, but as Tornquist and Tharakan (1995) asked, "... did taking a principled stand against everything preventing the productive and sustainable use of land... together with radical arrangements ... to help those who would like to make productive use of land if they had access to..." cause "even more problematic divisions among already established leftist supporters?" (p. 72). M P Parameswaran admits that while the formation of neighbourhood groups happened rapidly in Kalliassery, political interference was evident in decisions about the position of the convenor in each group: "...decisions were taken at party committees and they were willy-nilly accepted by citizens." (2005: 160). Thus what emerged was certainly no neutral civil society, but rather the subordinate level of 'local governance'.

17. Indeed, such submission to higher authorities is noted to be characteristic of panchayats now. Go K (2009) notes that the panchayats' capability to coordinate between different agencies is not negligible, and finds evidence for this in their work during non-normal times such as during epidemics: "...when the local governments prove their capacity in inter-agency coordination, the trigger comes from a guideline or instruction from the state government. This seems to be disturbing as the local governments tend to 'prefer' to be agencies of the state government." (p. 102)

18. Olle Tornquist (2007) raises the issue of non-transparency of politics in the Kerala experiment—the espousal of participatory deliberative democracy on the surface, but the actual continu-

ation of earlier models. He notes that no social movement in favour of democratic decentralization has emerged; people continue to come together on the basis of "special interests". (p. 35). Many groups are still unable to articulate their collective interests—especially women, Dalits and others. And the very possibility of these groups engaging in independent internal deliberation on what these might be is also prevented.

19. And, equally erodes the earlier 'political societies' of informal sector workers harnessed by the communist parties, one may add. 'Political society' action that challenges the seams of legality is now not very palatable to the CPM (Mannathukkaren 2010). The new welfarism does not usher the poor into civil society, however, neither does it foster the kind of political society-formation that Partha Chatterjee (2008) mentions as happening currently in India. Rather, a hybrid that may perhaps be called the 'civil–political society' seems to be taking shape mainly through the vast network of self-help groups of women from below-poverty-line families (BPL) sponsored by the state, known as the Kudumbashree network (CDS 2008). The poorest are often outside this formation. The arguments current in Kerala about the unsuitability of the central government's norms for identifying below-poverty-line households—it is pointed out that in Kerala, poverty is of a different sort, not captured by the central government's norms—illuminate this scene quite well (Williams et al 2010). Indeed, Williams et al (2010) note that in their field sites, those groups that displayed intense poverty were often excluded from the BPL list—they note that only the poorest were willing to carry the label 'destitute'. "'BPL' by contrast was a desired status—and the contests over inclusion indicated that any flexibility within its definition was being fully exploited." (p. 19).The 'civil-political society' does resemble 'political society' in some crucial ways; nevertheless, it is hardly amenable to collective action being still a collection of individual rational agents (representing families with low consumption capacity) reacting to extremely narrow local impulses. Hence its reliability as a 'vote-bank' is decidedly low, as the recent elections to the local bodies proved. The CPM has indeed been attempting to integrate the Kudumbashree women into its women's organization; however its failure to seriously challenge upper-caste gender values (that require women to

be 'civil') prevents it from politicizing these new entrants. It is nevertheless clear that the civil-political society is far from being passive (CDS 2008). Indeed the tendency to equate depoliticization with passivity needs to be qualified heavily, and it may be also possible to imagine ways of ' re-politicization' (Williams 2004). In 2008, a new by-law was adopted for Kudumbashree which radically restructured it, allowing for the participation of above-poverty-line women. Since 2008, interesting changes seem to be afoot, which appears to confirm the possibilities indicated by Williams 2004.

20. K N Harilal, however, remarks that "The new experiment of democratic decentralization cannot be traced to the same kind of popular pressure from below as in the case of land reforms and other such progressive initiatives. There has not been a major struggle or mobilization of the people to realize participatory decentralization. But it has been for long a prominent slogan and electoral promise of almost every political party in the state, which indirectly reflects the public opinion in favour of participatory decentralization." (Harilal 2008: 75). Also see Subramanian (2004).

21. Rashmi Sharma remarks about how cynics interpreted the PPC as a ploy to strengthen the CPM's presence in Kerala, taking, apparently, a leaf out of the West Bengal CPM's book. The invitation sent to S B Sen to head the Committee on Decentralization of Powers in Kerala seemed to confirm these fears further. Sharma points out that this was strange, for as far as social development was concerned, West Bengal had more to learn from Kerala than vice-versa (2003: 3835–6). However, the point we are making here is a more nuanced one—we consider political decentralization and local planning exemplified in the PPC to be not a short-term strategy aimed at the capture of political institutions but a long-term one of shaping hegemony.

1

Women in Dominant Left Politics

'Participation' in the PPC: Dilemmas of KSSP Women

Despite their huge numbers, especially within the dominant left, women occupy a woefully small corner of the domain of high politics in Kerala. The apparent consensus within the CPM in the mid-1990s (up until then dominant sections within the Party had displayed little sympathy towards women's struggles for autonomy and citizenship, either as individuals or as a group) over the special and highly visible emphasis on welcoming women into governance and local development as participants was perhaps to be expected. On the one hand, as mentioned in the previous chapter, feminism had to be 'transformatively' adapted. On the other, such assent seemed entirely suited for the project of rejuvenating the left with a new group of activists. Women looked particularly fit to be chosen as the latter. One, here was a substantial group of people who had already proved their mettle as agents of change within families (as the Kerala Model theorists claimed) and also within local communities, as was evident in the Total Literacy Campaign, and who possessed the necessary skills and time. Two, the fact that women were largely devoid of strong political affiliations, as also the fact that the category of 'women' was itself largely not politicised, may have made them particularly attractive.[1] But neither of these features had anything necessarily to do with working towards favourable conditions for locating women as agents not within the family/local community, but within the political. But neither did they close off that possibility. At the outset at least, the ambiguity of 'participation' was probably useful—it could have been either the extension of the active familial agency already conceded to women into the realm of the local community, or their active articulation of both practical and strategic gender interests on behalf of 'women' as a group with its own claims. This was probably crucial in garnering *general* assent for incorporating women in an unprecedented way in the PPC.

As may be evident later from Chapter 2, the KSSP's perspectives on gender were crucial inputs in its imagining of decentralized governance and local planning. Some leading women activists of the KSSP did try to actively give a feminist interpretation to 'participation' in the PPC. However, in our interviews with many of the women in that group, the sense of failure was palpable and the recognition that the odds had simply been too much was evident. As one of them pointed out, raising the question of gender within KSSP, defined as a 'science movement' was almost self-defeating, for this required that the question of gender injustice had to be posed and resolved within the framework of science: "...and so we had to argue that gender oppression must be opposed because it was unscientific and that gender relations must be reinstated on a scientific basis." This limited the range of questions that could be posed. Besides, there was the huge burden of distrust to be tackled, especially from those who considered this a divisive issue. Several of these activists recounted how male activists would intervene to bring the focus on 'both men and women', and the 'community', and how they were forced to re-route their tactics via precisely the 'community'. One of them remembered a citizenship training camp during the PPC where she was part of a group asked to create a new framework to view the woman question:

> It was this citizenship training camp at Mundoor that brought a huge change in my thinking. The question came up, why do women not break their chains. It is those women who comply who get accepted. The question was raised whether even within

the organization there was a limit up to which a woman was allowed to rise—why were there so few women in the leadership? We felt that the discussion was faltering when these questions were raised .... We were convinced that nothing was possible unless there was fundamental change. The injustice within the family was most responsible for this state and it all started from socialisation. So it finally appeared to us that Man must be dethroned from all positions of power, and that democracy must be established both outside and at home. When this was put up for discussion, some felt that it was against men. The framework was accepted only after those parts were deleted. That's not what we had wanted.

Another activist recalled how they had to resort to 'community' as the last resort to convince others about the centrality of the gender question to democracy:

There were meetings at the IRTC to understand the notion of 'gender'. But somehow it was as if the organization was not ready to accept it. We tried indirect ways. Let's hold family get-togethers, we said. When I was in Malappuram, we got together 28 families and requested the husband and wife to speak frankly—this was effective ... in a way, here too we were discussing the 'gender question'. It works well only when men and women come together ...

Clearly, when the community entered the scene, the object of discussion changed. However, the flexibility of 'gender' as a notion is precisely what allowed for the impression of continuity though the object of discussion had changed. And the discussion was rendered into less of a political act of communication and more of a confessional exercise, a kind of counselling. While many admitted that the KSSP was far more democratic than other left organizations, most of these activists recounted rather bitterly the entrenched masculinism within KSSP (many complained how committees are still held in the late evenings, a time very inconvenient for most women), the silent messages conveyed to women that they should prioritize the family above public work, how they could not break middle-class constraints in even their own lives as the organization was either indifferent or hostile—and most importantly, how 'feminism' was a bad word within the KSSP, such that most women activists declared right at the outset that they were not 'feminists'. It looks apparent that the eclectic political vocabulary of the PPC did not favour these women; rather, it seems to have served a conservative interpretation over what, according to them, could have brought significant change. The general disillusionment with the trajectory of people's planning is very palpable in these interviews. Strikingly, most of them harbour an unmistakable dislike for high politics as lacking in ethics and obsessed with power. A KSSP activist who was also a Block panchayat member declared:

> I will never fight the elections again. The party [CPM] will not invite me again. The party does not need people who will state the facts directly, especially if they happen to be women. It will never consider with sympathy the inconveniences and difficulties that a woman has to face. It is also not happy that I work with the rationalists' organization and the KSSP!

Nevertheless, the KSSP women also widely acknowledged the fact that the freer discussion on gender within the organization had opened their eyes to gender injustice elsewhere. This was especially true of women who were also members of the communist parties, who had been included in the local committees. Their exposure to KSSP, they admitted, has made them take a more critical and independent stance within the party committees, which was often disliked by their male colleagues. An activist who had been active in the student and youth organisations of the CPM and is presently a local committee member of the party reminiscences thus:

> The frameworks of the SFI and DYFI are rather rigid. Many times, even if you are totally right, your view won't be accepted. There was gender in such behaviour—though I didn't feel it that way those days ... the committee would go on till midnight, but Father still wouldn't call me out. But there is a measure of

freedom—only a certain measure—in KSSP. It is only now that I realize that there is gender in the Party.

And besides, paternal protection and some opportunities for leadership are apparently offered by the KSSP, as was evident in the words of many interviewees. To quote a senior woman leader:

> KSSP is more hospitable to women, it gives them more space. And it expands our knowledge considerably too. Importantly, it gives them official positions—I have borne important offices at the District-level, and for more than one year. I am sure I will be made State President if I express the wish to do so. Compared with service organizations, this is much better…Activism with a kind of family feeling is possible [in KSSP]. The discipline in this [organization] is that one can interact with [men] as though they were your own brothers.

This relative calculation leads KSSP women into a certain kind of passivity: almost all our interviewees were certain that they were willing to remain rather circumscribed and endure the more benevolent patriarchy of KSSP rather than gain a wider field but face the starker version prevalent in the CPM. Over and over, KSSP women mentioned how there was silent surveillance inside the organization on women activists' family lives and on whether they were discharging their domestic roles properly. And sometimes the ugly face of Kerala's Reformist patriarchy comes into view, which an ex-KSSP woman activist revealed to us, retelling her bitter experiences of moral policing within the KSSP ("Fourteen years of activism—overcoming domestic problems, without making excuses, without claiming exemptions as a woman—but KSSP did not stand by me in this personal crisis. Instead, I was victimised and 'tried'") which finally made her leave it. However the relative perception that KSSP was 'much better' than either service sector trade unions or the communist party makes women endure reformist patriarchy and limit their rebellion to angry words laced with pessimism.

The AIDWA in High Politics and Local Governance

In contrast, many activists of the All-India Democratic Women's Association (henceforth, AIDWA), the women's organization associated with the CPM, are decidedly upbeat in their tone even when they feel that women are not being politicized well enough by the party. A district-level AIDWA leader from north Kerala made this point forcefully enough:

> In the earlier days, the basic class in our communist movement was the agricultural proletariat. But now that class is declining in numbers because of progress in education. There we need to mould a new basic class instead, powerfully shape them. This can be fulfilled only if women are strongly politicized. That is not happening, it's not being prioritized.

The shift away from conventional Marxism is striking indeed and probably indicates the rising confidence of AIDWA within the CPM in Kerala. The AIDWA's present prominence in Kerala is probably related to the fact that it operates within both the domains of high politics and local governance. In the latter, it organizes BPL women who have come together in the Kudumbashree self-help-group network; it also does grassroots work in taking up women's complaints with the police and other authorities. In the domain of high politics, the AIDWA shares the moral authoritarianism of the CPM and its actions are most often belligerent, if regressive, thrusts against opponents. This has brought it much visibility. For instance, the 'symbolic purification' that AIDWA activists performed in protest against the alleged 'sexual anarchy' of protestors who held a night-vigil in support of the Dalit land struggle at Chengara in March 2008 (Bhaskar 2008). Through this act, AIDWA activists sought to occupy the position of women as the protectors of 'national purity', which calls for sexual self-discipline and submission to the demands of national pride.

Besides such public acts, the the AIDWA in Kerala continues its implicit endorsement of upper caste gender norms, which was noticed in an earlier study focussed on Bengal. Though this study (Basu 1992) was about the AIDWA in West Bengal of an earlier decade, many of its observations are valid for present day Kerala. The question of 'respectability' continues to dog women in politics even in the present.[2] This is admitted by most women party workers. One of them, from south Kerala, told us about the candidacy of a locally respected, senior woman trade unionist in the 2006 State Assembly elections. She is a rare female figure in party circles—single, a full-timer by choice living in the party office, which is a space normally controlled by men, and a woman who managed to gain entry into the CPM-affiliated trade union's upper echelons—but who has only school-level education. Her chances were apparently dismissed secretly by her own co-worker (our interviewee) who said, "she didn't stand a chance with the general public with her [lack of] qualifications—just wasn't acceptable. And besides, she has no home of her own—someone who literally lives in the party office." However, these calculations are entirely driven by new elite[3] socio-cultural norms, and may not be accurate seems to be evident from the fact that despite the reluctance in her own party, she won nearly 46 per cent of the total votes polled.

This notion of respectability clearly leaves the sanctity of the patriarchal family untouched. Indeed, the notion of the family was not so much critiqued as expanded by most AIDWA women we interviewed, in which the party is perceived as the senior-most and most revered guardian. Amrita Basu's observation about the CPM's women's wing in West Bengal seems relevant here too: that there was a connection between the democratic centralism of the CPM in Bengal and the ethos of the Bengali Hindu joint family which "...mystifies ...inequality and projects itself as a solidaristic unit whose members share identical interests." (Basu 1992: 54). This is evident from the words of a district-level activist from south Kerala about groupism within the party:

> ...Suppose there are four members in a family, there will be four different approaches. This is something similar. In such

situations, the father takes a decision, that's how decisions are made. Everyone will have to accept that. The Party is just like a family. Disagreements between members of the Party are exactly like disagreements between members of a family. One can't call it groupism ...

The same woman also claims to be living in a gender-equal family, one in which the husband willingly looks after family affairs and agrees that his wife is the better public worker. Interestingly enough, while she spoke at length about the need to democratize the family, it appeared as though she still retained the faith that it was the woman's duty to be integrated into the family she married into. She told us that this indeed had been her story; her daughters' stories were not different, and it did not bother her. Both girls who were active in the students' organization of the CPM—the Students' Federation of India (SFI from now)—are now completely inactive because "the families they married into are not political." Here, it appears, there are enduring structures. The recollections of a very senior and respected leader of the AIDWA about the early days of her marriage to a committed party worker in the militant 1960s reveal the same relation: the terms of marriage are set by the man and the woman accepts, merging her will seamlessly with that of her husband and the party he belonged to:

> I saw my husband only on the third day after our marriage. He had informed me earlier; there was a strike on. He came home and asked, are you angry? No, you had told me of this, I said ... Then he told me two things. One, in this family, this is the woman [his mother] who gave birth to me and raised me. I am her youngest child. You should not do anything that may hurt her. Secondly, be part of the politics I belong to if you can, if you can't, at least don't obstruct me. If you do that, I will have no option but to abandon you. I have kept the word I gave him. One must take forward the family and politics equally well. One must share one's problems with the family...

Therefore women fall back on claiming superior moral ground –selflessness—as a means of coping when faced with

disappointments in rewards and recognition of their work—
echoing the strategies of women within bourgeois-domestic
ideologies. One of our interviewees, a district-level leader
of the AIDWA who had first been tipped to be mayor of a
city corporation in Kerala expressed her disappointment in
precisely such terms. She characterized her political activism
as a form of public altruism to help "ordinary women and
the poor", taking care to stress that a good job would have
brought her financial security at least, but she had abandoned
that option to serve the party. Any other expression of dis-
content is evidence for the presence of individualistic and
non-altruistic intent. As another district level AIDWA leader
from a northern district, reportedly an active critic of male
dominance within the CPM, remarked: "... the duty of a
disciplined party member is to comply fully with the party's
decisions. If you fight for it [i.e. your views] beyond expressing
your opinion [on the party's decision] then it means that 'I
want it'. This should be avoided."

Such secularized brahminical norms colour the AIDWA's
participation in CPM's moral authoritarianism, and this probably keeps alive its claim to space within high politics. Much
of this destructive energy is directed at 'feminists',[4] who they
continue to actively misrepresent. An AIDWA leader from a
northern district in Kerala distanced AIDWA from 'feminism'
quite briskly:

> We have no connection at all with feminist organizations. They
> claim that men are women's main enemies. We believe that
> society consists of both men and women and that only if they
> work together will women's enslavement end. We are not a
> feminist organization. We have no women's perspective. Women
> and men should work together to create social change, we believe
> that change can occur only that way. Women will be liberated
> only under socialism. This activism is only temporary relief; only
> for the time being ...

The contrast with the earlier quote, in which women
were perceived as the new fundamental class and therefore
potential bearers of socialism, is striking. What needs to be

noted is that here the concern is with warding off an 'enemy', feminism, which accords central importance to women's agency in bringing about social change. This prompts an immediate retreat; women's agency is declared subordinate to class struggle and the arrival of socialism. Thus within party circles, activists may well stress the importance of women's agency to keeping the movement alive, but when the spectre of 'feminism' is afoot this must be set aside. Feminism is dubbed as an 'anti-male' stance though these activists are usually unable to clarify what this might mean. The most common answer refers to feminism's alleged identification of men as the primary source and agents of women's oppression. Nevertheless how 'anti-male' interventions may be identified in practice remains vague; therefore, potentially, any intervention that accuses men of perpetrating gender-based oppression may be dubbed 'anti-male'. This imposes severe practical limits on anti-patriarchal activism by the AIDWA and the very flexibility of the notion of 'anti-male' creates a loophole through which particular men may be exempted from censure.

The price paid for such dissociation with 'feminism' may be actually much higher. First of all, given the strict limitations under which 'women's rights' are to be perceived, the party's efforts to induct more women into committees and as full-timers do not seem to have borne much fruit. A senior woman activist who has been a district committee member since the late 1970s from central Kerala, known for her staunch advocacy of women's rights within the party pointed out that her presence in the district committee was proof that the party wanted to offer enough space to mass organizations. This was to be achieved through inducting the area committee secretary of the AIDWA into the party's area committee, the district secretary and president of the AIDWA into the party's district committee, and so on. She noted that this gave them the chance to advance women's issues, but too often, they were woefully outnumbered. In our interviews, panchayat members, KSSP activists, and also

AIDWA activists—who were also local committee members of the CPM—admitted to feeling isolated and marginalized in these committees. "When I get up to speak," a young local committee member, an activist of the KSSP and a panchayat member, said, "it looks like a big joke many a time. The feeling that a man's position is lost when a woman is inducted into the local committee is very strong." Women activists in left trade unions and service sector unions were also utterly candid about the unquestionable grip of male dominance in these organizations. A senior trade union activist claimed that she was still unmarried because her colleagues preferred a domestic-oriented woman and not a full-time activist as a wife. The induction of women into committees in service sector organizations does not seem to have made much difference in the timings (interestingly enough, a woman activist of a rival trade union associated with the Congress told us that they did participate in committees but male colleagues would ask them to leave by five-thirty or six in the evening. "When they tell us this we leave simply because we don't want them to feel that we are defying them. But then 'women's empowerment' had never figured permanently on their agenda"). Within the CPM and the CPI, women had begun raising the demand for reservations from 1998 and it developed into an internal struggle (Erwer 2003). Susheela Gopalan openly voiced this demand at a public meeting, pointing out that "women needed reservations in people's organizations and not just in the Parliament or the panchayat" and indeed stressed the point that "All positions in all fields are monopolized by men. They will not relent. How many women are to be found in the leadership of peasants' and service organizations?" (*Kerala Kaumudi* 29 September 1998). Similarly, in the CPI, several women were demanding reservations, though the party leadership did not approve then (Erwer 2003: 220). Such resistance was quite palpable within the CPM as well, where male leaders often stressed the importance of 'merit' in assigning positions in party organizations (Erwer 2003: 221). The struggle seems very much alive in the present. As a woman leader who has worked hard to establish a women's branch in her locality noted, she argued successfully for it as a means to induct more women. However, the women's branch seems to be discussing more of AIDWA work and besides, they have been faulted for not maintaining enough secrecy. She continued:

> I am also a member of the Area Committee—the only woman in 22 members! ...This time I have demanded to the Secretary that we induct another woman into the Committee. If this doesn't happen, I have declared loud and clear, I will leave. Either induct one more woman, or let me leave! If the panchayat president is a woman, she should be in the AC as well. A woman who occupies such an important role in government should also have direct access to the party's local level decision-making body.

More serious, it appears, is the fact that the cooption of women into committees is often perceived as not one secured through a discourse of rights, but a handout from above. This was particularly pronounced in our interviews with women leaders in service sector organizations. A senior woman politician of the left who has displayed keen interest in gendering political parties through reserving positions for women in party committees pointed this out, "These days, the positions set apart for women inside political parties cannot be used to full advantage, precisely because they have been handed down to us...". Women's concerns and interests, she observed, are then too readily defined by the male party elite. The very real limits imposed by the overarching patriarchal control are very evident in many experiences that the more assertive of our interviewees shared with us. The patriarchal structures and hierarchy within the party relies upon generalized patriarchal norms to silence recalcitrant women. An AIDWA activist from central Kerala who was also a local committee member of the CPM recalled how she had been hounded out of the party by a hostile Area Committee Secretary. She had challenged him on several grounds including corruption and intolerance of difference in inner-party debate. The inner-party struggle seemed never-ending and she opted out:

> My family was fine with me coming home at two or three at night. The Area Secretary called my brother and told him, she is not in any activism; she's just gallivanting with men. I had to speak of this in the party branch... Then, in a case in which an SC girl had been cheated by a man, my party branch stood by the perpetrator, saying that there were more votes in his family. I had to really fight and managed to obtain a resolution, somewhat. But I felt terribly isolated and decided to leave the party. My father and brother were not happy at all with my decision.

Another AIDWA activist from north Kerala, who came across as an exceedingly outspoken woman, also pointed out that the articulate woman's presence on committees was always extremely precarious because her colleagues often regarded it as a favour she had received, for which women were expected to be grateful—and silent. An Area Committee member of the CPM, she admitted that though all the committee members were expected to be silent outside about discussions in committees, "... one has to speak openly about certain matters to one's husband. Otherwise, when other events happen and then we have to reveal many things all at the same time, he may be terribly shocked." This reveals the considerably vulnerable position of the woman-committee member: in order to prevent hostile elements within the party from taking advantage of patriarchal family norms through the husband, she is forced to share committee discussions with him; such disclosure is against party norms and affects her claim to be a diligent party worker.

The experiences of the woman quoted above—an extremely articulate person who does not conform to the reigning upper caste norms of femininity—clearly revealed the massive hurdles in the path of women who utilize their presence in party committees to further gender justice. She admitted that her position was quite precarious and that there were serious efforts to get her expelled, mainly in retaliation against her protests against male members' sexual exploitation of inexperienced women party workers:

> The fellow who had done this went scot-free because he was influential, but she complained to the higher committee ... I was accused of having trumped up this charge against him. It was so painful a charge that I really was totally restless for a whole year. The inquiry proved him guilty. If this fellow was of the other party, it would have been so much easier—we simply had to scream.

Nevertheless it was clear that this woman's non-adherence to feminine gentility was often strength than weakness. Even well-established successful women legislators of the CPM complained about sexual slander in their interviews with us and mentioned how they were left without means to hit back for "fear of prolonging the discussion." However, this particular woman leader, who is active in politics at the local level—refusing to be corralled in local governance, though she is a panchayat member—told us that her strategy was to be completely open—"...state the truth as the truth, and that will be the end of it. I take the straight route. 'Brothers,' I say, 'I am asking for your votes not because I want to sleep with any of you.'" She told us of an incident when she had to accompany a male member to an office in town. They were delayed and had to wait for a while. The man was a chain smoker and the smoke irritated her. So she proposed that they go to a movie to while away the time. This, she says, was reported back to the party committee and there was a huge scandal:

> I refused to lie. Why should I? The fellow [i.e. the man who accompanied her] is as brittle as a joss-stick, I said, are you all mad? By now they all know. I get into the bus, and if there is a seat vacant next to a man, I sit. Last time a religious leader, a Muslim man, was most offended. Why didn't you get a taxi, I asked him. This is public transport. I've paid for my ticket just like you. I will sit, even if it is Pinarayi Vijayan [the State Secretary of the CPM] in the next seat because I have paid my

fare just like him. Now everyone here knows, no scandal is going to work on me!

Such voices are rare. This activist warned us that her outspoken nature was irritating many powerful men and indeed, "...next time you come around, well, you may not find me in this position. But I am fighting, and I do have some support. All local men aren't bad, you see." However, the words of a senior party activist and district committee member, who is also an AIDWA activist seemed to indicate that women who reach the upper committees are relatively free of control. Known for her outspoken defence of women's strategic interests, she pointed out that this was possible only because she was a very senior activist and in the higher committees since long:

> Me, as the district secretary of the AIDWA, and xxx as the president, we intervene in most issues quite forcefully from a women's perspective. They don't dare tell us to be quiet. But the ones in lower committees, they aren't that stern... when we say that we are going to take up some issue or the other, they'll urge us on saying yes, women's morale needs to be boosted ... but the ones in the lower committees, they are intimidated and made to stay silent. They'll comply. If you want to fight an election, or bid for a position in a cooperative society, or even survive within the party, you need the support of the party leadership. They won't have the guts to defy what that leadership orders. In any case, the attitude is the same: women should take orders from men ... leaning upon something is easier than standing straight on your own two legs ...

Secondly, the dissociation with feminism does affect the ability of the AIDWA to politicize the women of poorer sections in local governance, who they have been organizing. Erwer quotes from her fieldwork in the 1990s, a senior woman leader of the AIDWA and the CPM claiming that members of the AIDWA are all from "party families and party people. Not one is independent." (2003: 262). However, this scene has changed quite drastically, with the large numbers of poor women of the Kudumbashree self-help groups who are certainly not all of 'party families', becoming members of the AIDWA. In many interviews, the boundaries between Kudumbashree and the AIDWA were almost imperceptible ("...Kudumbashree has been a great boon for us," remarked an AIDWA worker, a panchayat member from north Kerala, "Muslim women have been empowered. Earlier it was hard to find 10 women for a self-help group; now a 100 will readily come. AIDWA has received a big boost—so many micro-enterprises, mushroom farming, orchids, saree painting..."). But AIDWA organizers are also confronted with the fact that they have been asked to organize not women, but the ungovernable 'consumer', a concern that is voiced in many interviews. Having shorn 'feminism' off from their discourse, AIDWA organizers are left with scarce ideological resources to politicize these women. As a CPM woman legislator remarked, the work of organizing these women is simply not translating into durable support for the left. To quote her:

> To give you an example, a meeting was organized by the Thrissur District panchayat when Subhashini Ali made a visit. What a large number of women gathered! I myself was astounded seeing the photos. The District Panchayat president, Vishalakshi teacher, was a very capable president who conducted government and struggle equally well. The neighbourhood groups were highly encouraged and all benefits were delivered on time. So what? After the election—we didn't gain a single legislator to the State Assembly from Thrissur—all the seats were won by the UDF! They took the welfare and voted Congress! ...I thought Subhashini Ali had attracted the crowd. No, the ones who came have nothing of that sort. They are not interested in anything except the welfare benefit that can be secured and the economic gain that is forthcoming... that's all!

In response to our question about how AIDWA hopes to politicize these women, most activists had little to recommend, except ruing the consumerism of present times and arguing that these women should be encouraged into productive activities. One interviewee, a young Dalit AIDWA activist and panchayat president, however, pointed to another direction:

> See, why do workers come when we create unions? They join so that they can secure their needs through unions, right? How? Through fighting for their rights. But what rights can these women [of the Kudumbashree] claim? Nothing! The Kudumbashree is being kept alive through welfare distribution... they come for loans and grants, and when those dry up, they will all break up. But they too have issues, after all they are also working for the panchayat—carrying out panchayat activities—and also engaged in negotiations with banks and others!

Why not unionize the Kudumbashree women, she asked. However, she also felt that this was a direction the AIDWA was not likely to take because the men in the party were not really in support of it.

The Kerala AIDWA's rejection of feminism reveals a greater conservative streak compared with the CPM's position on women's induction into politics, or that of the National AIDWA.[5] Here the document titled 'Party's Perspectives on Women's Issues and Tasks' which was adopted in 2005 by the CPM's Central Committee is of particular interest. It reproduces the stereotype about 'feminism' that we encountered in our interviews in more sophisticated terms: "In contrast to current feminist theories, Marxism does not see patriarchy as an autonomous system, unconnected to the basic economic organization of a given society." (CPM 2005: 7). Nevertheless, in the later parts of the document, there is significant acceptance of insights and positions from feminist thought that does not rely upon an economic-deterministic Marxism. It argues that the social oppression of women must be given equal importance along with economic oppression and observes that "There was a tendency to underplay the oppression of women within the family sphere to dismiss it as a 'non-class issue' and one that is of concern only to 'bourgeois feminists'" (p. 20). The view that centralizes women's economic oppression is one "that fails to recognise the multi-dimensional oppression of women including of women from the basic classes. It does not appreciate the importance of struggles against the gamut of socially oppressive and anti-woman practices, and the need to project alternatives founded in the practice of democracy, equality, and the rule of the law." (p. 20). It also advises caution against the common view that women's issues are 'divisive', especially issues like domestic violence and dowry. The document also strongly criticises the "feudal" gender norms which it admits to be rampant among both men and women members and strongly recommends that these be removed from the everyday business of political work (p. 26). This is an interesting, if limited, appropriation of the feminist political charge, which first misrepresents 'feminism', so that 'true' and 'false' activism around women's issues may be distinguished, and that sponsored by the Party may be set up as the 'true' model.[6]

In comparison, the 'transformative' adaptation of feminism in the PPC and the Kerala AIDWA is far more limited. The Kerala AIDWA participates only in the stereotyping and rejection of 'feminism', and unlike this document, it does not absorb its radical charge—the critique of the bourgeois family that it advocates seems completely unheeded in the Kerala context.

Respectability and Political Work

As these efforts to induct women into committees and women's own strategies to gain visibility, if not influence, in high politics, unfold, earlier ideals of women's liberation through their participation in militant class struggle seem to be waning. This is evident in the contrast between the recent entrants—of the 1990s—into politics, and those who entered it in the mid-20th century decades, a difference palpable in both leftist and non-leftist parties. Leading women activists of the senior generation of the left have moved away towards mobilizing workers in other modes without necessarily moving out of the party. C.K. Sally, one of the most prominent senior activists of the CPI, perceived a striking change in political activism in recent years; she mentioned the loss of 'willingness to sacrifice' as the major perceptible change. This reflects in the waning of mass mobilization, which she felt, was irreversible. Her present work therefore is of organizing women mat weavers not into a trade union, but into self-help groups. She thus seeks an in-between space between mass mobilization and the new forms of association-making.

There is also a sharp division in how these women perceive of politics and the possibilities they see in it. Almost every interviewee from the older generation stressed the risk that they took while choosing a career of public-political activism—it was an act of defiance against family and community and often meant the loss of sources of security. It also meant the sacrifice of jobs or other kinds of individual goals, for the sake of the movement. [7] This sentiment was echoed by women of both the communist and the national movements. More recent entrants in both the left and the Congress, in contrast, do not often perceive politics as such a decisive break—they are second-generation—or even third-generation—members of political families and hence politics means the extension of family, in many ways. Women activists of both the CPM's (and the Congress's) students' organizations were clear that the question whether they would stay in politics or not can be answered only after marriage, since this depended on the views of their future husbands. "But I would like to marry someone who will allow me to be in politics, or at least in public activities," said a woman district-committee member of the CPM's student organization, echoing the words of her peers in the same organization and counterparts in the rival one who we spoke with. The stress on marriage and primary commitment to the family reflects the current social scenario in Kerala in which marriage remains the key channel for women's social membership (Kodoth 2008). There is also a clear perception of politics as a career which the future husband should sanction ("since family life will be very difficult for the woman politician if her husband did not cooperate", said the student leader quoted above) not a passion or a calling, to which one is drawn despite all odds, so evident in the words of the earlier generation.

Career too, is now hugely valued. A district-level woman leader of the SFI from north Kerala argued very forcefully that when "everything gets fast, we too have to get fast." This young woman valued the students' movement for the security it gave her ("Even if I am lost while travelling somewhere I don't have to worry. There will be a party office somewhere around! I can go and tell them of any problem—they regard me as their little sister!"). Nevertheless, she continued:

> Nobody respects those who engage in party work alone—such people are almost extinct. Today one must move ahead in politics also keeping in mind one's family, the Party, and one's future, also concern for a career. Otherwise we are sure to fail. That's for sure.

This attitude was condemned by a senior woman activist from the 1940s, who is at present a senior leader of both the CPM and the AIDWA. She admitted that attitudes such as the above were very pervasive among the new female entrants and was sharply critical of it:

> Many come with a clear material goal. Now the present structure of governance offers many opportunities and these women have an eye on those. Either a job or some opportunity through the avenues opened up through governance. Now, this is from their view that to take life forward, a job is necessary ... why can't they write the public service commission exams and gain entry through the proper way ... this is a sign of these times ...

Yet just how pervasive this feeling is was revealed in the words of another senior women activist from the 1950s, who related proudly her decision to give up a permanent and well-paying job for life as an activist, inspired by the legendary communist leader, A K Gopalan. However she ended her interview musing that "if it were now, I wouldn't have taken that decision. Those were the times. It looked so right then. Now I'd have needed the job."

An aspect of the earlier ideal of the militant woman activist that has been transformed in the present relates to the 'sartorial performance' of left activist-womanhood. The earlier generation, both communist and nationalist, favoured a style of dressing and self-presentation that conformed to upper caste norms of decency but remained strikingly austere, true to their chosen sacrificial mode of activism. Erwer's interviews with AIDWA leaders in the 1990s revealed the extent to which they located themselves within the terms of a cultural nationalism informed by the modernizing and reformist impulses identified widely with Kerala's social development achievements (2003: 251–2). The femininity privileged by this narrative did not challenge dominant representations of upper caste genteel femininity in Kerala that was shaped in and through early 20th century community and social reformisms. The dominant style of the present that emphasizes new elite female sartorial code that produces a specifically elite (and non-austere) 'secularized' upper-caste 'Malayalee female' is however criticised by a small minority of younger women activists. A younger AIDWA activist, earlier a very visible student leader, was outspoken in her criticism of this style, which she feels has become a norm:

> …all this emphasis on long hair, the cotton saree, the demure posture, soft voice … that's the style followed by xxx [refers to a prominent leader of the AIDWA in Kerala]. Why, they are all aping her! This style is so conformist and conservative—most men are delighted by it! I find the salwar-kameez much more convenient—and you know, senior AIDWA women have been telling me, you ought to wear the saree to be respectable, not the salwar!

Dilemmas of Feminist Politics in the 1990s

The first efforts to articulate an autonomous feminist politics in Kerala were in the 1980s, and women dissatisfied with both the dominant political society as well as with the new forms of politics in the new civil society of these times were involved in these efforts. Unlike the AIDWA which built its foundations on the leftist national-popular forged in Kerala in the mid-20th century, the autonomous women's movement here drew actively on the Indian feminist movement. The brief history of major women's groups also clearly reveals that these were marginal to both dominant political society and the emergent oppositional civil society of the 1980s. As mentioned before, the dominant left was intensely hostile to feminism. On the eve of the fourth conference of the Indian Women's Movements in 1990 at Kozhikode, a campaign was unleashed by the CPM's newspaper *Deshabhimani* which accused the conference of having received U.S. imperialist funding. This implied the workings of the 'imperialist hand' to destroy the left and let loose a furious string of accusations, which called feminists "sexual anarchists, destroyers of families, and American spies". The barrage of accusations, it appears, was successful in decimating the fledgling efforts in Kerala (Erwer 2003: 207). They were certainly perceived as a challenge to the dominant left for they struck at one of the pillars of the 'Kerala Model' and the sort of Malayalee national feeling it engendered: the claims of the 'high status' of Malayalee women, central to the narrative of the triumph of social development through leftist struggle in Kerala.

However, this was not the only challenge feminists faced: the new formations in civil society which were critical of leftist political society and sought to reinterpret left politics differently were also quite hostile. Many of the leading women activists had indeed broken with these movements in protest against their insensitivity to gender power and women's issues (for example, see Nayak and Dietrich 2002). Speaking with Erwer in the early 1990s, a leading feminist activist who had been part of the independent fish workers' movement noted that her first exposure to feminism was at a workshop organized by women's groups, of the autonomous women's movement at the national level, in the early 80s (2003: 192). She and several other women activists who entered the women's movement through the fish workers' movement told

Erwer that they were soon identified as 'feminists'—trouble-makers (2003: 194–5). However, feminists have been very small in numbers, though they have indeed been able to make their presence felt in Kerala's very active and diverse public sphere, a presence quite disproportionate to their numbers. The numbers were and are few: as Erwer notes, only seven women took part in the preparation meetings for the fourth UN Conference on Women in Beijing (1995), compared with fifty each from other states (2003: 226).

Nevertheless, the heightened interest in gender at both national and global levels in the 1990s seems to have benefited women's groups in Kerala. By the mid-1990s, the gender mainstreaming efforts were also on locally, through political decentralization and local planning. Women's groups formed the network of women's organizations, the Kerala Streevedi in 1996 and much emphasis was placed initially on respecting diversity, as the earlier brochures and pamphlets indicate. And crucially, the Streevedi sought to maintain clear distance from politics—in 2000, there was a debate on whether an elected co-convenor at the State level who was also an active member of the CPM, should be allowed to hold office, which culminated in the decision that office-bearers of the network should not be party workers (Erwer 2003: 234).

But in some ways, the transformation of the dominant left in the 1990s has also eased the pressure on women's groups, for example, on issues of funding. The greater openness of the dominant left towards external funding, for example, in the District Primary Education Programme, which received World Bank funding and the Asian Development Bank loan of 2002 (Raman 2010) also leaves it less able to voice moral outrage at women's groups which receive funds from external agencies. Also, the 'transformative articulation' of issues raised by feminists at the level of local governance required some participation of feminists at that level. While the distance between feminists and 'high politics' did widen through a series of confrontations between the two around cases of sexual violence in which high politicians were implicated (Devika and Kodoth 2001), feminists participated in local governance, mainly as gender experts and trainers.

This, however, has had serious consequences for feminist politics itself. These confrontations with 'high politics' seem to have trapped the feminist movement in Kerala in a certain conservative sexual politics which may well shade into right-wing positions. Sexual violence had been a dominant concern of feminist politics in Kerala since the 1990s (Chandrika 1998), and the sharpening of this concern in the late 1990s when feminist groups fought sex-rackets (Erwer 2003: 242–5) brought them considerable visibility and more acceptance. However, this did not challenge bourgeois sexual morality, nor did it allow for new alliances and dialogue. This did work against the broadening of alliances which would have strengthened Streevedi, despite its stated commitment to diversity and debate. This flaw came into the open when feminists had to encounter other forces that were pluralizing feminism in the 1990s, such as the mobilization of sex workers by NGOs in the late 1990s (Menon 2005; Devika 2006). The issue of sex workers' rights in Kerala led to an acrimonious debate in which the positions of leading feminists betrayed deep conservatism.

On the other hand, feminists were hardly able to influence the gender mainstreaming agenda in local governance at any depth. Their work as gender trainers has been largely marginal; their efforts to influence planning, too, have been relatively unsuccessful. Observers have noted that the State's appropriation of part of the feminist agenda may not always be entirely disempowering to women (Banaszak et. all 2003). Rather, they have urged feminists to treat the State as a "site of struggle" and not as evenly and irreversibly invested with male interests (Waylen 1998) and perceive of institutionalization as a process that lets dissidents air their claims and allows states to manage, rather than stifle, dissent. However, as Amy Elman points out, this does involve a loss of political charge to feminists: management of feminist dissent by the State can compromise the latter's ability to "launch a credible threat of disruption to "normal politics". This is indeed a serious loss—"Given that any movement's raison d'etre relies on its capacity for commotion, there is cause for concern, though not for alarm (Elman 2003: 97)

Upward Mobility in Political Parties: 'Merit' or Favour?

As it will be evident from Chapter 2, historically, women who aspired for the upper echelons of the party and public-political power could distance themselves from new elite norms of femininity to a considerable extent. Therefore, the women on the left who were inducted into the political-public were not expected to be shy of wielding public-political power, especially 'power over'. There is no doubt that this was a form of masculinism and required of female aspirants a certain 'un-gendering'. However politics was indeed a space in which 'un-gendered' women could occasionally seize power reserved for men, and their (undoubtedly partial) rejection of new elite feminine norms was even perceived sometimes as a heroic act (for instance, in the case of leading communist women like K R Gouri or Koothattukulam Mary). The numbers of such women have always been few and the 1990s has been no exception to this. There were a few women politicians who aspired for upward mobility in high politics, for example, the young (now ex) communist politician, Sindhu Joy Chakkungal, the first woman to become State President of the SFI in Kerala and very visible in student protests braving a great deal of police violence, and in fact, suffering serious physical injury (which often figures as a qualification for promotion in the rhetoric of high politics). Sindhu Joy herself was fielded twice as a candidate by the CPM, but in constituencies she had no chance of winning; she was bypassed in the recent nomi-nation to the Rajya Sabha seat as well. After being denied candidature in the State assembly elections in April 2011, Joy left the CPM and joined the Congress, complaining of unfair practices. Does this mean that greater conformity to new elite feminine norms is becoming a requirement for women to gain upward mobility in high politics as well?

Responding to our question whether this was merely a casual impression, a middle-level woman activist admitted that the party seemed to prefer "refined" women for candidates, defending this as a pragmatic measure given the rise of the moneyed middle-class in Kerala and their cultural clout:

> Women candidates should look educated and refined nowadays, and they should be well-behaved and cultured in their speech and gestures. Unfortunately, those qualities are lost when one gets used to shouting slogans and inquilaab in the middle of the road in the searing hot sun! This is the reason why many senior women activists, though they have sweated and toiled with party work, never get into the limelight these days!

However, another young woman, a very prominent student leader of the SFI of the 1990s felt that this might be more than a response to changing class power. She cited the context of the internal power struggles in the CPM of the 1990s to bolster her view. Young, highly individuated women were more numerous on college campuses by the 1990s according to her; however, they are not politicized:

> When I first entered college in 1991, girls were still very shy and reticent and made themselves most inconspicuous on campus. But by the time I left in 1999, they had changed much. By that time the desire to stand apart from the crowd was evident in most girls. Somehow or other ... through dressing or in some other way ... just to get noticed. This was true even of women from the basic class. The truth is that student organizations, including the SFI, failed to recognize this chance. That energy should have been redirected into the public and politicized. Girls remained steeped in apolitical ways. That's why women's numbers are growing in membership but they are not present really.

She was trying to sketch out the trajectory of gender politics in the SFI in the 1990s in which women leaders who showed signs of independent judgement were flatly denied opportunities for upward mobility in the internal hierarchy of the left. This she connected with the heightening of factionalism within the party: women who were less challenging of male dominance could portray themselves in feminine terms, and this now received additional value.[8] For men, promoting such women was one way of displaying their adherence to the progressive goals of the party, while continuing to enjoy the advantage of dominant new elite/secularized brahminical gender norms. As for the AIDWA, its straddling of both 'high politics' and 'local governance' does not break down those boundaries. Rather, a few top AIDWA leaders are 'promoted' up while the rest stay well-below in 'local governance'. The entry of some AIDWA women into 'high politics' also seems to have had no impact whatsoever on either diminishing the male-centredness of 'high politics', or alleviating the domination of 'high politics' over 'local governance'.

By and large, then, strategic opportunities continue to determine the chances of women politicians' upward mobility.[9] Upwardly-mobile women politicians in all parties, all the more, seek to utilize strategic opportunities to enter and establish themselves in high politics. The 'strategic opportunity' may vary—it could be a 'crisis', such as the sex scandals involving politicians in which many women politicians were either silent or preferred to take completely unjust positions alongside their male colleagues (as was seen with women politicians of the CPM and the Muslim League), or party factional wars (recently in the Congress, the BJP, the CPM), or communal agitation (such as the BJP communal mobilization at Marad, Kozhikode, in which women took a very visible public role). In such opportunities women openly declare their loyalty to new elite patriarchal norms to establish their claims as candidates capable of appeasing the majority.

Another, relatively recent, group of women who have been promoted by the CPM are the beneficiaries of the party's new efforts to build alliances with new challenges from marginalized groups or contain the influences of such movements. Women activists of these groups have often gained extraordinary upward mobility. This is particularly true of many women politicians from the Muslim and Adivasi communities—both groups in which the CPM has been struggling to establish influence. A CPM legislator, a Muslim woman, reminded us that the CPM was the only party that was willing to field a Muslim woman without reservation for women in the State legislature. She admitted that she was relatively quite junior in the party and perceived of her candidature as recognition for "having worked harder than men." Such relatively-faster mobility is also noticed for some prominent Adivasi women leaders as well. It is also worth noting that these are also the relatively rare instances of women who entered through the lower tiers of local governance and then gained mobility into high politics. The other women who are now legislators, who also have experience in local governance, tend to have considerable prior experience in the party's mass organizations and/or wield considerable influence through family connections within the party.

Despite the fact that women aspirants have sought their way up through multiple channels, the elections in the new millennium did not see the major political parties in Kerala field more women candidates.[10] Women entered the fray more frequently as candidates supported by the less influential parties or as independents: in the 2001 elections to the Kerala State assembly, out of the 52 female candidates (out of a total of 676 contestants for 140 seats), 20 were such. In the 2006 elections to the State assembly, the number of women candidates went up to 70 out of a total of 931, out of which 36 were either independents or representatives of minor parties. The numbers of winners fell from 9 in 2001 to 6 in the last State Assembly. The candidate list of the 2009 elections in Kerala to the Indian Parliament presented an even more dismal picture: 15 women candidates out of a total of 217, in which no one won and 9 out of 15 secured less than 1 per cent of the votes in their respective constituencies. Nor is there greater attention to women's issues within political agendas of progressive parties. Even though the CPM has made a much more explicit commitment to treating women's issues as central to the party's political agenda, there is the admission that such integration has not really taken off. The political-organizational report of the 19th Party Congress of the CPM (2008) admits that much headway has not been made with joint action by women's, youth, and student organizations on issues like dowry and female foeticide; it also points out that "there has to be much more discussion with the CITU on the issues of anganwadi workers and domestic workers." (2008: 112)

In the next chapter, we try to recount a fuller history of women's struggle for citizenship in Kerala, and it is hoped that it will remedy at least partially a major gap in our historical understanding of women's struggles here. Besides, we also hope to flesh out the intimations of the title of this book through this chapter. 'New lamps for old?', as is well-known, is from the tale of Alladin in the Arabian Nights. It is the cry of the evil magician dressed up as a street-vendor who persuades Alladin's princess to give him the old, smudged, but powerful Magic Lamp and instead, take a shiny but utterly powerless new lamp in exchange. The questions then, are these: the largesse of seats in local governance, are they the equivalent of the shiny toy of Alladin's tale, which we are being given? Toys that guarantee to keep us largely, as a group, out of 'high politics'?

Notes

1. Shirin Rai 1999 points out that such a motivation could also underlie the political parties' recent attention to women's representation in Indian politics. However, the higher realms still seem inaccessible as the stalemate over women's reservations for the Parliament continues while in local governance, space has been further extended through the sanctioning of 50 per cent of seats for women.
2. This, and almost all the observations below, are confirmed by Monica Erwer's earlier study of women's politics in Kerala in the 1990s (2003). Obviously, change has been slow to come.

3. By 'new elite' we refer to those social groups which wrested a great deal of advantage through the economic opportunities opened up by the integration of Malayalam-speaking areas in the late 20th century into the capitalist World System, the political opportunities provided by the modernizing princely states, and the wave of community reformism in the early 20th century. These include not just upper-caste communities but also the lower caste Ezhavas. The power of the new elite has rested on secularized caste and naturalized gender.

4. The anti-feminist posturing of CPM in Kerala goes right back to the 1970s when EMS Namboodiripad identified "bourgeois and petty-bourgeois feminism" as one of the "chief threats to the emancipation of women", arguing that it was only superficially different from "male chauvinism". Because it wore "radical" garb, it was "... therefore even more dangerous to the integration of the women's movement for their equality with men and the common movement of working people for ending all forms of pre-capitalist exploitation..." (Namboodiripad 1975: 7). On the eve of the all-India conference of the autonomous women's movement at Kozhikode in 1990, Susheela Gopalan, known as a top-level leader with deep interest in women's issues, warned women against joining these groups that were separatist and too small to achieve anything. Another senior woman leader Bhargavi Thankappan, went further, calling feminists 'vulgar feminists', who aspired for "free life". *The Hindu* 30 December 1990.

5. Erwer notes that the National AIDWA conceives of patriarchy as foisting triple oppression on women—and this indicates that the AIDWA is "...open to the fact that power relations are multiple ...which challenges the party's class analysis." (2003: 264). She points out several members have contributed to key AIDWA documents which spell out this position, but none of these authors is from the Kerala AIDWA. (2003: 264). Party documents of the CPM and CPI reveal that there has been a slow but discernible rise in the visibility of women's issues since 2000 (Erwer 2003: 272–5).

6. Susanne Kranz, interviewing a leader of the AIDWA in Delhi, notes that the AIDWA's position is not clear on either feminism or Marxism. She quotes this leader who appears to craft an argument for a feminism that is indigenous and different from

first-world feminism but is not really able to specify this clearly. And she seems anxious to avoid 'feminism' as a description of her political work. Kranz surmises that this may be because "It appears women are still fighting for acceptance within the party itself. The problem of non-acceptance might have to do with the general misapprehension between Marxism and feminism. ... Many Marxists typically argue that feminism is at best less important than class conflict and at worst divisive of the working class." (2008: 5). In other words the document is trying to forge a difficult compromise that would allow women in the CPM and its mass movement to articulate feminist politics without being stigmatized as 'feminists' while precisely perpetuating such stigma. Erwer's interview with Brinda Karat, one of the most powerful national leaders of the CPM also clearly reveals that the distancing from 'feminism' shrinks at the top-level leadership—Karat does not dismiss either feminism or the international women's movement as 'western' (2003: 265).

7. Erwer quotes a woman leader of the communist movement of the 1940s: "There was a difference I feel in the old times. Women were coming out; there were *real revolts* ... Now people have a comfortable life. So women prefer to follow the husband. The fighting mood is not there." Erwer 2003: 255.

8. Though it is usually argued that under-institutionalization of political parties is a key reason for the exclusion of women as members and candidates for public office (Norris 1993), the CPM remains a better-institutionalized party even now and therefore the paucity of women as members, office-bearers, and candidates has to be explained. Nevertheless, it is not easy to perceive of factionalism in the CPM as a recent phenomenon, though there can be little doubt that the present war is less concealed. There have been stories about hidden factional strife within the CPM for almost the whole of its history, and women leaders were also frequently reported to have been keen players. K R Gouri's exit from the CPM in the 1980s does confirm this. However, the better-institutionalization of the CPM has been a key reason why women leaders of the CPM were better protected than those of the Congress from accusations of corruption and sexual slander, which is however, waning with the rise of factionalism within the CPM.

9. Studies of women politicians and legislators in India reveal the strength of family connections in women's entry into politics, and the relatively easier access enjoyed by the middle-class or affluent groups (Bhatt 1995 ; Kumari and Dubey 1994). In a study of women legislators from Uttar Pradesh from 1952–1996 (Singh and Pundir 2002) the authors note that while the age of women legislators has gone down across the decades, the requirement that they be married and located in the domestic has not.

10. The situation is equally bleak at the central level. Deshpande (2004) points out that the percentage of women parliamentarians has been below 8 per cent, a trend that continued in the 2004 elections (p. 5433). In 2009, it rose marginally to 8.3 per cent (Kazi 2010: 18). See also, Randall (2006) who notes that the most vigorous champion of women's reservations in Parliament has been the CPM. While the number of women candidates it fielded in 2004 was not large, it was marginally better than other parties. Of all the candidates it fielded in the 2004 elections, 11.6 per cent were women, compared with 10. 8 per cent for the Congress, and 8.2 for the Bharatiya Janata Party, and 4.6 for the Bahujan Samaj Party party (p. 73).

2

Inhabiting Inhospitable Space

Introduction

For the citizens of Kerala, the road to the twenty-first century has been paved with several 'paradoxes' in politics and development. The 'gender paradox', it is now admitted, is one such (Erwer 2003). Stated very generally, the 'gender paradox' refers to "women's low participation in politics and the public sphere despite high human development" (Erwer 2003: 130). Of interest in this chapter is a 'sub-paradox' of the gender paradox: the fact that women's lack of access to political power was despite their formal admittance into the field of modern politics quite early. In other words, the franchise as well as the eligibility to sit in legislative bodies was achieved as early as the 1920s in the princely State of Travancore. At a time when women activists in British India were launching a campaign to extend the franchise to women who met the qualifying standards set for men –which was not completely successful (Forbes 2000: 100)—the electoral reforms in Travancore (1919) not only granted voters the right to elect members to the Travancore Legislative Council, but also lowered the franchise qualifications and extended it to women (Menon 1972: 60). Besides, in 1922, women were made eligible to sit in the popular body, the Sree Mulam Popular Assembly (Menon 1972: 63). The official chronicler of the freedom movement in Kerala notes in a footnote: "Even in England and the USA, women got enfranchisement only as a reward for their service rendered during the First World War" (Menon 1972: 63).

Indeed, the reasons advanced against extending the franchise to women in British India, that there was conservative, 'religious' opposition to the move, or the restrictions of the 'purdah', did not seem to apply to the women of Travancore, as this official chronicler proudly points out (Menon 1972: 60). Equally important, perhaps, was the fact that women of matrilineal communities, quite common in Malayalee society of those times, did freely own property, as was frequently pointed out in official writing from Travancore. As the *Travancore State Manual* claimed in 1940:

> Thus the women of Travancore enjoy rights and privileges which have not yet fallen to the lot of their sisters in other countries. In India, the right to inherit, irrespective of sex, according to the rules of natural relationship, and the right to unfettered enjoyment and alienation of property have still to be recognized. In England, until recently, it was impossible for a woman to hold property in her own right or to recover money from her debtor or even buy things for household use except as the implied agent of her husband. (Pillai 1940/1996: 44)

Nevertheless, women did not gain easy admittance into the domain of modern politics even as it was progressively broadened and considerably democratized in the course of the 20th century. In this chapter we briefly trace the history of women's participation in politics in Kerala and the debate around it through the vicissitudes of the 20th century.

'Women's Politics' becomes Impossible

From the early 20th century onwards, a clear divide is perceptible between the Travancore government and the newly-educated male elite active in the nascent civil society on the question of women's role in public politics. For the former, fostering women's presence in this new domain was linked to the Travancore kingdom's need to convince the British rulers of its 'progressiveness'. For the latter, however, public politics was the arena for the modernizing communities of Travancore to compete for resources and make demands for rights upon the State. Advancing the interests of women as a separate group was read as undermining the internal unity that communities required in these contests.[1]

Thus, as far as the modern educated new elites in late 19th century Malayalee society was concerned, 'politics' was delineated, early enough, as a terrain unfit for women, in early discourses on modern gender ideals in Kerala. The first Malayalam magazine for women, *Keraleeya Sugunabodhini* (1892), stated this at the outset:

> We will publish nothing related to politics. Principles of physiology, entertaining tales, writings that energise the moral conscience, stories, Womanly Duty, the science of cookery, biographies of ideal women, the history of nations, book-reviews and other such enlightening topics will be published... (Raghavan 1985: 141)

This was also the case in Malabar, where the newly educated male elite discussed a range of issues pertaining to the public and the private, especially matrilineal family and inheritance. The well-known novel *Indulekha* authored by O Chandu Menon (1889/1991) emerged from, and was an intervention in, such debates. Perhaps it is no coincidence that it is precisely the two topics shunned by the *Sugunabodhini*, religion and politics, which figure in the all-male discussions in *Indulekha*. In the novel, both these discussions are conducted in a place far away from the community, region, and the wrangling of domestic relationships. Early attempts by women to organize associations were not treated kindly. In Travancore, the efforts of Chellamma Raman Thampi to form a women's association in Thiruvananthapuram in the early 20th century were greeted with contempt by the educated male elite, and its founder was lampooned mercilessly by the well-known novelist C. V. Raman Pillai in a farce, *Kuruppillakkalari* (Pillai 1973). However, by the 1920s, the scene had obviously changed. The pressure put on the Travancore government by women's associations, journals like *The Mahila* (Saradamoni 1999: 132–33), and individual publicists, was enormous.

This was to a certain extent, a contrast to medieval notions of rulership in Kerala, in which political power in the major Swaroopams—the ruling houses—was not necessarily the preserve of men. For example, in the royal house of Attingal, senior women ruled in their own right. In this *Swaroopam*, the oldest woman held the senior position (*moopu*) and was referred to as 'Rani' by the Dutch and the English, and remained so until Attingal *Swaroopam* was annexed to the emergent kingdom of Travancore in 1730 by Marthanda Varma, the founder of modern Travancore (Nair 2005: 161). According to Dutch sources, the Attingal Rani had enjoyed full control over a territory of some 15,000 acres, and negotiated independently with the English and the Dutch in the 17th century (Nair 2000: 138). Umayamma Rani of Attingal (1678–c.1700), who allowed the English East India Company to set up their first factory at Anjengo, is remembered for her spirited moves in the power struggles of the *Swaroopams*. The Dutch commander Van Rheede mentions her to have been a major player in the succession intrigues of the times and a powerful ruler.[2] The Ranis of Attingal could also reign as full potentates in the neighbouring *Swaroopams* of Deshinganad and Trippappur in the absence of male heirs; the Ranis did hold power there (Nair 2005: 120; Nair 2000: 144). However, from the 18th century onward, the possibility of female members succeeding to full political power steadily receded, even though Travancore was ruled in the early years of British dominance (early 19th century) by two 'Regent-princesses', Gauri Lakshmy Bai, and Gauri Parvathy Bai (Menon 1878/1983). Attempts to reassert the right of the senior female member of the Attingal royal house to succeed to the throne and undivided power after the demise of Maharajah Sree Mulam Tirunal in 1924 were unsuccessful, and the Rani was treated as a regent only (Editorials, *Malayala Manorama* 30 August 1924; 2 September 1924) And interestingly, in *Umakeralam* (1913), a fictional poetic rendering of the 18th century intrigues in south Kerala by a major Malayalam poet of early 20th century, Ulloor S. Parameswara Iyer, Umayamma Rani figures as not the "young Amazon" that the Dutch commander Van Rheede encountered but as a passive and pure tragic maternal heroine!

While women were deemed less fit for politics in the emergent new elite-dominated public sphere, the government of Travancore, drawing upon the image of 'progressive Travancore' and the 'Model State' (Pillai 1940), and the fame of Travancore's women who were projected as 'more advanced' than their sisters elsewhere, conceded women's political rights more easily. Nomination was used to secure a spokesperson for a class or community which would otherwise go unrepresented (Kooiman 1995: 2128)—and Women and the 'Depressed Classes' (Dalits) gained access, most frequently, through nomination. In the 1920s, women were nominated to represent 'Women' in legislative bodies in Travancore and Cochin. Tottaikkattu Madhavi Amma was nominated to the Cochin Legislative Council in 1924 and Dr Mary Punnen Lukose, as Head of the Medical Department, to the Sree Mulam Popular Assembly—the appointment of the latter was described as 'Feminism in Travancore' by the *Madras Mail* (*Malayala Manorama* 4 October 1924). Appeals began to be made to 'Women' as a separate group in the political public which could make legitimate claims to the State. The demand that 'Women' must be treated as a separate constituency with representation proportional to the numbers of voters along with other constituencies such as 'Industry and Commerce', 'Jews', or 'Planters', was made in Kochi in 1925 (*Malayala Manorama* 28 March 1925). In the wake of the elections to the Sree Mulam Popular Assembly in Travancore in 1927, the women's magazine *Vanitakusumam* published an editorial, which exhorted the Travancore government to nominate a woman to represent 'Women'. Specifically, the editorial identified 'women' as a separate and legitimate political constituency, responsible for pressurising the government for fulfilment of their demands.

> The work of intrepid struggle and sound bargaining to secure legitimate rights is the responsibility of women themselves. Any complacency on their part, induced by the hope that the government—which has displayed its conservatism in all affairs—will concede their rights and authority in full recognition of justice, and the mood of these times, would be most foolish. In all the countries of the world, women have won their freedom and rights only through agitation. These struggles have made it evident that 'only the infant that cries will have milk'... In these circumstances, all we can say to the women of Travancore is this: You must not while away anymore time in idle slumber. Open your eyes to the realities of the world, ascertain your needs, recognize your rights, and move to secure them. (Editorial, *Vanitakusumam* 1927–28/2005: 109–11)

Elizabeth Kuruvila was nominated to represent 'Women' and in 1931, five women from five communities—representing Nair, Ezhava, Araya, Syrian Christian, and Protestant Christian—were nominated (Mrs G Sankara Pillai, Meenakshi, Rudrani, Anna Chandy, and Penina Moses). It is interesting to note that the political field in Travancore of these decades was characterised by extreme competition between communities (Chiriyankandathu 1993). However the nomination of these five women was frequently interpreted not so much as heralding the entry of women into the political field, as an apolitical gesture towards 'communal unity'. Women as a group, it was hinted, are less disposed towards competitive politics than men. Such a reading echoes, for instance, in the comment made by a leading women's magazine, *The Mahila*: "If anyone was to opine that womankind as a community, being different from men, needed to speak only their needs and grievances and not make communal arguments, then one cannot but agree that this is a superior thought." ('Panchavarnakkilikalo?', *The Mahila* 1931, 3–9)

In 1932, women and men were given equal rights in voting and membership in the Council as part of electoral reform; two women were to be nominated to the Council. The rising numbers of women, mostly of the dominant communities, in higher education and increasingly, in government employment, was the backdrop against which the demands of 'Women' were framed and advanced. In 1928, women graduates in Travancore formed the 'Travancore Lady Graduates' Association' with the intention of pressurising the government to end their unemployment through reservations (Devika 2007: 181). A furious debate on government jobs for women was raging in Travancore then, with prominent male intellectuals like T K Velu Pillai arguing against granting government employment to women, and first-generation feminists like Anna Chandy vigorously contesting him (Chandy 1929/2005: 113–129). The first-generation feminists also explicitly connected women's political rights with other kinds of rights, for instance, legal and reproductive rights, an effort especially palpable in the writings of Anna Chandy. In 1935, for instance, Chandy was arguing for legal equality of women with men, which meant not just the removal of the exemption of women from the death penalty in Travancore law, but also the removal of brutish anti-woman provisions in the Travancore Civil Procedure such as the husband's right to file for restoration of conjugal rights (Chandy 1935: 23–4). In the same year, she was also arguing for women's reproductive rights as body rights in a discussion on contraception:

> Many of our sister-Malayalees have property rights; voting rights; employment and honours [from the state]; financial independence. But how many have control over their own bodies? How many women have been condemned to the depths of the feelings of inferiority because of the foolish idea that the woman's body is but an instrument for the pleasure of men? (Chandy 1935a: 14–5)

Such advocates of women's interests in the public, when they entered legislative bodies, worked actively to champion these causes. By 1932, nominated women legislators worked together to demand proportional reservation in government jobs, for better educational facilities and concessions, livelihood and better health care. Importantly, proposed marriage restrictions on employed women were stoutly challenged by members nominated to represent 'Women'.[3] Indeed, it is interesting to see that the mandate to represent 'Women' was crucial here: when, in 1925, Dr Mary Punnen Lukose defended marriage restrictions on nurses as a 'practical consideration' in 1931, T Narayani Amma, who represented 'Women', attacked the same restriction for Assistant Inspectresses of Girls' Schools, pointing out that domestic responsibilities affected both married and unmarried women (Devika 2007: 198–99). Women legislators were also quick to oppose the argument that women did not deserve reservations and special claims because they had not yet transformed themselves into a publicly-mobilized, homogenous group. They pointed out that the lack of public voice of any group cannot be cited to deny them social justice—making special provisions in employment, health care, and other government allocations for women was a matter of social justice, irrespective of whether or not they mobilized as a homogenous group in public. Responding to Dr N Kunjan Pillai in the discussion in the Sree Mulam Popular Assembly on the proposals of the report of the Public Service Recruitment Committee, T Narayani Amma made this clear, arguing for the proportional representation for women in public services:

> I am sorry that I cannot go all the way ... [with the] view that the communal principle should not be recognized in the matter of appointments of women in the public service. I grant that there is no communal spirit among women. But taking things as they are, I cannot see how, without some sort of communal representation for women, the claims of qualified candidates can be satisfactorily met. (*Proceedings of the Sree Mulam Popular Assembly* Vol. II, 1935: 950)

Though their pleas were not often effective, women in the legislatures of Travancore and Cochin continued to make demands on the State on behalf of women both inside and outside legislative bodies. Anna Chandy, who was also the editor of the women's periodical *Shreemati*, which campaigned for women's status as a distinct group with claims on the State, criticised the disadvantages to women arising from male-centred legal and administrative machinery, the male-centredness in emergent popular politics, and actively debated with proponents for community reservation, who argued that caste inequalities were primary.[4] In 1940, T Narayani Amma successfully introduced and piloted legislation in the Sree Mulam Popular Assembly, the Travancore Child Marriage Restraint Act, the first in the history of that institution.[5] In the Cochin Legislative Assembly, a woman-member, Mrs Joshua, introduced a Dowry Prohibition Bill, which was staunchly opposed by the male members. In many of these debates the tension between 'Women' and other categories came to the fore. For example, in the discussion on the Cochin Child Marriage Restraint Act in the Cochin Legislative Council in 1940, the question whether a member representing 'Women' could rightfully introduce a bill affecting the lives of mostly Brahmin women was hotly debated. Many male members, including those who took an explicitly anti-caste stance, argued that the Bill should not be passed without the consent of Tamil Brahmin members, as they were most affected. However, Thankamma G Menon, who introduced the Bill, argued that as the representative of 'Women' she had the right to introduce the bill since the deleterious effects of child marriage were borne largely by women, and since most women approved of the provisions of the bill.[6]

Yet these efforts were not really encouraged by emergent forces that would shape the democratic politics of the future. Indeed, on the eve of the first universal adult franchise elections of 1944 in Travancore, T N Kalyanikutty Amma noted with regret that the prominent parties did not support women candidates wholeheartedly, and therefore their collective strength as voters did not count much. She continued:

> Therefore we feel that no matter how unquestionable the personal greatness of women candidates for general seats may be, the support they receive is questionable. Even though the percentage of women voters is decisive enough to ensure victory for women candidates, we do not feel that they have been given enough information and encouragement beforehand to vote exclusively for women candidates... it must be said that the scarcity of vehicles and petrol since early this year and the relative vastness of general constituencies have made women candidates' election campaigns almost impossible. (Amma 1944: 102–4)

She then went to articulate her own critique of the recent electoral reforms, which did not concede special electorates to women.[7] The article ends with requests to the Maharajah and the Dewan to increase the numbers of women nominees in the legislatures to represent 'Women' so that proportional representation will be attained. It appears that Kalyani Amma's position maintains the same distance from both the emergent 'progressive' forces in the field of politics, and the entrenched powers. She placed her trust in the Travancore monarchy, which had persistently used nomination as a means for ensuring the representation of 'Women' in legislative bodies.[8]

The 1940s was of course a period of intense agitation against the establishment in Travancore. No wonder, then, that the advocates of the rights of 'Women' were identified, with much hostility, as 'westernized' (because of their insistence that political rights were as important to women as social rights) or 'elitist' (because they were generally distant from the working classes and marginalized communities), and closer to the oppressive Dewan (because the establishment seemingly favoured their demands) by community movements, nationalists and communists.[9] Many first-generation feminists pegged their arguments in favour of full citizenship not on sexual sameness but on sexual complementarity (see for instance, Amma 1924/2005: 75–82) and indeed, on

'Indian Womanhood'.[10] But they still looked suspect in their unwillingness to merge the interests of 'Women' with the nationalist or communist cause. Added to this was the insistence on separate electorates for women by many first-generation feminists well into the 1940s. These are perhaps important reasons why they were wiped completely off the historical record unlike their peers in other parts of India whose memory has survived slightly better.

In hindsight, T N Kalyanikkutty Amma's plea for increased numbers of nominated women-members may not be read as support for the anti-democratic regime in Travancore. Yet in the context of heightening anti-colonial struggle, it could be read only as a 'sectarian' or 'self-seeking' demand that continued to repose faith in the oppressive monarchy in Travancore. Further, the communists' adherence to the primacy of class struggle—as well as their commitment to masculinist Leninist vanguardism—led them to devalue the 'politics of presence' demanded by women intellectuals. This ensured that such a demand would never be repeated in post-independence Malayalee society until the late 1980s and 1990s.

In short, the defence of 'women's interests' ended up doubly denied its claim to be a politics. Many of its advocates saw in it a non-divisive agenda uniting all women around specific 'feminine' capacities that would direct women into non-competitive, non-political endeavours of social service. Its opponents perceived it as an unnecessary and divisive distraction that could weaken what they perceived to be proper politics—community competition over resources, nationalism, or communism. This fear arose from the perception that the demands made on behalf of 'Women' implied a militant politicization of women, the shaping of an independent women's movement. And indeed, this seemed evident in some writing by women in the 1940s—for example in the exhortation by A. Bhageeraty Amma, a first-class Magistrate in Thiruvananthapuram, that "Women must get into the legislatures and Municipal Councils in large numbers to fight for their rights...Let us organize a women's movement and chalk out our programme for progress in all directions. It is man, not God that tells you that you are intended for the kitchen. " (Amma 1944: 208)

Women in Politics and Community Organizations

By the 1940s, the advocates of 'Women' as a politicized group were pitted against the dominant forces in the political field—powerful new elite communities, and the nationalist and communist movements. Even women who contested on behalf of 'Women' did not escape community dynamics. When Anna Chandy entered politics in 1931, she earned the hostility of the Nair newspaper, the *Malayalarajyam* which attacked her, and the support of the Christian *Nazrani Deepika* which defended her as a "Syrian Christian candidate."[11] In the 1930s, women in community movements sought to both represent their collective interests within their communities and represent their communities in the political public. There were instances in which women of specific communities raised sharp criticisms of the failures of their respective movements to address women's rights within communities— and indeed faced threats of violence for their outspoken stance.[12] Women were really not very visible in the leadership of community movements, but were prominent in representing the 'social' aspects of community reformism— thus K. Chinnamma was revered by Nair reformers for her philanthropic and educational efforts; Devaki Narikkatiri, Parvati Nenminimangalam, and Arya Pallam were respected as reformers of social and family arrangements among the Malayala Brahmins. These women often took pains to emphasize that they represented not just the community, but also, often more prominently, its women. For instance, in 1937, K. Devaki Antarjanam, a Malayala Brahmin woman nominated to the Sree Mulam Popular Assembly, thanked the Travancore government for nominating her, who represented not just a member of the Nambutiri community, which she claimed "has been suffering from superstition and evil customs", but the "*antarjanasamudaayam* [the community of Malayala Brahmin women], which suffers all the misery that afflicts the Nambutiri community".[13] The evocation of women's 'special interests' continued to be raised even within the nationalist struggle for example, during the Civil Disobedience in Malabar, the Provincial Women's Conference held at Vadagara in 1931 resolved to form the Kerala Mahila Desa Sevika Sangh to carry on constructive work in night schools and handicraft training for women. But it also reiterated the commitment to gaining proportional representation for women in all government jobs (Menon 1972: 232–33).

However when women were invited to participate in political struggle by community movements, the nationalist movement, and the communists, they were often asked to abandon their championing of 'women's interests' and carry forward the virtues of the 'domestic' and 'social'. This seems to have been a shift: in an earlier struggle in Travancore, the nationalist-led anti-caste Vaikam Satyagraha (1924), a call issued (by a woman satyagrahi) to 'the Hindu women of Kerala' had emphasized the struggle against caste as also a struggle on behalf of 'Women'—since caste restrictions denied many women their basic civil rights (Kalyani 1924/2005: 83–5). However, in the exhortations to women to join the 'Abstention Movement' led by three major communities against the Dewan of Travancore in the 1930s, women's agency in public was clearly tied to community self-assertion, and in particularly gendered ways. In a public appeal to women of the "Christian, Ezhava, and Muslim communities" to actively enter the 'Abstention Movement' in Travancore organized by the Christian, Muslim and Ezhava communities against the reforms announced in 1932 in Travancore (Kooiman 1995), the author, K Gomathy, wrote:

> Women are not to sit in their kitchens. They have the responsibility to render service alongside the men for the country and the community. Even our educated sisters do not recognize this need

and act appropriately; the shame that results falls, indirectly, on the whole of Womanhood.

The early 1930s, it has been argued, was also the period in which Gandhi reformulated his thoughts on 'Womanhood', displacing his notion of non-violent courage on to the idealized woman, not as a solution to women's marginalization in society, but as a response to larger developments in nationalist politics, such as the widening communal gap (Mondal 2002). As many have pointed out, the Gandhian argument for the entry of women into politics was conditional on their active participation in the anti-colonial struggle, and their presence in the public was pinned on to rendering service to the nation—in either instance, women's issues were to remain strictly subordinate to nationalist goals (Katrak 1992; Mondal 2002). Nevertheless, women's commitment to the nation/community was privileged, in situations of active conflict, over their domestic responsibilities.

In Malabar, where the national movement was stronger and women were active participants in Civil Disobedience, nationalist women did raise objections to politics centred on women's rights. Equally, they were urged to set aside their immediate domestic concerns for the sake of the nation. E. Narayanikutty Amma, a leading Congress activist in Malabar, wrote during Civil Disobedience, "The times in which we were required to speak of women's education or independence are almost gone. What is the duty of educated women today? ... They have a duty towards the Nation, which is as, or more, important than their duty towards their home." (Amma 1930/2005: 131). Women's early participation in the national movement in Malabar had been through khadi and spinning, and in the wake of Civil Disobedience, large numbers of women joined it, including many modern educated women from Cochin (Menon 1972: 182–233). They were also urged to participate in public protests. Such participation of women was solicited from the earliest days, for instance, in a call issued by T C Kochukutty

Amma in the *Mathrubhumi* which exhorted women to leave aside their daily cares to join the protest, and take part in the Gandhian constructive programme (Menon 1972: 182). But within the nationalist movement, the emphasis continued to be equally on constructive work, located in the 'social', rather than in the political, and indeed, several prominent women in the national movement—Mukkappuzha Kartyayani Amma, A V Kuttimalu Amma, E Narayanikutty Amma —combined political work with Gandhian social work.

However in Travancore, politics seemed to be more open to women. In the anti-Dewan struggle in Travancore in which Akkamma Cheriyan and Anne Mascrene played a prominent role, the association of women with constructive social work was not so strong, and the possibility of women becoming leaders in their own right seems to have been conceded. Akkamma Cheriyan and Annie Mascrene were not merely involved in public protests and jailed several times between the late 1930s and mid-40s, but were recognized as full-fledged leaders and activists in their own right (Cheriyan 1977; Varkey 1948/1999: 91–96). The radical literary author Ponkummam Varkey described Anne Mascrene, a leading woman politician in Travancore thus:

> She has made many sacrifices for the State Congress. She will not admit any feminine weakness in her courageous love for the nation. She equals Man in courage while taking up troubles and burdens for the sake of the nation. She has given a large portion of her blessed youth in jail. It is not during peace, but during times of conflict that she shines in her services.... To any foolish ones who try to suggest to her, we have raised you up, she will reply: not you, my service alone will raise me high. (Varkey 1948/1999: 94)

In other words, a woman's bid for positions of leadership and power was not necessarily dismissed. Many non-Left women politicians continued to actively bid for power in the post-independence scene and claim distance from the domestic as well as constructive social work. The writings of

Annie Thayyil, a prominent woman politician of the 1950s, illustrate this in striking terms. In both her autobiography and other writings, she claims to have left behind the trappings of domesticity to a significant degree. Nor does she shy away from baring her ambitions—as evident in her detailed account of playing the political game in which she was outclassed by Leela Damodara Menon, another leading Congresswoman (Thayyil 1954) (from Malabar). Congresswomen attempted to draw on the Gandhian legacy of the ideal of Woman the Renunciator (Patel 2000)— which allowed them to claim greater mobility and greater ideological resources against sexual slander provoked by their crossing of gendered boundaries. They did believe that being 'ungendered' and desexualized also exempted them from the community's surveillance—though this confidence was to deteriorate rapidly. In a recently published interview, the veteran Congresswoman Padmam S Menon reminiscences that women activists [of the Congress] in the 1940s and 50s enjoyed considerably higher mobility, moved around on bicycles, and were much freer of social shackles (*Mathrubhumi Weekly*, June 14, 2008: 14–5). Women politicians of this generation did not take recourse in claims of chaste wifehood when faced with slander; nor do they cite understanding husbands or families. Rather, they drew upon their gender-neutral public identity and asserted their equal status in their parties to shield themselves against the sexual double norm. Confident that they had indeed excluded threatening sexuality, women politicians often rebutted the allegations they faced as inevitable 'thorns' in the path towards political power. As Mary Thomas Alakappilli declared at the inauguration of the women's wing of the Congress in Muvattupuzha in 1954: "Those of us who ventured into organizational work were greeted with many bitter experiences. But we are still moving forward. We know well that political work is no bed of roses here."(*Nazrani Deepika*, 8 June 1954: .2). Secondly, these women considered themselves spared of the obligation of projecting themselves as essentially domestic beings. Referring to her lack of domesticity, Thayyil declared: "[M]y books are my children…Your children will die. Mine will not. I will not allow people to forget me." Thayyil 1954: 38).

Nevertheless, the tide turned almost completely against women activists in the post-independence scenario, with several male politicians voicing open hostility towards their attempts to transform themselves into politicians within a field of competitive democratic politics. The Gandhian argument could not aid women in their transition from activists to politicians; while activism was associated with 'pure service and sacrifice', the politician's role was associated with ambition and strategic action, which fell outside the ideal public role of nationalist activism. Politics in Travancore lost all aura of idealism in the immediate post-independence years, and intense competition over power-sharing between different groups broke out. In this context, it was easy to declare women who stayed on in politics 'unfeminine'.

In fact in these years, both women's bid for leadership and their claim to represent the interests of women as a group were severely curtailed, and all the more so when the former was tied to the latter. This is particularly evident in the post-independence political career of Akkamma Cheriyan, who had emerged as one of the most prominent leaders of the Congress in the south and who was returned unopposed in Travancore's first adult-franchise elections of 1948 (Jeffrey 2003 : 47–9). Indeed, among Akkamma's many differences with her male colleagues in the Congress was her rejection of the latter's view that women in Kerala had played a relatively minor role in the national movement compared to their peers in the north, and hence deserved much less representation in the legislature (Jeffrey 2003: 47–8). The trials that she faced in the 1950s revealed the challenges that lay ahead for women in politics, now that the heady days of anti-British and anti-Dewan public protests were over. She resigned from the Congress in 1952 protesting against opportunism. In the elections of 1952, there was not a single woman in the Congress candidates list. The senior Congress leader from

Travancore, Kumbalathu Sanku Pillai, declared in 1951, in response to Jawaharlal Nehru's call to include more women in the Congress candidate list:

> Here [the common practice is that] once a woman is married, even if she is educated, the burden of her life is borne by her husband with a sense of moral duty. The woman usually stays at home and rules the man.... Women haven't yet felt that they have been enslaved by men, and that it is necessary to enter into competition with them in politics.... In this land where women enjoy all kinds of rights with a moral understanding, and where women rule their husbands as wives, no harm is to be expected from women not attending Legislative Assemblies. (*Nazrani Deepika*, 29 October, 1951: 1)

Some of the arguments used by the *Travancore State Manual* in 1940 to justify women's "prominent part in public life" in Travancore were being deployed to the opposite end here (Pillai 1940: 43). These statements endorse different understandings of women's rights to participate in public political life. For T K Velu Pillai, author of the *Manual*, (in the earlier quote) these rights follow on other rights, especially 'market rights' and the right to education. For Sanku Pillai (in the above quote), implicitly, political rights lead to the latter kinds of rights—and since women already possess the latter, they do not apparently require political rights. Equally important is the surfacing of gender as a consideration for the requirement or non-requirement of political rights. Velu Pillai's account does not find women's participation in political life inimical to their gender; Sanku Pillai, however, emphasizes "moral understanding"—gendered 'appropriately' for both men and women—that leads these groups to respectively require and not require political rights. In other words, 'properly gendered women' do not demand political rights, and conversely, those women who indeed demand these, are, by implication, lacking in gender.

Several Congresswomen protested openly at Sanku Pillai's statement, notably, A V Kuttimalu Amma, who pointed at the discrepancy between the Congress candidate list in Travancore-Cochin and the achievements of the women of Travancore in public affairs and education.[14] Since the Congress was closely allied with community interests and organizations, women in community politics were no less vocal in their condemnation of the exclusion of women from political power by the male elites in the Congress and the powerful communities. For instance, in 1951, Mariyakutty John who delivered the presidential address at women's meeting held in connection with the All-Kerala Catholic Conference's Annual Meeting at Aluva endorsed conservative Catholic positions on family roles and contraception—and then voiced her deep protest at the exclusion of women from the government, against the denial of a ministerial berth for Mascrene, arguing that these were the reasons for the "sorry state" in which the Congress government of Travancore-Cochin found itself. She also presented a detailed review of the international situation and exhorted women to develop an interest in public affairs (*Nazrani Deepika*, 15 May 1951: 2). Akkamma Cheriyan, however, defied the Congress by contesting the 1953 by-election as an independent candidate supported by all the opposition parties—the most prominent of these, was of course, the Communist party. She was deluged by slander—something that Anna Chandy had faced as a candidate over two decades back—and powerful communities made concerted efforts to campaign against her (Jeffrey 2003: 48). Akkamma appealed explicitly to women, and in her campaign meetings she highlighted the Congress' neglect of women in their candidate list. She won 43 per cent of the votes but lost the election.

For Congresswomen, a second chance to enter the public as 'Guardians of Inner Space' emerged in the context of the mass anticommunist agitation of the late 1950s, the 'Liberation Struggle', widely projected by the Congress and the Catholic Church as one to protect the sanctity of the community and the 'purity' of public life. A very large number of women, of all classes, participated in massive street-protests. According to the supporters of the 'Liberation Struggle', the numbers of women who participated in street protests and were jailed exceeded 40,000 (Gopalakrishnan 1994). Women's hope for entry into the higher levels of the political field seems to have been highly raised by this. Prominent women who had led street-protests formed an organization called the 'Akhila Kerala Vanitaasangham' at Kochi at a meeting presided by Dr O K Madhavi Amma, which aimed at the forthcoming elections in August 1959, and a branch was formed at Kozhikode in September 1959. At the Kozhikode meeting, participants declared their determination to stay in politics and discussed their strategies in the forthcoming elections (*Nazrani Deepika* 22 August 1959). These hopes, however, did not bloom into actual gains. They were not endorsed by the party and community leadership. Even as these efforts were on, the *Deepika* wrote an editorial which congratulated the women who were active in the struggle, but also gently shooed them into safely apolitical 'social work' (*Nazrani Deepika*, 20 September, 2 August 1959). However, articulate women politicians in the non-left like Annie Thayyil, continued to claim their rightful share of political power, now that their influence in politics was indisputable.[15] But in the State elections of 1960, the Congress fielded just 7 women out of a total of 80 candidates, out of which 5 won (out of a total of 63 winners from the Congress).[16]

In any case, as mentioned earlier, the protection accorded by Gandhian ideals was waning rapidly: Padmam Menon herself was embroiled in a massive 'morals controversy' in the 1960s, involving a prominent leader of the Congress, P T Chacko. The controversy was over Chacko's alleged involvement with a 'mystery' woman, and finally, Padmam's name was made public. She revealed in the interview that though she was not the 'mystery woman', she had permitted the Congress to use her name to protect Chacko's reputation, because she was confident that as a well-known woman activist, she would not be suspect in the eyes of the public. But her expectation—

that as an 'ungendered' politician she would not have to face sexual allegations—was clearly misplaced. Such was the barrage of accusations that she finally left public life. However, (the very few) women who could overcome such hurdles could well rise to political heights—those who were skilled at alliance building, manoeuvre and negotiation.[17] Leela Damodara Menon, active in politics since the 1950s, was one of the most successful women politicians in Kerala. She was a member of the Kerala State Assembly twice and of the Rajya Sabha once, and also the Indian representative at the UN. Her rise in Kerala's political scene was, as she herself put it, in the shadow of her husband, the powerful Congressman Damodara Menon. Through her political career, Leela switched political loyalties, and effectively steered herself to power, attaining prominence in the debates around the first communist ministry's education bill (Leiten 1977)—and earned for herself in many quarters the name of a ruthless player, something reserved for male politicians. But the stigma against the 'unfeminine'—the 'street woman'— was always the underbelly of such success. Indeed Congress woman politicians in Kerala, especially those who entered the scene in the post-independence decades have had to face precisely such stigma ever since. This was confirmed in most of our interviews with women active in contemporary Congress politics. One of them, a district-level leader, even remarked that such stigmatizing was commonly encouraged by men in the Congress against their women colleagues if they were assertive and popular.

Under such circumstances, a great many women activists of the national movement retreated into constructive social and developmental work.[18] This was a national pattern (Roy 2002: 491). This retreat was thus often perceived of as a rejection of selfish and worldly power games. Swarnakumari Menon, active in the nationalist movement in Malabar remarked to an interviewer that in her understanding of 'politics', "There was no personal interest like becoming a minister, or getting hold of power. Politics had only one meaning and that was 'get rid of the British and attain Swaraj'" (Anandi 2001: 46). B Hridyakumari, the noted educationist, who hails from a well-known nationalist family in Travancore and is presently a prominent opponent of campus politics (of all hues), in an interview, touched upon the criticism of politics as a 'space of self-seeking and corruption', when she explained her decision not to enter politics in the 1950s:

> I was indeed keen to enter politics in the 1940s; I had decided to study history precisely for that. Most of my father's friends expected me to become a politician—in school I had led nationalist protests in the late 1930s and 40s. But it was not to be. The fire and the joy of winning independence were followed by a terrible flood of selfishness and infighting, which tore all the illusions from me. I then chose to become a teacher, where I felt I could mould minds away from the ugliness of politics.

The legacy of 'ungendered activism' also seems to have been available to leading women activists in the communist movement who would become politicians. By the 1940s, the communist party had a handful of active and articulate women, some with extraordinary leadership abilities. Of these, K R Gouri Amma was the most prominent—in the 1948 elections in Travancore, she lost, but won 35 per cent of the vote (Jeffrey 2003: 214). Also, communist activism provided many opportunities for women to overcome the strictures imposed on new elite women and take up active public roles. Koothattukulam Mary, an early communist, who was the secretary of the Communist Party during the difficult years of 1948–49 when it was banned, went underground to avoid arrest but continued to be active dressed up like a man (Josephine 2007: 21–22). Further, domestic expectations informed the communist ideal of the woman activist not directly but in mostly surreptitious ways and inevitably linked with her presence as a transformative force, opening up the space of the traditional family. The heroine of the communist novelist Cherukad Govinda Pisharady's widely-read novel

Muthassi, Nani 'Mistress', brings thrift, order, hygiene, and neatness to her husband's home, besides being a capable schoolteacher and disciplined, fearless political activist (Cherukad 1989). The former is no less important as the latter in the construction of Nani 'Mistress' as the heroine of those times. However, given that the family was also reimagined in communist discourse as an institution open to the public—and so Nani's successes at home could be read as proof of her rationalizing abilities—the communist woman politician could also claim to be 'ungendered'—pursuing the same goals and methods as her male peers. KR Gouri reiterated this in a recent interview: asked whether she faced any problems as a woman in the legislative assembly, she replied: "Such problems must have been there. I haven't even thought as a woman. So what to do?" (Sahadevan 2007: 77–8). Similarly, Koothattukulam Mary argues that she felt nothing strange about sharing her existence underground with men—"there was only the thought of being a comrade. Of revolution." (Josephine 2007: 23).

Women on the left who entered party activism and legislative politics as the wives of prominent politicians had to project themselves not as possessing abilities gathered from being good wives or mothers, but as dedicated political activists engaged in radical mass mobilization. K R Gouri, arguably the most successful, powerful, and popular woman politician in Kerala's left, was a successful woman leader who could play both the roles (equally masculine) of the militant protestor outside the government, and of the decisive administrator inside. She often raised questions on behalf of women in the Kerala Legislative Assembly—which were sometimes quite against the gender-wisdom of the times—for example, when she publicly proclaimed that women did not really need four months of maternity leave, and that women should be appointed as bus-conductors, an exclusively male job (*Nazrani Deepika* 28 January 1959: 3). She, however, refused to be projected as primarily their representative.

Susheela Gopalan's entry into the public was heavily mediated by the prestige of her husband, A K Gopalan. However, despite being cast widely in the role of the 'comrade's wife', she did not feel obliged to couch her political ambitions and aspirations in public-altruistic terms; her later fame rested entirely on her work to further the agenda of communist mass mobilization. She was instrumental in advancing the cause of women workers within the trade union movement (Meera 1983), and especially in bringing into their fold women hitherto unrecognized as 'workers', specifically, anganwadi workers.

It may be remembered that claiming distance from the domestic involved submitting to sexual puritanism—and this was relevant for both women and men (Devika 2007). Women, however, may have taken the greater burden of assuring the sexual purity of the political party they belonged to. On the Congress side, in the 1940s, nationalist women's demands for women's suffrage increasingly leaned upon the linking of "the home and motherhood with the emergent national state [which] represented women as citizens with equal rights who would exercise virtuous responsibilities." (Pearson 2004: 214) Clearly this involved pinning women's citizenship to the disciplining of female sexuality into procreative familial roles. Padmam S Menon [above], O K Madhavi Amma and others drew upon the earlier Gandhian legacy of the asexual Woman the Renunciator. Sexuality came to be excluded in the communist vision of women's political activism as well, though women's association with 'Indian tradition' did not apply here. In communist discourse, evident, for example, in Cherukad Govinda Pisharady's novels, as well as in many autobiographies of early communists, the exclusion of the body and the enthroning of the mind was an integral part of the self-disciplining of the 'ideal comrade'. This involved, for women, the careful adherence to 'respectable and self-restrained', though not always domestic, ways in their social interaction.

This was a common thread that bound many of the first-generation feminists with the first-generation women politicians. Women who appeared to be risking their 'purity' voluntarily were silenced in the discourses of both. For instance, in 1929, the nominated representative of women in the Cochin Legislative Council was vociferously arguing that women should be prohibited from the production and sale of liquor (*Malayala Manorama*, 4 August, 9 August 1929). Examining the interventions of women legislators in post-Independence legislatures in Kerala, a direct continuity is often evident in the early years, especially when the female body is involved. Interestingly, K R Gouri, whose views on maternity leave and women's work were iconoclastic as far as the ideal of sexual complementarity by now entrenched among the new elite was concerned (*Nazrani Deepika* 28 January 1959: 3), took a position less so when the female body was at the centre of the discussion. In 1953, she argued in the Travancore-Cochin legislature that a greater number of seats should be made available to women in the medical college because women needed more gynaecologists to care for them in pregnancy and childbirth. And only female doctors could, apparently, serve this end, "...surely more lady doctors are necessary".[19]

The Question of Women's Full Citizenship

Akkamma Cheriyan's defeat was the defeat of a campaign strategy that projected women's equal rights within formal political institutions, and appealed directly to women voters. She had forcefully challenged the separation between 'being a woman' and 'being a politician' throughout her campaign, arguing in effect that one was not opposed to the other, in the face of tremendous opposition. Henceforth, women in politics would strictly decouple the two identities—and pursue exactly the same goals and methods as the male politicians. Exclusive appeals to gender difference, of either the conservative or the modern kind, seemed invalid and defeating. Women politicians were keen to establish that they addressed and represented women and men alike (or at least that their championing of women's causes did not outweigh their 'general' commitments). Thus they rarely challenged the instrumentalization of women's citizenship to other ends.

If the concern for women's full citizenship was to be overshadowed by concerns about authentic tradition, national and community interests in Congress politics, the problematic of class set the terms of understanding women's citizenship in the communist movement. As evident from the earlier discussion, both avoided problematizing the new consensus on gender roles shaped by late 19th and early 20th century community and social reformisms in Kerala. Contemporary women commentators did notice this. In a sharp critique that appeared in 1955, a woman commentator in the popular journal *Kaumudi*, Kumari Saraswati, pointed out that the neither communist nor Congress efforts to organize women were really geared towards addressing women's issues. Referring to the communist women's organization as *Vanitamunnani* (women's front), she says:

> [Their meetings] are usually presided over by an active woman worker of the Party. The speakers will all be staunch Communists or fresh converts. The speeches will mostly be about the oppressive measures of the government or the exploitation of the capitalist. I won't say that no word is uttered about women. A few words will be said, rarely. A few words of advice: "Women should not stay inside their homes like in the old. [They should] boldly enter, alongside Man, in their husband's and brother's struggles... [You] must oppose the capitalist's wicked acts..." ... More than burning questions that affect women, it is the issues in politics that get addressed...
>
> ...The official activists of the Women's Front are usually young women who are in close contact with the Party. The men are usually in charge of its propaganda work. This Women's Front actively participates in the Party's strikes and organizes demonstrations. They also hold public functions on occasions like the May Day... In other words, this Women's Front is merely

the women's wing of a political party. It cannot resolve any of women's problems because its growth is dependent on male support and protection... [This Front can represent] only those who have blind or half-faith in the Communist Party. There are also many who are active in it because they believe that it is beneficial to work for a party that is adhered to and loved by the husband, brothers, or lover... (Saraswati 1955: 39–40)

But the Congress' women's organization is no better. Saraswati launches a scathing critique of the *Vanitasangham* (women's association), which, according to her, is full of educated elite women who think that the reformist solutions about social work, cottage industry and good housewifery dished out in their meetings actually address women's issues: "Are these the burning issues that trouble Woman? Does she not have no other problems? But they have no eyes to see those. They are not brave enough to challenge Man who rules the land." (ibid.: 40–41). Saraswati rues the reduction of women's issues to 'social issues' resolvable through social development—and the formation of 'women's associations' supported by the government in the 1950s—pointing out that this does not move even a finger against male dominance in all walks of life (ibid: 41). This not only excludes women from politics, it refuses to recognize male dominance as an outcome of patriarchal power, and hence as an issue for public politics.

Communist women and Non-elite women

The legacy of 'ungendered activism' does not seem to have been shared by all women activists in the communist movement alike. Indeed, this was enjoyed only by a few who reached the top leadership—either through a combination of political work and privileges available to the new elite woman (like K R Gouri) or through a combination of political work, new elite privilege, and family connections (Susheela Gopalan). Below this level, there were women political organizers from the lower middle class who were active labour organizers often shouldering key responsibilities in the turbulent decade of the 1940s when many male leaders were arrested or underground. One such notable instance was that of K Meenakshi, one of the earliest women trade union organizers in Travancore. Meenakshi worked in the Travancore Coir Factory Workers' Union in Alappuzha and played a key role in organizing women's factory committees and ward committees after the general strike of the coir workers in 1938. In the early 1940s, the women's factory committees took up a range of issues on behalf of women workers, from arbitrary dismissal to securing maternity benefits, successfully (Velayudhan 1999: 508). She also took over the position of General Secretary of the union when the male leaders went underground, representing the union in the tripartite conference called by the Labour Commissioner and organizing strikes and picketing against retrenchment (ibid.: 507–8). However, after the crisis was over, the men who returned took over key positions.

These women, however, seem to have been subjected to a greater degree of gender disciplining; many of them seem to have retained strongly gendered notions of women's role in the political public in the course of their activism. This is clearly evident from the biographical and autobiographical accounts of the women who entered communist politics through marriage, or were later integrated into the movement through marriage to communist activists.[20] Take, for instance, K Devayani's *Chorayum Kanneerum Nanajna Vazhikal* (1983), which, arguably, is the most popular of autobiographical texts produced by woman activists in Kerala's communist movement. Clearly, it belongs to that genre which G Arunima calls "biographies of marriages" (2005). A long list of well-known autobiographies of new elite women in Kerala, from B Kalyani Amma to Rosy Thomas, belong to this genre, which is of women writing about their marriages to famous men, yet asserting themselves in the process. The early chapters are about Devayani's growing interest in the public, and soon, her induction into the communist movement. But midway through the narrative, she marries a communist activist, later a prominent leader, A V Kunhambu. Suddenly, in the midst of an eager account of her growth as a public activist, an identity that she had ostensibly left behind—that of the new-elite woman marked by her gendered 'essence'—surfaces and takes over. She reveals that she was so enamoured of public life that she would have stayed unmarried, but Kunhambu proposed and reminded her that "it often happens that rumours circulate when unmarried girls engage freely in public activism" (p. 20). From then on, the narrative of self-development is inextricably intertwined with the 'biography of the marriage', and indeed, in the end, when Devayani quits public life to care for a growing family, the two merge into one. As in many other 'biographies of marriage', this one, too, ends with A V Kunhambu's demise, and contains a longish biographical appendix on him.

Through her long account of life under police repression in Karivallur in Malabar, Devayani narrates a time in which the public/domestic distinction was violently suspended by the State, in which women's suffering and sacrifice could be counted as equally political as communist public activism. But the suffering brought about by State repression does not efface gender. Rather, the suspension of the public/domestic division by the State is seen as producing particularly gendered forms of suffering, mainly of women stripped of the cultural and social respectability of socially-sanctioned domesticity, which exposed them to police violence. Thus while declaring the different suffering of women and children a valid and important aspect of the political suffering that the communists underwent, the text subtly relies upon and reinforces gender difference understood within dominant terms. And notably, the restoration of the public/domestic divide is central to her characterization of the post-repression political peace. Not only is the questioning of the public/domestic divide usually associated with the left more or less absent in her account, the faith that certain features of the public may be assimilated smoothly into the domestic without upsetting the divide is palpable. At the end of her story, in her narration of the 'domestic peace' finally achieved, she says: "Even today we [the family] meet together from time to time to engage in debate over ideas, for the perfection of the ideal of the communist family he so desired." (p. 65). In her account of communist women's political work in Travancore, Meera Velayudhan mentions that women activists had to be accompanied by trusted male activists—this probably qualifies the claims about the mobility of women activists made by some activists of that generation to Erwer (2003: 184). Mobility, it appears, did increase, so long as the women were appropriately escorted (Velayudhan 1984: 71–2).

Perhaps more poignant is the fact that when such middle-level women labour organizers entered the wider political scene from trade union activism without the comforting shadow of male relatives, the cost they had to pay was much more. In 1948 P K Mary and P J Aleymma, both organizers of factory committees in the Alappuzha district, were chosen along with two male comrades to stage a spectacular protest in the newly-built Legislative Assembly building in Thiruvananthapuram. They raised slogans against the oppressive Dewan of Travancore and his 'American-Model Constitution' for an independent Travancore within the Legislative Assembly, and demanded responsible government and universal adult franchise, and were arrested. "This unusual act also produced some negative consequences. When the women were released, the husband of Mary drove her out of his house. The emotional shock affected her health and she died shortly afterwards." (Meera 1983: 56).

As for working-class women, precisely because the discourse on 'Women' in mid-20th century Kerala was powerfully undergirded by new elite gender norms, the largely lower caste working class women figured in it only as junior participants who were to be reformed by new elite women. Communist trade unions, however, organized them in the 30s, 40s, and 50s as members of the proletariat endowed with the historical agency attributed to the working class by Marxism. These women often were a very visible presence in trade union struggles and those of agricultural labourers; they also held public protests by themselves (Lindberg 2001). There are many stories of how women provided care, food, shelter, and protection to communist leaders in hiding; how they facilitated secret communications, and so on. Anna Lindberg's interviews with the first generation of unionized women workers of the cashew industry reveals the enormous extent of their participation in left trade union struggles. She notes that despite the fact that women workers were indeed the majority participants in these struggles even leftist newspaper reports of strikes from the 1960s to the 80s do not convey this. If the perspective of the Communist Party of India's newspaper, *Janayugam*, may be treated as representing the general leftist discourse (as Lindberg does), the shift towards treating women workers as not fully workers but more as 'housewives' appears evident (Lindberg 2001: 274). She notes that for newspaper reports of the 1940s, it was the participation of men in strikes that was remarkable (for the workers were often largely women), but in the later decades, it became the reverse. She remarks:

> It appears from these accounts that, in spite of the greater numerical presence of women in the factories, they had become less prone to take an active role in trade unions as time went on. To continually stress that "women, too, participated" is to express the uniqueness of this experience...in the reports of demonstrations and other trade union activities, the *true* activists, the women, have been portrayed as the exceptions, the Others. Males—in most instances not even cashew workers—have been regarded as the true activists. (p. 275–6)

Lindberg's account carefully traces a process of 'effeminization' of the woman worker through which she was relegated to the domestic sphere and subjected to new elite forms of femininity, effectively removing her from the public and politics. The rights demanded on behalf of women workers, thus, tended to be maternity rights and other such demands that eased the woman worker's double responsibility, but affirmed her status as 'secondary earner'. Lindberg's powerful account of the emergence of the 'family wage' discourse within trade union discourse which approved of higher wages for men and subsumed women under the 'secondary earner' category is revealing indeed (pp. 178–214). Other accounts, too, note the disempowered status of women workers in Kerala even when they were in a majority. T K Oommen's study of the militant agricultural workers' struggles in Kuttanad region in the late 1960s notes that the despite the fact that women constituted 60 per cent of the membership of the agricultural workers' union of the CPM, and not less than 40 per cent of other unions in the region, they were completely absent in the leadership. He writes: "Paradoxically, no women occupied any office in any of the unions, even at the lowest level and no union had yet seriously put forward and consistently pursued the demand for parity of wages between male and female labourers" (Oommen 1985: 156–7).

This appears to have been a regression from the 1940s. The 1940s offered glimmers of hope, and it appeared as though the interests and needs of working class women would be integral to the demands raised by the workers' movement. The fact that there were more women in the leadership of the trade unions in Travancore in the 1940s, for example, K Meenakshi among the coir workers, may be important here. In 1943, the question of equal wages for women and men was raised in the Travancore Coir Factory Workers' Union, and the union was willing to settle for a lower wage in return for a uniform rate (Velayudhan 1999: 508). These years also saw the formation of factory committees for women and efforts to link left trade unionism with women's organization outside the factory—K Meenakshi was the leader of both the union and the women's organization, the Ambalappuzha Taluk Mahila Sangham (1943). As is clear from Oommen's account, these efforts petered out into insignificance progressively in the post-independence decades.

In the 1960s, dominant left mobilization was questioned from within the projection of Naxalite radicalism as 'truly radical' left politics in Kerala. In this case, the challenge was from within a highly masculinized politics. Not surprisingly, the Naxalite intervention in Kerala was largely a dispute about the nature of 'truly radical left politics' between men. Though women were certainly involved in such political work, barring a few, like Mandakini Narayanan, (who has been promptly recuperated as a maternal figure) and K Ajitha, who later went on to carve space for feminist politics and a few others who were active in cultural forums, the Naxalite movement produced no prominent women public or political activists. Though it idealized the radical political public for both men and women, it did not produce a critique of the conditions that prevented women from accessing it on equal terms. In fact, the sacrificial idealism of the Naxalite movement demanded certain 'purity' from dedicated cadres which appeared to render questions of gender inequality irrelevant. In any case, the question of gender was quite firmly subsumed under the question of class in the Naxalite ideological horizon— and women's wings of radical left groups which are now part of the political mainstream continue to follow this line even now.

In other words, by the end of the 1960s, the handful of new elite women who entered the upper echelons of politics and power could still claim some space through a fragile 'ungendering', while their working-class and lower-middle-class counterparts remained outside power despite their visible presence in militant struggles in the streets. The possibility of representing 'Women' as a distinct group waned in the political sphere; it was relegated to the social. The articulation of 'women's issues' was in strictly gendered terms—as Lindberg points out in her analysis of the wage-fixing negotiations of the 50s and 60s, in which factory owners, government officials, and trade union leaders were all convinced of the secondary status of women's workers and of the wisdom of the family wage (Lindberg 2001). This was questioned only in the 1980s.

Women and the Oppositional Civil Society: the 1980s

The divide between idealistic public mobilization and oppor-
tunistic political manoeuvre seems to have widened within the
mainstream left further around the 1980s—a period which
saw strong challenge to the hegemony of the ideologies of the
organized left from the oppositional civil society in Kerala,
but also one in which the middle-class began to assert itself.
Three developments of this decade are important for our pur-
poses. First, several women moved from the dominant left
parties' trade unions and mass organizations to more 'flexible'
platforms. Secondly, subaltern women, especially the women
of coastal communities in southern Kerala, entered public
struggle outside the mainstream political parties—in the
oppositional civil society, represented by the independent
fishworkers' movement, fighting the depredations of capital
on the coast (Nayak and Dietrich 2000). Thirdly, feminist
groups emerged in the late 1980s, later than in other parts of
India, as this was a part of this new oppositional civil society
(Erwer 2003). These developments were not unconnected;
indeed, the reverse would be true, and women who entered
public activism in this decade frequently moved between the
spaces opened by these strands.

The movement of middle-class women on the left from party
forums to the more flexible KSSP was not really a result of the
politicization of gender issues at least to begin with, though
the latter did clearly influence it especially towards the end
of the 1980s when women activists within the KSSP began to
take an interest in feminism. The civil social space of the KSSP
which they moved into was perceived, at least initially, not
as a renewed political space, but as a pedagogic one. It also
held out the promise of a new universalistic public activism,
that of 'development'. 'Development activism' was perceived
as distinctly different from its precursor, social work. 'Social
work' carried the stigma of association with the 'society
lady'—the stereotyped upper-class woman for whom 'charity
work' was a mere excuse for philandering. This figure had

emerged in the 1930s itself, in humour magazines that attacked the first-generation feminists. It migrated into leftist cultural discourse (the women who participated in the 'Liberation Struggle' were widely dismissed by leftist commentators as *kocchammamaar* (fine little ladies), (Gopalakrishnan 1994: 188) and continued to be lampooned mercilessly in popular discourse during a period of left hegemony. 'Development activism' (*vikasana pravarthanam*) carried no such stigma; nor was it exclusive to women. It was gendered only insofar as its practices were to be civil—conducted with civility—unlike the militant and sometimes law-breaking practices of political society. However, the middle-class educated woman socialised in new elite gender values was indeed advantaged in this domain of civility and could claim active agency and visibility there—since she was identified precisely as the bearer of civility.

In their interviews with us, such women who migrated to the KSSP justified their decision to move to other platforms as a way of getting away from 'corrupt' politics. They clearly found the civility of KSSP more conducive and this space appeared more hospitable to them. A well known KSSP member from Thrissur, active since the 1980s and very prominent in People's Planning, remarked thus in an interview:

> There were many like us who are interested in social activism... [KSSP] held out an opportunity to us. What it offered was not mere political activism. We organized women around issues of health and education and did what we can. [This activism] was not ideological but practical. It could attract women and ordinary people. Most importantly, it offered a platform for learning and teaching—changing society through knowledge.

Nevertheless, women's issues were raised in the KSSP in the mid-1980s and the interventions were now more complex than the efforts to raise the numbers of female members. There was more systematic effort to address the question of patriarchal restrictions on women's active presence in the public now (Erwer 2003: 197). However, the interest of these women activists seems to have been in a pedagogic role within the new space of civil public activism—the question as it appeared to them seems to have been whether women's citizenship may be secured through a new culture of learning without violently disrupting but gradually eroding patriarchal social arrangements, especially the modern conjugal family.

However, women entered the KSSP in larger numbers not at the height of its thrust against women's second-rate citizenship—during 1987—but in its Total Literacy Campaign in 1990, in which gender issues were certainly not central: 18,000 women took part in it as activists and teachers (Erwer 2003: 199). The brief effort to question reformist gender values in the late 1980s seems to have receded later. Monica Erwer, who interviewed women leaders in the KSSP in the 1990s remarks that they did have a consensus by then that "the struggle for women's liberation had to be along with the men, as part of the whole struggle. Further, it was recognized that gender issues need to be raised in every area of activity and not left alone as entirely a responsibility of women" (Erwer 2003: 198). On the one hand, this seems to be an effort to reinterpret the familiar position of the left on the women's question, which viewed women's efforts to work independently towards a politicised collective identity as a divisive enterprise. Therefore the demand that women's issues should be treated as a 'general' question, and not as representing a group interest. Interestingly, this was the dominant way in which a large majority of our interviewees made sense of the notion of 'gender'. And very often, they posed it against 'feminism', which was understood as a narrow and undesirable group interest. On the other hand, this conciliatory position was tied to high faith in the power of pedagogy. Erwer notes that the women leaders clearly indicated in their interviews with her that literacy activism attracted many women because it did not demand the breach of new elite gender norms and respectability, and indeed, built on them (ibid.: 200). This seems to have been carried into the post-literacy campaign women's groups, called Samata, which were intended to train women to utilise opportunities that were to emerge in political decentralization (Erwer 2003: 200–1). While the KSSP aspired to be a bridge connecting the AIDWA with the feminist groups/ideas (Erwer 2003: 298–300), it ultimately ended up as a space in which feminist political goals and strategies were recast in non-threatening moulds so that they could be readily re-appropriated by the dominant left parties in the discourse of the PPC in the mid-1990s.

The second development of interest in the 1980s was the possibility of the re-politicisation of women workers through the independent fish workers' movement and organizations like the SEWA Kerala. The women fish vendors' struggles were particularly prominent. Historically, the impoverished coastal communities in Kerala have been counted among the 'outliers' of Kerala's well-known success story in social development; they have also been among the least politicized. But it was they who offered the first organized resistance to certain aspects of economic exploitation that would later grow to predatory proportions in the late 90s and after. The fish workers' movement on the coast strongly resisted mechanised trawling demanding protection from their State of their right to survival (Dietrich and Nayak 2002). After offering resistance to moneylenders in the 1970s, the fisher folk in south Kerala launched a major struggle in 1981, demanding the banning of trawling during the monsoon months—which culminated in the breaking away of a group of activists from church-sponsored activism to form the independent union, the Kerala Swatantra Matsya Thozilali Union (KSMTU) in 1983. The continuing struggle saw the participation of several nuns especially Sr. Philomene Mary and Sr. Alice who undertook fasts in protest against the inaction of the government. As early as 1979–80, women fish vendors had taken to the street demanding the use of public transport to take their produce to the market and had learned the ropes of public protest by then; they also began to resist aggressive male merchants and tax collectors (ibid.: 133–4). Fish worker women became a very visible presence in the fish workers' movement and began to assert their demands within the union—and by the end of the 1980s, an unofficial grouping, the 'Coastal Women's Front', the *Teeradesha Mahila Vedi* (TMV), became active in women's struggles in the state (ibid. : 136).

Thus in many ways, the fish worker women's activism clearly raised a model of women's participation in politics and the public significantly different from that of the new elite women. Demands were raised by the TMV on behalf of 'Women', but without reference to a femininity informed by new elite gender norms. In other words these women had not yet been 'effeminized' (Lindberg 2001: 338). It is not that these women were entirely free of new elite values—indeed not, since the Catholic Church exerts enormous influence on coastal communities especially in south Kerala. Nevertheless, they put up active resistance to the male leadership's efforts to keep them in their place—and their strategies appear to have been quite like those of the early women in the communist movement and labour unions (Erwer 2003: 135).

The report by Gabriel Dietrich and Nalini Nayak (quoted above) was submitted in 1990 (it was published only in 2002, though). Nearly twenty years later, both the shape and the content of activism among the women who formed the base of the TMV seems to have changed considerably. Recent research on the coast notes that the women's groups that formed the units of the TMW are now overwhelmed by micro-credit centred self-help groups of women which are clearly tied to new elite domestic ideals and gender norms. Fieldwork done in 1996 revealed that the economic condition of women fish workers in south Kerala had not improved; indeed the burden of dowry seems to have worsened (Samuel 2007). Women have steadily coped with challenges in the market, devising new strategies to deal with the heavily patriarchal odds stacked against them (Hapke 2001). Nevertheless, the spread of the new self-help and micro-credit centered State welfare which carries the halo of new elite respectability (by raising the possibility of earning an income from within the vicinity of the home and gaining social presence without crossing community norms or physical boundaries) which young women on the coast have taken advantage of has apparently correlates with the displacement of a discourse of *avakasam* (rights) with that of *aanukoolyam* (welfare benefit/handout) as the desired end of struggle with the State, as recent research notes.[21] There is indeed a huge difference between these:

> The language of rights has a politically normative subject whose fundamental sense of "natural" justice includes the right to challenge the state, to wage a struggle against the state, and to question entrenched relations of power that the state represents. In contrast, the language of handouts denotes a subject that is fundamentally ambiguous about its political position as to whether it is within or without the state's realms of power even as it is uncertain about its own power to wage a struggle to secure the handout. (CDS 2008: 159–60)

The third significant development of the 1980s was the emergence of feminist groups, later than in other parts of the country, which has been discussed in the preceding chapter. Not surprisingly, feminists seem to have differed quite drastically with the women politicians in their understandings of power. The latter tended to stress 'power over' as the empowering dimensions of political participation which would enable all other forms of power; while they do not dismiss or devalue 'power over', our feminist interviewees ascribed equal value to the generation of collective power through the coming together of women in public politics. This came up quite strikingly in the words of a feminist activist from Alappuzha who had tried to actively support K R Gouri in her bid to challenge the CPM after her expulsion from the party in 1994. She was among the many civil social activists who flocked to the new political organization—the Janadhipatya Samrakshana Samiti—that Gouri had floated after her exit. Interestingly, the feminist involvement in this effort marks perhaps the most serious effort in Kerala to transform women's presence in politics into substantive representation by feminists. She recollects:

...[We] had tried to view Gouri Amma's issue as, indeed, a woman's issue. I was never close to her but became close after she formed her new party... in the early phase, it held out the possibility of a third front. All those who felt that a different politics was necessary flocked around it—Dalits, women, all others. We were all inspired by the prospects of a political party headed by a woman ... but that's not how it took shape. We were insistent that this new party led by a woman should have a woman-centred perspective. We were against holding meetings and committees at night [which would be difficult for women to attend]. But things worked out in such a way that I was soon convinced that just having a woman at the helm will not lead to a woman-friendly perspective ...

The differences between her and Gouri were most clearly revealed over the manner in which the latter sought to exercise her power, which were unacceptable to those who dreamt of recasting politics in new, non-hierarchical ways:

... And then, she called me and announced that she had made me the District Secretary of the party's women's wing. I can't take it, I said, if she just built some kind of shelter and made me its office-bearer ...

A Story of Closures?

This chapter has traced a long story, from the early 20th century to its last decade. In one sense, it is a story of closures, specifically, of two kinds—of the effacement of the possibility of politicizing 'Women' as a specific social group, and of the exclusion of women from the political public. No wonder, then, that the 73rd and 74th Amendments of the Indian Constitution appeared to hold the possibility of reversing these trends. The reservation of 33 per cent seats in the local bodies for women seemed to support the conception of women as a specific social group with special interests and eligible for a distinct share in the pie of state power at the local level; in that sense it also appeared to hold the possibility of women entering the political public.

These hopes notwithstanding, the preceding discussion indicates that by the end of the 1980s, the specific shape of the gendered governance that was to emerge in the mid-1990s through the PPC had already firmed up in the 'civil' space of the KSSP. It was to be informed by a specific version of liberal feminism that emphasized the automatic-liberatory effects of women's participation in political and economic institutions. Meanwhile, women's presence in State-wide politics and in the higher tiers within political parties continued to be poor.[22]

Reflecting on whether the model of the 'ungendered' woman politician was really a 'magic lamp' (albeit an old and soiled one) through which women could gain entry into the world of political power, one cannot help concluding that it was not really so. No doubt, the magic was real. But, in the first place, Masculinism was often the genie in the lamp, which shaped the fortune and the life of the woman who summoned it up. As is evident from the discussion above, masculinism not only separated women leaders from 'Women' in the collective sense, but also ensured that the very presence of 'empowered' women in the public-political domain itself remained contingent on their ability to assume the masculinist stance. Secondly, it was largely available only to new elite women. Even when they voiced the interests of non-elite women in the political public, the privilege of new elite women politicians remained more or less intact. The question remains of the 'new lamps', the positions opened up in the newly-delineated space of 'local space'. What kind of power, what sort of agency do they confer on women? The chapters that follow seek answers to these questions.

Notes

1. The only 'group rights' that women could possibly demand, then, came to be tied closely to modern notions of gender. The demand for maternity rights would not be considered 'divisive', but a call for political representation would be condemned.

2. The Dutch commander, Van Rheede, described Aswathy Tirunal Umayamma Rani thus: "... Along with the old princess lives a younger one, but of such noble and manly conduct that she is both feared and respected by every one ... she not only rules Attingal but also Travancore itself within whose bounds no princess may set foot according to their laws, nor pass the river Karamana on pain of forfeiting their rights, but this young Amazon has lately violated those customs and made even the king fly before her." (quoted in Nair 2000: 144).

3. See for instance, Demands for Supplementary Grant—Education, November 15, 1933: 98–99; Demands for Grant—General Administration, 26 May 1934: 950–51; *Proceedings of the Shree Mulam Popular Assembly* (Hence forth, *PSMPA*), Vol II, (Government Press: Trivandrum, 1935); also, see, T Narayani Amma, Motion No 391, Demands for Grants, Cooperative Department, 3 August 1937, *PSMPA*, Vol X, 1938: 862; Demands for Grant –Medical Department, 31 July, 1937, *PSMPA*, Vol X, 1938: 689.

4. The *Shreemati* was edited by a group which included V M Katherine, C P Saradamma, A.Vijayamma, and Bhagavaty Lakshmy Ammal, all graduates, besides Anna Chandy. For criticism of the argument that women will be less communal by the rationalist social activist Sahodaran K Ayappan, see 'Malayalarajyam Kanda Suvarnarekha' (The Silver Lining Espied by *Malayalarajyam*) (1935), and qualified approval of reservation of jobs for women, see 'Shreematiyude Vaadam' (1935), (The *Shreemati*'s Argument) in Ayappan 1965, 11; 8.

5. 27 January 1940, *PSMPA*, Vol XV,1940: 449.

6. Discussion of the Cochin Child Marriage Restraint Act, 5 April, 1940, *Proceedings of the Cochin Legislative Council* Vol IV, 1940: 1439.

7. It appears that compared to elsewhere in India, women activists in the national movement were much less directly involved in framing demands made on behalf of 'women' in Travancore and Cochin. The Indian women's movement's reluctance to press for separate electorates in the early 1930s (Roy 2002) does not seem to have resonated strongly in Travancore.

8. Pitching the appeal for special provisions directly to the state was a strategy followed also by women of minority communities in Travancore. See Haleema Beevi (1938/2005).

9. For a sample of such veiled hostility, see the sarcastic response to an article in the *Shreemati* published by the 'humour magazine', the *Naradar*, which advised women not to heed *Shreemati*'s advice to 'return to earlier ways': "In the old days you had no bodice, no blouse, no jumper, no saree, no face powder, especially no hanging ear ornaments. You weren't supposed to appear before brothers and heads of the household. You had to remain in the kitchen. Now there is freedom; you can go anywhere; you can wear a sleeveless jumper; you can hang ear ornaments on your earlobe, big or small; there are concessions and facilities for education; you have employment in every department, even in the police. Why should you return?" *Naradar* 1, 9, 1940: .4. Interestingly the perception that woman's demands as a special interest group and equal citizenship were divisive of national or radical politics echoed elsewhere too. In Bengal, for instance, the cause of women's suffrage was won in the 1920s mainly because a powerful political party, the Swarajists, offered staunch support. See, Barbara Southard 1993. The feeling that the advocates of women's rights did not represent 'poor women' was also present elsewhere. See Roy 2002.

10. This falls into a national pattern, in which women advocates of women's suffrage internalized this formulation of 'Indian Womanhood', which served to both emphasize their 'common cause' with male nationalists, and as a rallying point to criticize conservative opposition to full political rights for women. See, Roy 2002. The negotiations between western feminism and first-generation feminists in India were similarly complex. See Mrinalini Sinha 1995. However, in Travancore, this did not always automatically translate into a rejection of separate electorates for women.

11. See, editoral, 'Jatimatsarattepattiyulla Malayalarajyam' (Malayalarajyam on Community-Competition), *Nazrani Deepika* 16 June 1931: 2; L.G. Beemar, 'Malayalarajyam Patraadhiparkku', *Nazrani Deepika* 2 July 1931: 5–6.

12. For example, outspoken women like Mariam Nidhiry (Mrs. I C Chacko), faced death threats for having vociferously attacked dowry and the unequal rights of women in family property from community platforms (Ulakamtara 1995: 112). See her speech 'Our Women', (1927/ 2005: 96–105).

13. Reply to President's Address, Joint Sitting of the Sri Chitra State Council and the Sri Mulam Popular Assembly 21 June 1937, *PSMPA* Vol X, 1938: 19–20.

14. See, statement by A V Kuttimalu Amma, (*Nazrani Deepika*, November 3, 1951: 5) and Mariakutty John, *Nazrani Deepika*, January 8,1952: 2 .

15. Report of her speech, *Nazrani Deepika* 25 May 1960: .4.

16. http://eci.nic.in/eci_main/SR_KeyHighLights/SE_1960/StatRep_Kerala_1960.pdf.

17. Interestingly, in the dominant discourse of modern gender in Kerala that began to accumulate and expand in the 19th century, these were often identified as characteristic of 'uncultured traditional women', who were found lacking in agency—of both the intellect and morality. They were understood as nothing but versions of lying and cheating, and thus figured as qualities that needed to be eradicated if the ideal of the morally superior modern woman was to be actualized (Devika 2007).

18. Examples are many: Parvati Ayyapan; Konniyoor Meenakshi Amma; Ambady Kartyayani Amma; Akkamma Cheriyan; Mukkappuzha Kartyayani Amma and others. Gandhi was often cited as an inspiration for this calling.

19. Demand for Grants, Medical Department, 21 March 1953, *Proceedings of the Travancore-Cochin Legislative Assembly* Vol. 2: 1821–22.

20. See, for instance, the accounts of early women activists, often wives or relatives of leading communists, such as Umadevi Antarjanam, Karthyayanikkutty Amma, Kalyani teacher, and Sarojini Balanandan. Josephine 2007.

21. It may be argued that the micro-credit based self help groups have often worked to manage the poverty of the 'outlier' groups to a certain extent and indeed, even the small additions to women's income have helped them cope with rising burdens of familial responsibilities that now fall upon them (as evident in recent research, for instance, Thampi 2007). However, as Shobha Arun argues in the context of tribal women in Kerala, while the self-help groups may be recognized as valuable—as 'interrupters' of vulnerability, the possibility that they may reinforce new forms of patriarchy is real (Arun 2008).

22. This is evident in the numbers of women candidates in the Indian Parliamentary elections in the 1980s and 90s. In the

1977 elections to the Indian Parliament, out of 64 candidates for the 20 Parliamentary constituencies in the state, just 3 were women; in the 1980 elections, out of 93 candidates, there were just 2. In 1984, the numbers rose to 7, but the total numbers of candidates had risen to 151. In 1991, there were 179 candidates in the fray, out of which just 10 were women. http://keralaassembly.org/lok/index.html [accessed, 30 April, 2010]

3

The Rise of Feminine Public Altruism

Probe Success?

A large majority of the women presidents of village panchayats who we interviewed may be characterized as 'successful women leaders'. By this we mean those women presidents who have gained for themselves widespread respect and approval in the local community. A good number from this group has been able to transform this goodwill into more durable support at the local level. They have often served as member or president either in the same tier or in the others for the past two or even three terms. At present this group is certainly not small even if we consider the whole of Kerala, and it includes women presidents of all social classes and communities, though the majority (at least in our sample) hail from new elite communities, entering the fray as candidates of the 'General Category'.

This focus has been chosen deliberately. The reasons why women fail in leadership positions are relatively better explored than the reasons for their success. Secondly, and perhaps more crucially, we feel that it is necessary to ask questions about the nature of 'success' itself. It is too readily assumed that women's 'success'—in the above sense—implies the decline of entrenched patriarchal gender norms. As we were increasingly convinced in the course of our interviewing, in the present case, 'success' is often contingent on women leaders' conformity to entrenched gender norms, which are not entirely disempowering, but part of a 'patriarchal bargain'

(Kandiyoti 1998). In Kerala, we find that successful women leaders are often the bearers of a specific form of power linked to the deployment of sentiment and affect which was associated with ideal femininity since the late 19th and early 20th centuries (Devika 2007). The same form of power, it may be noted, has also been projected as crucial for the smooth functioning of local governance. This is perhaps only to be expected in a society in which women are most often directed towards the domestic and the sentimental as true domains of femininity which they may legitimately claim, and from which they may derive resources to make sense of and deal with the world in general.

However, successful women also attribute their success equally to *knowledge*—of official norms and procedures, which is certainly not associated with sentiment and affect but with the rule of the state, clearly beyond sentimental considerations. This is an advantage that arises from the superior level of education that women leaders often possess, and their practical experience of working in government institutions, often in positions of leadership, such as that of the school headmistress or government official. An intriguing question however is why these latter advantages, which are doubtless of key value in public life almost universally, are nevertheless not powerful enough to enable women to get beyond the 'patriarchal bargain' in Kerala. Also, that this is most frequently and effectively available to new elite women than to others, can scarcely be missed. There are successful women from the working-class, Dalit, and tribal groups, but their 'success' is hard-fought and indeed, sometimes comes at considerable cost.

As mentioned earlier, the opportunities for women opened up by political decentralization in 1995 were presented as a channel through which women could possibly enter the field of development and democratize it.[1] In hindsight, it appears that even though the panchayats were expected to accord top priority to productive activities, the emphasis has been largely on welfare disbursement. Thus 'development' has meant the highly expanded disbursal of welfare, more than the expansion of production.[2] This, has prepared the ground for the flourishing of a certain 'feminine public altruism' which draws upon new elite gender norms, and rings quite differently from the militant class politics of the mid-to-late 20th century Kerala. This chapter probes the new elite femininity that has received a fresh lease of life through the institutions of local governance. It draws upon eighty-five interviews with women presidents from all the three tiers.

The Interviewees: A Description

The large share of our interviewees—49 of them[3]—are middle-aged women were of the Malayalee new elite—the powerful communities of Kerala: the Ezhava, Thiyya, Nair, and Syrian Christian. Two were Malayala brahmins—the traditional elite. They were overwhelmingly of the LDF, especially the CPM, and this is especially true of the Ezhava and Thiyya women, which happen to be powerful OBC communities in Kerala. Dalit women are roughly one-fifth of the sample (17), and Muslim women, roughly one-fourth (19). Considering the total sample, our interviewees were mostly aged 36–45, and the middle-aged groups, 36–45 and 45–55, constituted the large share (56.26 per cent) (Table 3.a.). We also noted that within these groups, individuals in their 40s were more in number.

Table 3.a. Interviewees—Total Sample: Age

Age Group	Numbers
25–35	13
36–45	29
46–55	18
56–65	16
65+	7
Total	83

Taking the Dalit women interviewees alone, it appeared that the age groups 25–35 and 36–45 predominated (Table 3.b.). While 50.60 per cent of our interviewees in the total sample were below the age of 45, 76.5 per cent of the Dalit women interviewees were below that age. This is not surprising, since modern education is now an important requisite for candidature. Among Dalit women, it is the younger generation that is better-educated. However, relative youthfulness has important implications for Dalit women's ability to exercise power, especially of the 'feminine' sort considered appropriate for women in Kerala. Age, as we will see, is one of the key factors that determine the kinds of challenge the woman president faces in her struggle to gain acceptability.[4]

Table 3.b. Interviewees — Dalit Women Presidents: Age

Age Group	Numbers
26–35	4
36–45	9
46–55	2
56–65	2
65+	0
Total	17

Also, when one compares the average ages of all women panchayat presidents who have won from SC/ST wards or wards reserved for SC woman/ST woman with the average ages of all women presidents who won from either the General wards or the Women's Reservation wards in the 2005 elections, a difference is apparent: the former are about 6–9 years younger than both the latter groups on an average (Table 3.c., below). The difference diminishes as we move to the Block level (where, except for women in the Women's Reservation group, the total numbers are really low for the others—9 and 11). But if we were to compare the incidence of women below the age of 30 in each group for the village panchayats, the difference is striking. Some 43.75 per cent of

Table 3.c. Women panchayat presidents at block and village level: Average age and numbers below the age of 30 in each category

Women Panchayat presidents	Village panchayat		Block panchayat	
Won from	Av. Age (total no.)	No. below 30 yrs (% of total)	Av. age (total no.)	Below 30 yrs (% of total)
SC/ST/ST woman/SC woman wards	34.77 (32)	14 (43.75)	38.55 (9)	2 (22.22)
General category wards	43.38 (57)	3 (5.26)	43.09 (11)	3 (27.27)
Women's reservation wards	41.17 (265)	20 (7.54)	43.46 (31)	1 (3.22)

Source: State Election Commission, 2005.

the former are below 30, while for the latter, the number is below 10 per cent.

In the age profile of Muslim women presidents in the sample (Table 3.d.), more of them tended to be below 45 (57.89 per cent) compared with the total sample (50.60 per cent); however, the share of the two middle groups, 36–45 and 46–55 was higher for Muslim women (68.42 per cent) compared with the total sample (56.26 per cent).

Table 3.d. Interviewees—Muslim Women Presidents: Age

Age Group	Numbers
25–35	4
36–45	7
46–55	6
56–65	0
65+	2
Total	19

Age is also important because it gives us a sense of the domestic burdens that women are expected to carry. Interestingly, the age of the youngest child for an overwhelming majority of our interviewees was above 21 (Table 3.e.). Freed of the burdens of childcare, these women were able to devote much greater time and energy to local governance, as they reported in the interviews too. However, here too there are interesting and significant differences. For instance, the numbers of unmarried women and married women with no children (taken as one group) were significantly higher among Dalit women presidents compared with the total sample— 35.29 compared with 12.04 per cent. Out of 19 interviewees from this group, 6 were unmarried or childless. As we may see later, this may not prove to be an advantage when combined with lower caste and class status—marriage being regarded as a key requirement for women's social membership in Kerala (Kodoth 2008). Of the remaining 11, the age of the youngest child of 6 interviewees was below 18—54.54 per cent of Dalit women have children below 18 compared with just 15.06 per cent of the total sample. This means that a significant number of Dalit women carry a relatively heavier load of domestic burdens—given the fact that childcare constitutes the major share of domestic burdens in contemporary Kerala (Thampi 2007).

Muslim women interviewees with children below 18 were more than half their total number—10 out of 19. However, their oldest children tended to be very close to or above adult

Table 3.e. Interviewees—Total Sample:* Age of Youngest Child

Age Group	Numbers of respondents
0–12	11
12–18	17
18–21	10
21+	35
Total	73

* Excluding 10 respondents who were childless/unmarried

ages, and for 6 out of the 19, the age of the youngest child was above 21. As a group, they seemed less burdened with childcare responsibilities than Dalit interviewees, since they were amply supported by extended families.

Examining education and employment profiles as well as the employment status of spouses reveals the large share upper caste or powerful OBC women have in the advantages of the Malayalee new elite: access to professional education, employment, and marriage with males with similar advantages. Professional work, however, does not mean high-income-high-status occupations, but mostly low- or medium-income jobs which, however, command considerable social respectability. And many women with diploma-, degree- and postgraduate-level education were unemployed, reflecting the larger pattern of women's unemployment in Kerala (Lakshmi Devi 2001; Mazumdar and Guruswamy 2006). Table 3.f. shows that 51 out of the total of 83 interviewees possess diploma-, degree- or post-graduate/professional education—nearly 61.44 per cent. However, as Table 3.g. shows, 26 out of 83 were unemployed—31.32 per cent. The high prevalence of diploma holders may hint that a large number of women who entered local governance were desirous of employment and salaried work. Most of the diploma holders have diplomas that grant them entry into the 'respectable' teaching profession.[5] (No wonder, so many of the women leaders in politics, across caste and community—and in fact,

Table 3.f. Interviewees—Total Sample: Education

Educational Level	Numbers
Lower than High School	8
SSLC	16
Higher Secondary	8
Diploma	19
Degree	12
Post-graduation/Professional degree	20
Total Numbers	83

the Minister of Health and Family Welfare in the last LDF Ministry, P K Sreemathy herself—publicly carry the suffix 'teacher' next to their names—so we have not just P K Sreemathy or Nafisa or Mary, but often, 'Sreemathy Teacher', 'Nafisa Teacher', or 'Mary Teacher'.)

It must also be noted that a sizeable number of interviewees classified as 'worker' happened to be anganwadi workers, a group that shares many of the features of the informal sector labour including exploitative working conditions, insecure tenure, low skills, and poor wages. Nevertheless in Kerala it enjoys the status of 'respectable work', something that adds weight to women's chances of entering local governance. Not surprisingly, out of the 9 women who reported themselves as 'workers', 6 were anganwadi workers.

Table 3.g. Interviewees—Total Sample: Employment

Type of work	Numbers
Labourer/Anganwadi worker/Service Sector Worker	9
Self-employed	6
Clerical	6
Professional	28
Fulltime Political Activist	6
NGO worker	2
Unemployed	26
Total	83

Considering Dalit women separately, they seem be less educated. Out of the 17 interviewees in this group, only 4 had degree-level and postgraduate/professional degree-level education—17.65 per cent, compared with 38.55 per cent in the total. Compared with 33.73 per cent who did professional work in the total sample, only 17.64 per cent of the Dalit women occupied comparable positions at work. A relatively smaller share of Muslim women, too, has acquired higher education: 5 out of 19 have degree/postgraduate/professional degree-level education, 26.31 per cent of their total, compared with 38.55 in the total sample. All five were employed as teachers. Among Muslim women, clerical and professional employment takes the larger share, 7 out of 19. However, in the share of unemployed women in the total sample, the Dalit, and the Muslim groups are equally high: 31.32 per cent for the total sample; 35.29 for the Dalit women; and 42.10 for Muslim women. The question of employment emerged as a crucial point in many interviews, as will be seen later.

A key determinant of social respectability for women in Kerala is the spouse's employment status. Having a husband well-connected in politics or well-respected on account of his profession is essential—and for widows, being the widow of a 'respectable' person matters. Often many successful women have husbands who are in respectable professions like teaching and are also very well-connected in political party circles. This does not hint that these women are controlled by their husbands; nor should we ignore the fact that the biographies of our interviewees revealed that many of them had a fairly long history of public presence before they entered local governance—as trainers in the Mass Literacy Campaign of the early 90s, health volunteers in the Mahila Swasth Sangh, party members and so on. A 'respectable spouse' indicates not just a source of control but also the strong presence of social respectability and political support—social/gender capital. Needless to say, it is middle-class and secularized-brahminical norms that set the terms of this 'respectability'. The large share of Dalit and tribal women among the unmarried (3 out of 4) thus indicates a disadvantage. Table 3.h., below, indicates that a large number of the spouses of our interviewees are indeed in 'respectable' professions and trades. Professionals form the single biggest share, and adding the fulltime party workers and those in clerical jobs to it, the share of 'respectable' spouses would be more than half (not counting the four unmarried women). This number is actually larger since among the self-employed, at least half are medium- or large-scale businessmen. It is also significant that not a single spouse was reported to be unemployed.

**Table 3.h. Interviewees—Total Sample:* Employment
Status of Spouse**

Type of work	Numbers
Gulf Migrant	8
Labourer/Service Sector Worker	14
Self-employed	15
Clerical (Public and Private Sector)	13
Professional	18
Fulltime Party Activist	11
Total	79

* Excluding four unmarried women and including widows, who reported about their late husbands.

The spouses of a larger number of Dalit women would also be counted as pursuing occupations 'respectable' in secularized brahminical terms—counting together fulltime party activists, professionals, and those in clerical jobs, they are 7 of 13 (leaving out 3 unmarried women and one widowed very young from the total of 17). However, a fair number are working class men or in petty trades: 5 out of 13. Thus among Dalit women interviewees, the percentage of spouses who are in occupations considered less 'respectable' is 38.46, compared with 17.72 in the total sample. This group and the unmarried/widowed group together form the larger share in the total sample of 17. This too has deep implications, which will be discussed later. Among Muslim women, the share of 'respectable spouses' is high indeed. Of a total of 19, 6 are professionals, 5 are fulltime party workers, and the self-employed spouses (3 in number) are medium-scale merchants. While not a single Dalit woman in the sample has a spouse who is a Gulf migrant, 3 of the Muslim women have spouses who work abroad.

Another distinguishing feature of successful women presidents is that the majority of them claim to be from 'party families', families with a history of stable allegiance to a political party for two or three generations (Table 3.i.).

Or they have been socialized into 'party ways' through marriage into a 'party family',[6] or it could be both. This would mean that the ways in which these women are linked to their parties may differ significantly compared with the experience of first-generation women politicians mentioned in Chapter One. While for the latter, entering politics often meant tensions with families and the labour of building up the parties, for the former, such pains are less intense. Both of these have interesting implications and point at distinct spatial configurations. This does not mean that these women have no position of their own within their parties—indeed they have, at least in the women's organizations. Considering women presidents of the CPM (the party which has tried to explicitly induct women into committees), more than 20 of our interviewees (out of 51) are Local Committee members; about 20 are in the Party Branch; 7 are Area Committee members. More women presidents in our sample are located at the lower levels of the party hierarchy. Only one is a district committee member. However, family connections do matter, as many interviewees were keen to stress.

Table 3.i. Interviews—Total Sample: Family Connections in Party Politics

Source of Connection	Numbers
Born in 'party family'*	26
Husband's influence more important	34
Family/Husband neutral influence	23
Total	83

* Some in this group did mention support from husband/husband's family, but not as the primary influence.

Dalit women seem equally to be of 'party families'—6 out of 17 are born in 'party families' and another 6 were married into these—more than 70 per cent. This compares well with 72.28 per cent of total sample. However, a slightly larger number of Dalit women reported that the family's influence was neutral, compared with the total sample: 29.41 per cent compared with 27.71. In the Muslim women presidents' group, all women were of/married into 'party families': 17 were married into 'party families' and two were born in them.

Here again, one needs to guard against falling too easily into a 'proxy' argument (Leiten 1996) (which, in any case, has been demonstrated to be too simplistic and fuzzy. See John 2007; Sundström 2008). Right at the outset it is evident that these women have served multiple terms in different tiers. Of the total sample, while the presidents who served in any tier for the first time are the single biggest group (38), those who served for the second and third times, put together, outnumber this group (45). This strength however is not evident in the Dalit women presidents' group: 12 served their first term in any tier, and only 5 have had a second or third term. The record is somewhat better for Muslim women: while 9 served their first term in any tier, 10 had a second or third term. Asked about future plans, an overwhelming majority expressed their desire to contest again—the women in the left parties used politically correct language, but they did make their interest clear (Table 3.j.). The distinction between 'will surely contest given a chance' and 'will contest if party calls' was decidedly thin. Many who said that they will withdraw from the contest but plan to be active in public life were in their third term; they also pointed out that their parties may not want them to contest again.

Table 3.j.   Interviewees—Total Sample: Future Plans

Future plans	Responses
Will be active in public but will not contest	13
Will surely contest given a chance	25
Will contest if party demands	27
Will withdraw from public life	15
Not decided yet	3
Total	83

Dalit women who said that they would surely contest either if there was a chance, or on the party's demand made a total of 13 of 17. Two of them expressed the wish to stay in public life even though they did not wish to contest. Just two expressed the desire to withdraw. This does not deviate much from the pattern in the total sample, but the Muslim women presidents' group appears to be more diffident: of the total of 19, only five expressed the willingness to contest either out of their own wish or the party's wish. Three were undecided—in fact, the only three undecided respondents were of this group. However, seven still expressed the wish to stay in the public even though they did not wish to contest—importantly, they preferred to stay in 'social work' rather than in politics. Also, of the three who wished to withdraw, two cited reasons of age and one, the inconveniences she suffered because of lack of domestic support, since her husband was a Gulf migrant. She intended to come back later.

In short, the larger share of our interviewees were women of Kerala's powerful new elite, and they clearly enjoyed several of the advantages available to new elite women, which did underlie their 'success' at least partially. Muslim women who have entered local governance clearly do share many of these advantages, some to a lesser degree. While these advantages were not entirely closed to Dalit women, the degree of their availability has been much less. This seems to have crucially affected the odds that they had to face, especially for those who were in their first terms. It also affects their access to that specifically 'feminine' sort of power, which very many of our interviewees found so efficacious in local governance. As may be clear from Chapter Four, Dalit women who achieve success do so against much greater odds and sometimes even in the absence of 'gentle power'.

'Gentle Power' and 'Knowing the Rules'

The single most common and striking theme articulated by the 'successful' women leaders was of 'gentle power': it seemed evident that they drew not so much on political, as on social power. However, they were also insistent that this must be combined with a sound knowledge of the rules of local governance and the legal framework of panchayati raj. In this section, we reflect upon this peculiar intertwined manner in which women leaders view their exercise of power.

First, examining their biographies, we found a common link: their previous public exposure was not of political agitation but of development activism, even though many who said so did hold positions in party committees at the local level before their entry into local governance. Secondly, they pointed to certain conditions that may be largely accessible only to new elite women, such as the presence of the husband/ male member as escort and guide, and interestingly, access to cash. Both these are linked to the women's need to maintain respectability in the local community. This seems to indicate a reinstatement of gender—the articulation of a feminine 'public altruism'. Even when they proclaim to be political, these women rarely identify themselves as politicians in the sense of handling or desiring political power. They perceive themselves as distant from both of the two common ways of the conception of politics: as radical mass mobilization-centred militant activism which is clearly partial to the poor and maintains a certain distance from the State, or as the building of alliances and retaining power for the defence of particular interests. Rather, they project themselves as altruistic agents of welfare disbursal who 'give' welfare to the poor, and manage their disappointments and anger though the deployment of the 'gentle power of persuasion', which of course is historically perceived as typical of the ideal feminine.

This perhaps was most evident when the interviewees spoke about the welfare functions of the panchayat. Interestingly, a very large majority cutting across caste and faith took pride in their role as 'fair distributors of welfare'—and voiced their immense pleasure at being able to fulfil the function of overseeing such distribution. These interviewees tended to view the resources distributed not in terms of 'people's rights', or 'group interests', but as governmental entitlements handed out to groups deserving uplift by the state. Given the emergent shape of local self governments in Kerala, this should come as no surprise. The relation of non-reciprocality between the State and these groups, and the shift of the aim of State welfare towards guiding citizens into self-help, looks extraordinarily similar to the relationship of power posited between the ideal mother, who disciplines through 'gentle power', and her children in the ideal modern family as imagined in Malayalee social reform of the early 20th century (Devika 2007). Politics seemed distant to them in other ways as well. Interestingly, many women leaders regarded differences of opinions among different party members not as stemming from ideologies or political and ethical positions, but from more individualized temperaments or mindsets. A senior woman president, also a CPM Local Committee member in her locality, remarked:

> I have never had a problem here, and that's because of [my] willingness to make compromises. Why do problems arise? See, when it is a family, the members, husband and the relatives will all be of different temperaments. Who leads them as one? We [women], truly! I have the maturity to lead in that way—that is, through advice that prevents quarrels and smoothens out disagreement. Young women these days are ... what am I to say, haughty and interested in power, that's why they have problems.

Given this, it is again hardly surprising that many women argued that their work was indeed 'social work', and in an exceptional case, a president serving her third term in a village panchayat remarked that this was her way of performing charitable deeds:

> My father had given us some property when he died which he wanted us to devote to charitable purposes. I'd planted rubber in that plot and it yielded well. It is that money which I use to fund my work in the panchayat. The honorarium is a pittance, you know, and as president, you have to attend to everybody ... marriages, sicknesses, all kinds of collections ... I had donated

the income from that plot to the poor much earlier, now I use it for this. Now the rubber's being replanted, and I'm a bit exhausted!

'Gentle power', thus, is the accompaniment of the new elite woman, and she does use it effectively in a variety of situations. Most frequently, it is evoked in attempts to pacify dissatisfied welfare beneficiaries. A considerable number of these women do project their 'natural' affability, approachability, their capacity to be empathetic, as factors that have enabled them to be successful in pacifying the dissatisfied. To quote from one of many such accounts:

> I'm happy and often satisfied by the fact that I could distribute the welfare benefits fairly across all sections of the panchayat community. However it is true that the same amount of assistance cannot be extended to all needy members at the same time. As the resources of the State are limited, some of them have to wait till the next time, and I could convince them to do so. After all, most of the welfare recipients are women and hence I can pacify them and persuade them to wait.

Such power allows the woman president certain closeness— an intimacy—with welfare seekers, especially women. Our interviewees, across party lines, very frequently identified this as the defining quality of women's presence in panchayats. Interviewee after interviewee claimed that women are blessed with 'natural talent' that makes people open up to them and reveal their most intimate issues, while with men, there will always be aloofness. "We are always different," said a young and very active president from central Kerala. "When someone comes to see us, we always ask them to sit down first. However angry or irritated the people may be, they always calm down at a kind word and gesture." Certainly, this involves considerable effort on the part of the woman leader herself. Explaining her success in a strongly left-dominated panchayat, a woman president of the Congress pointed to her successful exercise of 'gentle power', reminding us, however, that it was not easy:

Self-control is most important. I was very careful and remained absolutely neutral. No matter what swear-words a person might throw at me, I never let myself forget that when he is in the panchayat, he is a welfare beneficiary, primarily. Never give anybody the tiniest excuse to start blaming you.

Though this seems hard enough, the results were often very satisfying. This is proudly displayed in many of the anecdotes they shared which were often demonstrative of the efficacy of 'gentle power' in pacifying the dissatisfied:

There was this really poor woman whose name didn't figure in the list for the EMS Housing Scheme. Her husband is a very violent man, beats her up regularly. That girl came in here and broke down. I sat down beside her for a whole hour, patted her on the back, helped her to calm down—women should not be weeping like this, I told her. I'll help you to get the money, it will take some time, but I surely will. The government is giving you this amount of 75,000 rupees. Build at least a small house of two rooms and be safe there ...

And as another woman panchayat president who vouched very strongly for the efficacy of 'gentle power' observed:

When women presidents give their word on something, there is an advantage. Because people feel we are more sincere, we are more forthcoming. Maybe that's because of our style. When it is a woman leader, she takes care to ask the person approaching her to take a seat. She speaks gently and sympathetically, reassuringly. She gives detailed reasons and assurances about the speediest disposal of the issue. Male politicians aren't like that. They will examine the issue and give a view, and the person usually has to withdraw and wait for further action. When it is a woman, they can approach us at home and there too, we will offer a seat and kind words.

Another situation in which 'gentle power' worked very well was to be found in panchayats where the traces of earlier militant working-class mobilizations of the left were still active. In these panchayats, welfare beneficiaries were impatient with the bureaucratic norms through which welfare handouts were administered and resorted more frequently to the older political language of welfare as 'people's right', the rules of which ought to be eminently bendable in the interests of the poor. Here, the women leaders especially of the left, had to mediate between the altered regime of welfare in the state and the militant poor. 'Gentle power' was found not only useful, but absolutely indispensable in such instances. As a woman leader from north Kerala, a worker with long experience in militant working class politics herself, remarked:

> I have had to be very patient and gentle ... There are so many rules in panchayati raj, the people have no sense about it. They want their welfare benefits really soon. What rules, they ask— aren't needs more important than the rules? Can't we change the rule according to the need? Our government is in power, isn't it? Then what's the problem?—This is how they ask. I try to persuade them most gently ... remain patient and keep talking even when they don't see sense after many attempts to explain.

The third and the most frequently encountered situation in which the use of 'gentle power' seems inevitable involved dealings with the staff of the panchayat. Women leaders are extremely aware of the fact that precisely because local governance involves considerable bureaucratic tangle, the cooperation of staff—especially the Secretary—is an absolute must for even the routine functioning of the panchayat.[7] Here, they felt, there was entrenched patriarchy which could be 'softened' only through the exercise of 'gentle power'. "The cow printed on the page doesn't eat grass," remarked a senior woman leader from central Kerala. "The training that we receive from the Kerala Institute of Local Administration advises us to keep the Secretary below us. If we try that, the panchayat is likely to simply stop. " A great many interviewees therefore felt that it was important to address the Secretary deferentially, as 'Sir', and to take good care not to display one's power as the head of a Constitutional body. This was peculiar to women, they felt. "Male panchayat presidents can be closer to the officers. After all they are men, they can all go off and have a drink or smoke together. But we can't do that." This feeling echoed through the large majority of interviews and seemed to indicate the limits of the intimacy permitted by 'gentle power'.

However, senior women found their age a convenient factor that allowed them to break through the distance with officers precisely through 'gentle power'. "The officials in my panchayat, Secretary included, are younger than my children. I treat them just like my own kids, I always call them *Makkale* [children], never scold them harshly, care for them like I would for my own. I always know when they are hungry, when they are tired. Nothing is cooked in my house which isn't shared with them," said a woman leader from south Kerala, who was widely recommended to us by all sections in her panchayat (they also deeply regretted the fact that factional rivalry in her party had forced her to step down early). She then gave us an account of how she reformed a Secretary (not a very young man) newly posted to her panchayat, who was addicted to liquor:

> There was a person posted here from north Kerala, a nice person, just 45 years old. Was terribly bound to drinking and would turn up here only occasionally, and that too with a bottle stuffed in his pocket. Sometimes he wouldn't come close when I called. The stink! His wife and kids were calling me on the phone all the time. He stayed by himself in a lodge, they said—they were so worried what he'd become here, all by himself. I would then console her, don't you worry, we will all take good care of him. So then I began to gradually speak to him, why are you drinking so much, Son, don't you see your wife and your twelve-year-old son are worrying to death? Well, after long persuasion, he turned over a completely new leaf, stopped his drinking and became such an efficient person!

Tight-rope-walking between Gentility and Subservience

As evident in very many interviews, the exercise of 'gentle power' in situations such as this involve careful strategic moves, such as not ringing the bell for the peon, and instead picking up the files, walking to the concerned clerk's desk, sitting down beside the clerk, and getting the matter settled. The thin dividing line between subservience and gentility was sometimes blurred—the challenge was to keep it sharp and clear, which was admitted to be a difficult one. The dilemma was stated clearly by a woman leader from central Kerala, who was in local governance for the third time:

> There will be a hundred and one things to handle at the same time. You're expected to answer a hundred questions. In the middle, you have to take all this forward in a very diplomatic way, without offending anyone. But you also have to be able to firmly discipline the rowdier ones. You have to fight with your words. You have to be extra-calm, look really superior in your knowledge and composed if your words have to be accepted!

The last point stated by this woman leader gives us a clue about the question why these women find 'knowledge of the rules' so very essential to gaining a foothold in the panchayat.[8] Almost every woman leader we interviewed stressed to us that while docile behaviour can indeed be turned strategically into a useful tool, ignorance can only disempower. This also probably explains the fact that a large number of our interviewees felt that inducting more women into local bodies through the reservation of 50 per cent seats in the term starting in 2010 would be a folly if these women are not suitably trained and thus endowed with 'knowledge of the rules' beforehand. 'Gentle power', they seem to think, comes naturally, but not 'knowledge of the rules'. Historically, the project of domestic-oriented female education was rejected in Malayalee society in the 1930s in the wake of the Great Depression, which forced many women of the emergent new elite into the labour market, especially into teaching and other professions deemed 'genteel'. More and more women sought to enter higher education in the 1930s and after, hoping to find such work (Devika and Mukherjee 2007). No doubt, it is this historical trajectory of education that works to women's tremendous advantage in local governance, which calls for handling a great amount of official paperwork and decision-making according to ever-changing rule and procedures.

As a great many interviewees reported, these skills have been vital in keeping the difference between docility and genteel behaviour sharp and clear. They have also protected them from censure from above and pressures from below—especially from false allegations of corruption and misspending. Some of the most interesting anecdotes we heard, retold by women leaders with a great deal of pride and pleasure, were about how they dealt with harassment from hostile bureaucrats and local politicians who were either envious or irritated by their uncorrupt and independent stance. The most striking one was told to us by a Muslim woman president, third term in local governance, about how a politically well-connected minor official had tried to bully her into approving a list of anganwadi workers. She resisted and had to suffer a long series of challenges—inquiries on allegations which were proved baseless later, denial of an anganwadi to the ward she represented, harassment of anganwadi workers who supported her, denial of crucial certificates to her family members, State-level auditor's visits. In the end, she emerged unscathed:

> These people think we do not know the rules. They are mistaken. We know procedures much better than them. This man [the auditor] was quite taken aback to see that I had kept the rules perfectly. He returned without a word. You can get a bill, a record here anytime, I told him. The four per cent commission is appropriated not by an individual but a semi-government institution ... . They think that these women from Malappuram [a northern Muslim majority district of Kerala, thought to be relatively 'backward' in social development] will pee in their sarees out of fear if they quote us a few rules. Well, he learned a good lesson—that women here are like rockets with fire in their tails!

This woman leader nevertheless insisted that she did not want to be known as a politician or even as a development worker, but as someone "capable of wiping the tears from the eyes of another". The combination of 'gentle power' and 'knowledge of the rules' worked well for her, clearly.

It is striking, however, to note that where women have tried to combine the latter with political and institutional power—the political authority conferred upon the head of the panchayat as a constitutional body—they have faced greater hostility. A three-time successful woman president of the CPM, with twenty years of experience in public politics, whose life reads like those of her female predecessors in the communist movement—a story of intense struggle against family loyalties to embrace her chosen politics—admitted that her success was hard-won precisely because she was "not *paavam*, but a woman who feels that presidents can and must rule."

> I know every single detail about my panchayat. All the members give me full respect. Nothing in this panchayat happens without my knowledge. If I settle a boundary dispute within this panchayat, no one dares to meddle with it after. The Secretary has to be kept below the President. There are many women who readily address the Secretary as 'Sir'. They are wrong to do so. The position of the president is a very important one. It should not be belittled. The Secretary in my panchayat will not sit down unless I ask him to do so. Only then can you be effective.

The knowledge of rules also helps her to fend off undue attempts by the CPM's local committee to interfere in the affairs of the panchayat. She was a member of the local committee but withdrew because she insisted on keeping the two apart—" ... in the panchayat things can move only according to rules. I have convinced my comrades that the party's interests in the panchayats are best kept when we correctly follow the rules." However, she also admitted to a great deal of hostility towards her, especially from elements interested in 'commissions' and so on. "And of course, they resent the fact that I do not bow my head but remind them constantly that as long as I am the president, I have power, I am in charge." Another senior woman leader from central Kerala with a similar style of functioning, a great believer in 'knowledge of rule and procedure" (quoted in the introduction)—and who declared that 'gentle power' was to be completely avoided—also mentioned considerable opposition to her especially from within her party. Yet their successes are as or more enduring than those of their peers who prefer to use 'gentle power'. Both concluded their interviews by saying that their experiences with colleagues were such that they did not wish to contest again, but their style of governing had worked so well and brought so many honours to their panchayats (both are rated the best in their blocks and districts), that they will probably have to. In the words of the first woman leader quoted here:

> This panchayat has won many prestigious honours ... Because I have remained firm I have created for myself a space from which I cannot be excluded. There are many in this panchayat, party members, supporters and many neutral folk, who will come out in open opposition if there is any effort to exclude me. That, perhaps, is the chief reason why a person like me continues to be retained in these times of moral turpitude.

However, women leaders such as the above may indeed have a more forceful career, with achievements even more enduring than those of women who combine 'gentle power' and 'knowledge of the rules', if they are able to develop a local agenda of development adequate to their panchayat. The example of a woman leader of local governance who enjoys well-deserved fame not only for being a fair distributor of welfare but also for having intervened in local development processes innovatively and effectively, convinced us of this. A retired school teacher, she had been active in the PPC and had worked hard at developing a local perspective in development. Her grasp over the rules and extraordinary ability to mobilize local panchayat officers, department officials, and the local party to her agenda brought her considerable credit *outside* the panchayat, in the press and development circles as well, something exceedingly rare for a leader of local governance. Such achievements in local development strengthen the leader's position by bringing fame to the panchayat as well, and this further improves her standing within the local party. In the case of the woman leader mentioned above, 'knowledge of the rules' was of key significance, but so was gaining space in local politics—she has been able to effectively contain rivals. Her success at the local level has proved enduring and her work attracted the attention of the press as well. Public attention has enabled her to garner significant support from senior leaders in high politics and draw upon the MLA and MP funds, and in turn, this has helped her to bring positive change in local development.[9] In short, there are clear synergies between the different sorts of approval she has managed to amass, which makes her look indispensable to local governance in her area.

It is perhaps important to note that a major limitation of women who prefer to stick to 'gentle power' is that while many of them have achieved considerable respect in their local community, very few have been able to influence local development priorities significantly.[10] The example above also seems to indicate that the support of senior leaders in high politics is necessary for women leaders to intervene effectively in local development priorities which are otherwise laid by the male-dominated party local committee according to the entirely non-local general policy of the party. However, this has proved no passport to high politics. Indeed, her upward mobility seems to have been seriously affected by the weakening of her supporters' faction within her party.

The Limits of 'Gentle Power' and 'Knowledge of the Rules'

Indeed, the limits of 'gentle power' are almost as immediately evident as its efficacy. One common thread that runs through the narratives of all our interviewees who claimed to be relying upon it was their very close identification with the local. This, many of them claimed, is a distinctly feminine quality. And besides, as middle-aged women, they had no plans to move away; indeed, there was a discernible anxiety about returning to the locality after the five years with a spotless reputation. Hence the concern was most intensely about preventing corruption in the beneficiary lists—interviewee after interviewee stressed the fact that she was adamant that the norms were followed in the preparation of beneficiary lists.[11] The same concern, however, was missing about intervening in local development effectively. Many of the women leaders, especially of the CPM, are members of the local committee of the party where such decisions are discussed according to the party's general policy.[12] Here, however, they are often the only women members and grievously outnumbered. The few women who said that they had tried to influence local planning also revealed that the local committee of the CPM in their areas had many members who were also KSSP activists interested in local development and addressing local issues and utilizing local resources. It was this support that allowed them to carry on. Not surprising then, that several women who preferred 'gentle power' tended to justify their inaction. "We should not insist too much, I think. After all we are not independent and we are here to implement the party's policy. And we should never forget that it was the party that helped us to win this position and so there is an obligation."[13]

However, it can be argued that such inaction actually costs these leaders dear, making them forfeit a chance to build vital sources of support more enduring than that afforded by 'gentle power' in the panchayat. Irregularities in the beneficiary list are real (even though not rampant), but it is also a fact that the average welfare beneficiary in Kerala is a well-developed rational agent who seeks out information and acts accordingly (Krishna 2006). Over and over, our interviewees did note that welfare beneficiaries—as individuals, not in a collective sense—were very well aware of their entitlements and of ways of accessing them.[14] They also admitted that welfare beneficiaries were often keenly aware of the various bodies that oversaw the work of the panchayats and of the possibility of approaching the rival party in the panchayat in case of the dissatisfaction with the efforts of the ruling party. Some even complained that impatient beneficiaries did not hesitate to issue threats:

> Can you imagine? I did so much, and personally, for that old lady despite the fact that there were so many deadlines pressing. And then, when it appeared that she may have to suffer a slight delay, she threw a tantrum and threatened to set the Ombudsman on me! Who'd have thought that the wizened old lady knew about the Ombudsman? No doubt, the opposition members must have told her!

It appeared to us that any large scale attempt to deny welfare according to set norms would be challenged by beneficiaries directly and indirectly. And, as Sharma (2009) points out, intense competition between political parties at the local level does reduce corruption and rent-seeking (pp. 125–26). However, the women leaders, driven by their anxieties to satisfy local interests, continue to focus on welfare distribution rather than on development priorities, where they could have attained more durable achievements. In that sense, they are trapped in the role of fair distributors of welfare, with only 'gentle power' to resort to.

Indeed, one gets a distinct sense of a frustration at confinement in many interviews. A woman leader, who had just waxed eloquent about how she was loved by welfare beneficiaries in her panchayat for being accessible,[15] suddenly mentioned her fear that this did not really empower *her*:

> The panchayat is always full of people. They are very free with me—they come right up to where I sit and speak to me, *mole*, *makkale* [daughter, child], I need this, I must have that … even if they see quite well that I'm hard at other work. I wonder, isn't all this a bit too much? If it were a man sitting in that chair, this kind of behaviour wouldn't happen … nobody would walk into the room without permission … men are identified mostly with the party, but we are identified with the panchayat and so people take this extra freedom with us. You need tremendous patience to put up with it! I have managed to keep them happy with diplomatic behaviour. But the former president who was a

woman with a lot of education, she had little patience. She was not liked at all!

Moreover, despite their espousal of 'gentle power' as the best way to deal with entrenched patriarchal attitudes among officials, many women were painfully aware of their sheer dependence upon the officials, especially when support from the local party was shaky. In other words, relying on 'knowledge of the rules' could not prevent the blurring of boundaries between gentility and subservience many a time. Also, some pointed out that if they knew the rules, male leaders and panchayat officials had 'knowledge of bending the rules'! Thus many admitted (often on second thought) that their use of 'gentle power' was really under compulsion: "They can harm you if they want. Men know all the shortcuts, and they don't have to fear a bad name. Those are not options for a woman, so I never displease officials too seriously." Of course, women leaders who combine 'knowledge of the rules' with political power are vociferously against 'gentle power', arguing that 'knowledge of the rules' is not of much help when gentle behaviour and soft-spoken manners serve only to reinforce patriarchal control. One of them pointed out:

> If a man replies sharply to a question, that will be regarded as evidence for his ability and power. If it is a woman, she will inevitably be dubbed as terribly bold and vain. If a woman speaks strongly, if she takes a decision and implements it all by herself and is able to argue clearly about its rightness (even if she happens to be the Prime Minister), it would be evidence for her being arrogant and conceited. This discrimination is alive and well today. This is the reality in the panchayats … .A firm decision is a firm decision. Putting it softly doesn't lessen its impact. Ticking off a troublemaker is something you do as a last resort, but you can hardly be gentle then … if you oscillate between being mild and being bold, then you will surely earn more enemies than if you were just either bold or mild...

Women leaders are also painfully aware of the fact that for all their knowledge of the rules, they can hardly change any.[16] Interestingly, very few even considered the solution of putting this up within their parties as a focal point of political struggle. One such woman leader, a longstanding party activist whose memories of militant struggle are especially vivid, remarked passionately that "… the Department of Local Self-Government should not forget that we, not the bureaucrats, are the elected representatives of the people. How come the bureaucrats trust us so little? How come our observations, which come from the ground, are not even considered when these rules are formulated?" She remarked bitterly that for all her knowledge of the rules, knowledge of how rules may be bent seemed to be the only way to ensure that enough reached the deserving poor. Another remark made by a woman leader from north Kerala captured the non-reciprocality of the relationship between the panchayats and the Department of Local Self-Government humorously:

> See, it is all a husband-wife affair, even now. The Department [of Local Self-Government] is like the husband. He hands over a certain sum for various expenses to the wife, the Panchayat, in this story. The wife must spend that money according to certain established ways. She isn't free to change that way—even if things at home demand a change. She has to wait for his permission first. And that is hard to get! There is no consideration of whether the woman is capable, or is healthy, or has enough support. Uhuuh! At the end of the month the money must be spent in the right way. If not, she will be shouted at! We haven't even got past the husband-wife system over here, and we are expected to behave like empowered women!

To gain more space for manoeuvre, women leaders need good ground support from their parties—and here neither 'gentle power' nor 'knowledge of the rules' guarantee anything, as most of our interviewees agreed. Rules are routinely bent, as many interviewees agreed, and knowledge of the rules alone did not allow one to challenge this. One young and enthusiastic woman president from south Kerala noted with bitterness how she had been persuaded to fight the elections on the assurance that the local party will not interfere in the routine functioning of the panchayat and encouraged to follow rules, but was forced to comply with gross violations later. She suspended a corrupt official fully complying with the official process; this was however a well-connected man and he managed to influence the local party, which forced her to reverse her decision. "I kept quoting the rules to the local committee secretary when he called us for 'talks'. He didn't care. The corrupt fellow was back, as corrupt as ever. Can you imagine how powerless and humiliated I felt?"

That the usefulness of these two weapons wielded by women is limited is also evident from the fact that women were relatively absent in those positions of power within the machinery of local governance which were, until the present term, not covered by reservation norms (and thus entirely subject to the control of political parties). It is widely perceived that considerable, indeed, decisive, power is exercised by the Standing Committee Chairpersons in panchayats, something also evident to us in the course of fieldwork. The pattern described above is well-discernible in Table 3.k., which represents the gender break-up of the three major chairpersonships of standing committees of Finance, Development, and Welfare, in the panchayat in July 2007.

Of 71 block panchayats (out of the 152 blocks in all), 69 had male chairpersons for finance standing committees, and only 2 had females; 62 of the 71 development standing committee chairpersons were male, and just 9 were female. However, in the welfare standing committees, women exceeded one-third the total numbers. In the lowest tier, though more women figured as welfare standing committee chairpersons compared to the other two positions, their presence was lower than in comparable positions in the higher tiers. Going by this sample, women's share in the total positions goes up from 14.03 per cent in the village panchayats, to 17.84 at the block level, only to fall to 11.90 at the district panchayat level—the third tier which involves considerable political influence.

Interestingly, as far as our fieldwork goes, it appears that a sort of 'reverse reservation' was also at work—the presence of a woman panchayat president often meant that the standing

Table 3.k. Numbers of Women and Men chairing Standing Committees (SC) in Village, Block, and District Panchayats

Panchayat	Finance SC		Development SC		Welfare SC		Total	% of women in
	M	F	M	F	M	F	(positions)	total positions
Village (%)	103 (90.35)	11 (9.65)	99 (86.84)	15 (13.16)	92 (80.70)	22 (19.30)	114	14.03
Block (%)	69 (97.18)	2 (2.82)	62 (87.32)	9 (12.68)	44 (61.98)	27 (38.02)	(342) 71 BPs (213)	17.84
District (%)	12 (95.12)	2 (4.88)	13 (87.80)	1 (12.20)	12 (67.08)	2 (32.92)	14 DPs (42)	11.90

Source: Fieldwork data

committee chairpersons would all be male. In a sample of 57 male- and 57 female-headed village panchayats of the former term randomly selected, it turned out that in 44 of the latter, standing committee chairpersonships were held exclusively by men (in July 2007) and just 12 showed a mixed pattern, of one woman and two men and in only one panchayat was 'more female' pattern evident (Table 3.l.).

Table 3.l. Gender Composition of Standing Committee (SC) Chairpersonships in Village and Block Panchayats with Female Presidents

Tier	All-Male	Mixed* (nos of women heading welfare SCs)	More Female† (nos of women heading welfare SCs)	Total
Village	44	12 (8)	1 (1)	57
Block	16	8 (8)	0	24

*'Mixed' refers to a 'one woman, two men' pattern.
† 'More female' refers to a 'two women, one man' pattern.
Source: Fieldwork Data

Exclusively male standing committee chairpersonships (Table 3.m.) were not infrequent in the presence of a male panchayat president, but 'mixed' chairpersonships appear to be more here compared to the sample of panchayats headed by women considered above.

Table 3.m. Gender composition of Standing Committee (SC) Chairpersonships in Village and Block Panchayats with Male Presidents

Tier	All-Male	Mixed* (nos of women heading welfare SCs)	More Female† (nos of women heading welfare SCs)	Total
Village	26	26(17)	5(4)	57
Block	9	13(10)	2(2)	24

*'Mixed' refers to a 'one woman, two men' pattern.
† 'More female' refers to a 'two women, one man' pattern.
Source: Fieldwork Data

In the male-headed panchayats, the all-male group was 26, and the 'mixed' (26) and 'more women' (5) groups together, 31—less of a difference between the two figures, compared with 44 and 13 for the women-headed ones. It is worth reflecting whether this pattern signifies 'reverse reservation'—did the acceptance of a woman as panchayat president often involve the tacit 'reservation' of the three major standing committee chairpersonships for men? The opposite scenario—of a male panchayat president and three women standing committee chairpersons—was almost unthinkable, though we did find one panchayat where this is true. Even instances of two women standing committee chairpersons were comparatively rare in our sample. It is also worth noting, again, that women were largely in welfare standing committees—indeed, the sole woman in the 'mixed' group, and one of the women in the 'more women' group was most often a welfare standing committee chairperson—a pattern that firmed up in the block level data too.

Our interviewees were also quite vocal about the tendency of the Vice-President, the Chairperson of the Finance Standing Committee, to usurp the powers of the president.[17] Indeed, most of them included the interference of the Vice-President, more likely to be a seasoned local politician with more experience and connections in local politics, among the dangers to be avoided through acquiring sound knowledge of the rules. Yet they were also clear that this weapon would be quite useless in the absence of strong support within the local party or from politicians located higher up in the party hierarchy.

Lastly, it may be important to gain a sense of male members' perception of the advantages to governance from women's presence, especially from 'gentle power'. This also probably helps us to understand why these women leaders continue to feel that 'gentle power' underlies their popularity, despite the above-mentioned disadvantages and tensions in their perception. The answer is that it does make them popular, but does not free them from the shackles of patriarchal expectations. Rashmi Sharma's (2009) observations regarding male response to women's reservation in local bodies in Kerala do help here. She notes that women members were regarded as less able than men, but were accepted. This was as a gesture of goodwill towards "empowering women and bringing them into the public sphere" and not as recognition of "their positive contribution to the GP" (2009: footnote 6 p. 152). More interestingly, "While a large proportion of PRs [panchayat representatives] (63 per cent) did not see the women PRs as having made a special contribution, some did say that women made a special contribution in women's programmes or issues, or increased women's access to the GP, or improved the GP by making it more peaceful or friendly." (p. 152). This, however, did not translate into greater empowerment of women members: "Women were viewed by both men and women PRs as having difficulty in working late, in travelling and mingling with people, or paying less attention to work because of duties at home and lacking training, experience, and influence, while facing discrimination and harassment by male colleagues. Many PRs said that women had problems within political parties also." (p. 116)[18]

Apolitical 'Empowerment'?

A significant sub-group of our interviewees saw career opportunities for themselves through their experience in local governance. This was especially pronounced among those who are better educated and young, who perceive their participation as a career opportunity, a chance to acquire new and marketable skills, and not as political activism. This may indeed be connected to the fact that these women who have entered local governance are second or third generation in 'political families', for whom entry into local governance does not signify a decisive break of any kind. Family connections now seem to ensure much smoother entry, both at the higher, competitive levels and at the lower levels. Most women panchayat presidents enjoy considerable support from their families, especially husbands. The justifications of women's employment now seem to have gained greater application here. Many of them asserted that their mobility has brought gains not only in the form of an income, but also as greater acceptability for the family. To quote one of the most successful women panchayat presidents in Kerala, with experience across multiple terms: "I have been successful for three consecutive terms and now everyone knows me. Though my husband is a local leader of the DYFI, he is known after me. My children too get this recognition."

Further, she views her long and successful career as a panchayat president not as a springboard to a higher-level political career or more intense political activism, but as valuable, marketable experience that could secure her employment:

> By now I have learned all the rules and guidelines of the implementation of development projects. I have coordinated and implemented the development projects of various other government agencies. I know that my party may not give me another chance to contest as I have been here for three consecutive terms. Hence I need to find another job, and so earned a Masters' Degree through distance education. I think I can work with an NGO and the skills and abilities I have so far acquired may be utilized well there.

Just how influential this view of working in local governance is, was evident from what we observed in interviews with two women of different generations in the same district. The first belongs to the earlier era of radical public action for redistribution of productive resources; the latter, to the 1990s. Both are very successful panchayat presidents. The latter however, sees it as training for a job—while she agrees that being president has brought her social respect, a job was always a 'dream'. The former told us how she gave up government employment to be a fulltime political activist in the 1960s, inspired by A K Gopalan and his agenda of militant mass mobilization. The distance between local governance and political activism could not be more apparent. Many of our interviewees stressed the need for more income "in these changing times" and hence mentioned that they were also selling life insurance and collecting savings for the Postal Savings Scheme—mostly managed by their husbands since they were busy with panchayat activities.

This may seem to indicate that women leaders in local governance, no matter how successful they may be in welfare distribution and development initiatives, and despite their party affiliations, are apolitical to a large degree. Now, there is much in our interviews that may reinforce this view. For example, it appears that very few woman leaders—almost none—of any political persuasion have a good grasp of the politics of neoliberalism beyond the rhetoric that circulates in party circles (quite unlike many of their male counterparts, whose public speeches and statements indicate otherwise). This was apparent in their responses to our questions about successful projects in their panchayats. Almost everyone spoke enthusiastically of the World Bank-assisted Kerala Rural Water Supply and Sanitation Project (*Jalanidhi*). Yet it was striking that few on the left had any critical awareness of its design or of the implications of rising beneficiary contributions and other aspects, though they did speak of the non-viability of the project for the really poor and regretted their inability to help oftentimes. Only one interviewee could speak at length about the problems of neoliberalized water governance and suggest an alternative and this was because the falling groundwater levels in her panchayat became a burning issue in the area and the focus of agitation by environmental activists and local people. There were instances which could be read as evidence for the deliberate avoidance of urgent political issues by women leaders in local governance: for example, the silence maintained, in our interview with her, by a prominent woman president from north Kerala, about a controversial pesticide which is believed to have led to serious genetic damage among people. Though the issue had been raised quite strongly by the oppositional civil social society with plenty of discussion in the press and visual media, and though she told us that she was involved with institutions that had endorsed the use of this chemical, she preferred to sidestep the issue by saying that "it didn't happen in our panchayat".

Yet, it would not be fair to conclude that women leaders in local governance are apolitical. It may seem that they are cut off from 'high politics' (as their own claims to be disinterested may indicate). It may also appear that they do not see the sense of 'politics' as involving struggles around non-sovereign forms of power. Nor do many of them perceive the older sense of struggling against encroaching predatory capitalism (as their ignorance of larger political contexts may indicate). However, these may be inadequate impressions. In the first instance, it must be noted that there are huge barriers in the way of their migration to high politics and women leaders in the village panchayats are acutely aware of this.[19] Besides the support of powerful (most often male) politicians in their parties, and indeed, 'permission' in the case of women members of cadre parties (discussed briefly in Chapter 1), the most frequently mentioned hurdle was of money. The support of senior male family members or other influential male politicians is crucial here, especially for women in non-cadre parties, when it comes to successful fund-raising. It is certainly not becoming of a 'respectable woman' in Kerala to be dealing in money with strange men. And respectability is now an indispensable eligibility condition to contest in local politics. As an ex-panchayat president of a non-cadre party in south Kerala, now a fulltime politician, put it:

> Women need more funds [than men] to stay in politics. They will have to travel at night; but we can't afford a bad name. I have myself asked auto rickshaws to wait, and paid 300 to 400 rupees. Men have many sources—businessmen, contractors, other organizations—who give them money. Women can't directly tap such sources, especially newcomers in politics.

And besides, many women leaders do have a sense of the intense depoliticization happening in their panchayats. This is particularly pronounced in interviews with women presidents who are more closely involved in party activism especially in the CPM. Their assessment of political issues in the panchayat often combined a critique of consumerist depoliticization with the refurbishing of radical left politics through renewing anti-capitalist struggles in the present. Intense unease was perceivable in many interviews, like in one quoted below:

> It is our fault. Why do people come to the panchayat? For securing their personal, individual benefit. Asking, do I get money for home maintenance, do I get money for a new toilet? Other than this, there is no will at all to fight for the common good, against forces that affect everyone badly. And nowadays, people can't get enough. We get to know that the roads are bad only when it starts raining. If two people disagree on something as petty as a by-lane, they come straight to the panchayat. And when we try to solve it, each pulls his own way. The panchayat should not be an institution to settle petty disputes; it must be able to take on larger issues that affect us all.

Most importantly, many women leaders did perceive their powerlessness when confronted with the new capitalism fostered through remittances from abroad, eagerly cultivated by key elements in high politics. When inquiring about local development in her panchayat, a woman president in central Kerala quipped with scarcely-concealed anger—"Why ask me? Please go and ask xxx (the name of a leading NRI businessman from the panchayat). He has bought all the land here and land prices have skyrocketed. The panchayat wants to find a five-cent plot, but it can't find any affordable land anymore." She however felt that the panchayat could do little about it as "my own colleagues laugh at my frustration. They'd rather have me close my eyes." Many others pointed out that the workload of local bodies was becoming unbearable because they had to constantly deal with the effects of processes that needed serious regulation from higher authorities or action by social movements.[20] They often ended their analysis of the situation with the suggestion that the panchayat ought to change—it was being too closely identified with welfare distribution but ought to be the locus of a new radical anti-capitalist politics from below. A young woman leader from central Kerala articulated her vision thus:

> Truly, the next phase of panchayati raj should be against the rotten consumerist lifestyle and the greed that has spread everywhere. Panchayats should actively join the struggle to protect the soil, water, and the earth. This suggestion does not go beyond the already-designated powers of the panchayat—the power to protect the soil, water, and earth already rests with it. Panchayats should become able to use that power more effectively, and mobilize people as citizens actively. The initiative against plastics that the panchayats had undertaken did have an immediate effect—though it waned soon. But we need to think of how panchayats can be made into the locus of struggles and interventions to protect the environment.

Such a consciousness was also apparent in the words of some women leaders from both left and the non-left who were also active in fighting illegal sand-mining and destructive construction activities in their panchayats. A CPM president of a village panchayat which was totally dominated by the CPM in north Kerala confessed that "though we are unchallenged in our panchayat, we have been unable to stop even our own cadre from breaking building rules and indulging in illegal activities that harm everybody." She was clear that this could be remedied only through a show of strong political will in the top-level leadership. Similarly a senior woman president of the Congress from south Kerala admitted that illegal sand-mining was an unstoppable force in her panchayat which had powerful backers in all political parties; hence it was suicidal to take them on. She attributed it to "decline of moral values and uncorrupted dedication to the values of the nationalist struggle and Gandhism."

However, there was considerable wariness in their words about all forms of identity politics, which were most commonly derided as 'divisive'. Most of our interviewees perceived no contradiction between representing women as a social group and representing the general interests of their panchayat. The prominence of the Kudumbashree self-help-group network of BPL women in welfare distribution seemed to be a key reason why the women felt so: by 'giving' to the women, they were also 'giving' to the panchayat. Most admitted, however, that they were largely unable to pursue gender justice beyond this: thus the formation of local-level institutions meant for speedy administration of gender justice was admitted to be lagging.[21]

And it was also apparent that even the relationship built by some exceptional women leaders who chose the BPL women of Kudumbashree as their major support-base (which sometimes irked their party colleagues) was deeply informed by their new elite status. In that sense, it reproduced the 'pedagogic relation of power' that bound modernized new elite women to their non-elite counterparts in the discourse of community reformism of the early 20th century—in which the unquestionable-'enlightened' new elite woman was to 'uplift' her less-advantaged sister. One such leader, who had braved a lot of opposition in the local party which felt she was focusing too much on women, described her efforts thus:

> Before my term, the women used to be terrified of male leaders ... Earlier, they were used mainly to fill halls when leaders visited and in the welcome ceremony. Now they can't be used that way. If asked to attend a meeting, they will ask what it is about, if it is a meaningless one, they won't go, even if I ask them to ... the worst sufferers were SC women. Now, these used to be undisciplined women, almost impossible to improve (*nannaakkaan pattata*). But I discovered that they had a certain talent, by virtue of being born in that community, and arranged for it to be fostered ... and it worked quite well ... now, it is a different matter with SC women members. One (*orennam*) used to be a domestic servant ... and started displaying airs ... The other one ... (*mattethu*) is better ... she has passed the pre-degree level. See, these (*ithunngal*) have certain natural bent. They should be directed that way. That's why my effort to develop their natural talent worked so well.

The language used by the president to refer to the SC women of the Kudumbashree (*orennam, mattethu, ithungal*) who she helped reveals the connection between her new elite status and her reformist zeal for 'uplift' of an apparently 'undisciplined' group. Though she claims that her support has been vital in enabling these women to resist patriarchal power in the panchayat, her own reinstating of new elite norms brings back reformist power. This is perhaps most apparent in her disapproval of the SC woman member who seems unmindful of the necessity of being re-formed through guidance of 'enlightened' new elite women. Reformist power does not disappear; rather, it flows, this time, through the agency of the woman president.

Conclusion

Clearly, our interviewees form a very diverse set. If there were some women leaders who perceived career opportunities as the gain from their participation in local governance, there were many who regarded it as an opportunity for social work and charitable activities, a few others who hoped to make interventions in local development, and also some who saw the possibility of repoliticizing the space of the local through the panchayat. This diversity is partly fostered from the ambiguous nature of the 'panchayat' as a discursive construct. On the one hand it was projected as an apolitical-civil space of local development; on the other, it holds the possibility of transformation into a powerful vehicle of intervention in local space, being a Constitutional body endowed with considerable power.

It is important to note that women leaders' marked preference for 'gentle power' as their key instrument of governing is neither a matter of simple choice or of 'false consciousness'. Rather, the hegemonic projection of the space of the local as apolitical and hypermoralized makes it the ideal instrument. Though our interviewees usually projected 'gentle power' as uniquely and naturally feminine, some male presidents of village panchayats who we had a chance to talk with, especially those who were associated with the KSSP, did feel that they too exercised 'gentle power' in dealing with welfare beneficiaries. This is probably true, for the space demands such power relations. However, the need to bolster 'gentle power' with 'knowledge of the rules' so that the dividing line between caregiving and subservience remains sharp and clear, is probably more particular to women leaders, given the nature of entrenched patriarchy in both the local party and local bureaucracy. Also, women leaders' propensity to gravitate towards welfare distribution rather than intervene in local development priorities cannot be attributed to merely 'ideological limitations'. This point needs to be stressed: it is the construction of local governance as an apolitical and civil, even intimate,[22] space that orients leaders located within it towards welfare distribution. Researchers have suggested that many male members of local bodies share this depoliticized view of public responsibility: 65 per cent of the panchayat representatives surveyed by Sharma (2009), when asked to describe their role, responded that it involved "helping people", "providing basic facilities", "fulfilling people's basic needs" and so on; only 28 per cent responded specifically that their mandate was to address the needs of the underprivileged (p. 119). Prevailing gender ideology does direct women more insistently towards a view of their public role as apolitical, civil, and intimate—hence the strikingly frequent evocation of such a construction by women leaders. But it was also observed that besides their ideological views, women leaders' relatively deeper bonds with the local community and their greater fear of accusations of corruption oriented them towards focusing on fair distribution of welfare, even though this meant sacrificing energy that may be better directed towards changing development priorities, and indeed, even though their efforts could often be only partially successful.

Returning to the question raised in the opening section of this chapter—why 'knowledge' does not help women leaders get beyond the patriarchal bargain—it seems that we need to note the fact that 'knowledge of the rules' seems to be not so much an instrument of empowerment as a tool of self-defense in the narratives of women leaders. This is probably one of the reasons why the sense of 'knowing' and 'knowledge' most often possessed by them relates to rule and procedure, and not to knowledge of political and developmental alternatives. However, from the example of one woman leader who did manage to utilize knowledge in ways that changed local development priorities, it is evident that knowledge alone does not help women get beyond the patriarchal bargain.

It is clear that these two weapons wielded by women leaders do not guarantee them full participation—as evident from the statistics of participation as chairpersons of Standing Committees. And neither does it guarantee stable ground, given the shifting and unstable nature of welfare beneficiaries—a fact that women leaders are quite acutely aware of. Besides the dominant projection of the panchayat as an apolitical-civil space, this may be yet another reason why a significant sub-group would seek career opportunities, rather than expanded political activism, through the panchayats. Local governance, our interviewees unanimously agree, is a difficult space for women from low-income families since costs were high (as one woman leader remarked, " ... intimate contact with party supporters has been 'outsourced' to us—the bigger politicians don't attend marriages and funerals in party supporters' homes anymore. All that is our job—and it costs a lot!") and honoraria, ridiculously low. Dealing with welfare beneficiaries who are essentially politically-uncommitted consumers does not offer stable ground for those who desire upward mobility through a committed support-base.

Thus among women leaders in local governance, those of low-income backgrounds tend to seek other opportunities, while women leaders with better access to economic resources seek to move to higher, more stable ground, often moving up through tiers to the District Panchayat-level, which is a proven launching pad into the state-level arena. Some of our interviews with women politicians confirmed the latter: many of these women had actually moved out of local governance into mass organizations of the party, seeking more stable ground from which to launch themselves into high politics.

Notes

1. It is important to note that recent studies do point out that at the moment women's presence is high in the village assembly, but as one moves up the various steps of decentralized planning in Kerala, it shrinks considerably. Isaac (2005), Harilal (2008) and Go K (2009) note that women's presence is decidedly poor in the development seminars and task forces which require greater technical inputs; Sharma (2009) and Chathukulam and John (2000) point out that the resource persons identified and trained for local planning are overwhelmingly male. Isaac and Franke (2000) mention that only 17–19 per cent of the total numbers of Key Resource Persons and District Resource Persons were women. The authors of Go K (2009) found this to be so in the local bodies they studied. In one such panchayat, "in the working group on women, eight out of nine members in the GP were men." Besides, "In Thiruvananthapuram Corporation too, men dominated all the working groups including the one for women. Under such a situation the role of women is but marginal and ineffective" (p. 129). George (2005) notes that women are not part of the process of beneficiary list preparation which takes place prior to the village assembly (p. 191).

2. The state's *Economic Review* for 2007 points out that the spending of the local bodies still follows this pattern: for the period 2002–07, local governments' spending in Kerala has been highest in the infrastructure sector (77.13 per cent), closely followed by the service sector (76.17), with the productive sector trailing at 60.53 per cent. The *Economic Review* for 2009 notes that counting together the allocation of a total plan fund of Rs 1966.94 available for the three sectors, viz. the productive, service, and infrastructure, in 2008–09, and the amount allocated by the LSGs (31 per cent of their total plan funds) for mandatory provision for schemes and projects stipulated by the Government as per guidelines, service sector

expenditure predominated " .... It is noted that the projects/ schemes included under this category [i.e. the latter] belong to service sector. If we put this into the service sector allocation, it is surprising to note that about 70 per cent of plan funds of LSGs in the Annual Plan 2008–09 was provided to the service sector. At the same time, no progressive increase is noticed in the productive sector allocation of LSGs during this period compared to the previous year allocation where it was 20 per cent. Also, the percentage of utilization in productive sector declined to 68 in 2008–09 from 74 in 2007–08. This limited performance in the productive sector is valid for all tiers of LSGs ... As far as the LSGs are concerned they have a vital role in eradicating poverty at the local-level by achieving local production. But the poor performance of the LSGs in the productive sector will affect adversely the implementation of this role." (pp. 516–7). The research literature on local bodies in Kerala confirms this, for example, Harilal 2005; Go K 2009; Subramanian 2004.

3. Out of a total of 85 interviews. Two interviews which were useful, but which did not contain crucial details necessary for the description of our sample were left out of this section.

4. Our findings are thus different from those of Isaac (2005) who claims that the relative youth of elected women members in his sample from a survey conducted in 1998, indicates the easing of gender prejudices: "A lower age profile signals the erasing of some restrictions and the need for more energetic and proactive leadership because of raised expectations from panchayats ... it possibly reflects an increasing acceptance of women with childbearing and domestic responsibilities breaking out of stereotypical and patriarchal roles." (p. 377). The empirical basis of this inference, however, is not apparent in his essay. Isaac and Franke (2000) claim that for the elected members in the first term (1995), there were more women below the age of 50 than men: while 79.05 per cent of men were below fifty, 88.88 per cent of women were below that age. More than one-fourth of women were below 30.

5. Isaac (2005) found that educational profile of elected women was superior to that of elected men (p. 377); also, he found a positive correlation between educational qualifications and high

levels of self-confidence among elected women representatives (p. 412).

6. Isaac (2005) cites a survey by the KSSP which notes that while nearly half of the elected women interviewed reported that husbands and brothers were closely involved in politics, the large majority of men had no close relations in politics—and when they did report, it was usually of a brother (p. 383). From a survey of 1998, he mentions that of the women, nearly 35 per cent reported that they were motivated to enter local governance by their family environments (p. 383). Also see Bhaskar 1997; ISI 1997. This is true for other parts of India as well. See Datta 1998; Kaushik 1998; Kudva 2003. This is also true for women legislators, as noted by Singh and Pundir 2002.

7. Isaac (2005) notes that in 1998, only 32.22 per cent of the elected women members he interviewed claimed that they could manage officials at an "average" level. Only 15.16 per cent said their ability to manage officials was "very good". In contrast, a large number had gained confidence in interacting with the public—55.38 per cent reported that their ability to interact with the public was "very good" (p. 409). Knowledge of rules seemed to have improved later—a larger number of women reported "average knowledge" in 1998 compared with 1995 (p. 408). Go K (2009) notes that the inefficiency of the working groups leads to greater reliance on the panchayat staff, and often projects are prepared not by the working groups but by staff (p. 76). For an all-India picture in 1995, see Mohanty 1995, which notes many similar hurdles elsewhere.

8. Isaac (2005) notes that there was considerable improvement in elected women members' knowledge of the legal framework of panchayati raj and the various guidelines and norms between 1995 and 98 (p. 408).

9. Rashmi Sharma (2009) observes from her fieldwork in Kerala that it is this path, of combining a good grasp of the legal framework of panchayati raj and building up influence within the party, that assures success to male panchayat presidents as well. In her fieldwork, she notes that political competition can prove utterly debilitating to local development, and therefore success as a president calls for strong leadership: "In all the three 'best GPs', the presidents were politically experienced, and were able to negotiate across political parties, and evolve

common agendas." (p. 123). All three had male presidents of the General Category (p. 116). She also notes that this seems to be working against women and SC/ST representatives (p. 122).

10. Strulik (2008) argues from her research on women leaders of local bodies in Himachal Pradesh who constructed the work of the panchayat president as "charity work", that these women's treatment of the community as the "extended (fictive) family" may lead to a situation in which "politics may eventually be transformed through the new meanings, because women and maybe even men may place new and different priorities in local politics." (p. 368). While women's identification of their public role as 'charity work' may not necessarily indicate the absence of agency (as Mahmood 2005, for instance, has argued), a consideration of the local context—the local dynamics of patriarchy—as well as the differences between women in the local context need to be carefully considered before such expectations are projected. As we may see in Chapter 5, in Kerala, such discourse has been enabling for a group that had been almost completely outside formal politics until recently—the Muslim women of north Kerala. However, the same cannot be assumed for all groups of women, especially considering the fact that the discourse is itself less available to Dalit women. For new elite women, the persistence of such a discourse clearly prevents them from overcoming current restrictions—the current shape of patriarchy—and thus corrals them in which they have been historically confined.

11. While some studies have found much less bias in beneficiary selection along political lines, and corruption, as well, in Kerala's local self governments, they do admit that a clear political affiliation to the ruling party is certainly an advantage. One study (Nair 2000), a comparison between a left-dominated and a non-left dominated panchayat, observed that party involvement at all levels was evident in the former, and while non-left people were not necessarily excluded, the power to include or exclude lay overwhelmingly with the local party. Sharma (2009) notes from her fairly extensive fieldwork that "There was dissatisfaction about the criteria of selection, and the potential beneficiaries were reported to provide wrong information, leading to wrong selection. In the latter case, other people did not protest because they did not want to make

long-term enemies." (p. 132). Go K (2009) also notes that the issue of inclusion in the BPL list is fluid and can lead to corruption (p. 147). Also see Vijayalakshmi (2006) who finds the control of women members in panchayat committees by party functionaries in Kerala quite similar to elite domination of panchayats in Karnataka.

12. Recent literature on decentralization in Kerala does reveal the extent to which the elaborate process of local planning designed to involve people, has considerably deteriorated. Most of this writing points out that Village Assembly participation in the planning process is markedly poor (Harilal 2008; Go K 2009; Sharma 2009); that working groups, technical support groups, and the District Planning Committee are weak due to a variety of reasons including the disintegration of communities (Harilal 2008). They also show that working groups are non-functional, sometimes stuffed with favourites who have no technical skill whatsoever or controlled by elected members (CAPDECK, CSES and CRM 2003; Go K 2009; Sharma 2009). Sharma (2009) notes how the panchayat committee seemed all-powerful in shaping local development: in 11 (out of a total of 12) of the village panchayats she studied, "it overshot its role, and identified priority projects and earmarked funds before the working groups began their deliberations ... . The central dynamic of the planning exercise was competition over the allocation of resources across different wards. In all the GPs, [gram panchayats] ward-wise allocation of funds was negotiated fiercely, and in at least three, funds were simply allocated equally among the wards." (p. 145)

13. While the beneficiary lists seem less open to corruption, there are other sources of corruption at the local level, which, it appears, are handled by male members, especially leaders of Standing Committees. Many women leaders admitted to such corruption while pointing out that they were often not even in the know regarding such transactions. However, some did admit that they did approach contractors for 'contributions' to the party though they strongly discouraged bribery in the panchayat office and did not accept gifts of any sort. Existing research on the panchayats in Kerala does point to the persistence of corruption (Harilal 2005; Sharma 2009; Go K 2009; Oommen 2010). The report of the Committee for Evaluation

of Decentralized Planning and Development (Go K 2009) notes that innovative practices to contain corruption that were fairly successful in the early years, such as the Beneficiary Committee System have been discontinued: "Apparently nobody seems to be worried about the continuation of the contract system and the archaic public works manual which have facilitated and legitimized corruption in the state." (p. 61). Studies also indicate that women members are often outside the circuits of patronage and corruption. Chathukulam and John (2000) hint that women members prefer less partisan style of politics as opposed to the male style of "distributing patronage to those faithful to the party" (p. 92).

14. Some of the literature does acknowledge that most of the BPL beneficiaries participate in village assemblies not as a group but as individuals, representatives of BPL families, seeking individualized benefits. Harilal (2008), for example, acknowledges the "disintegration of local communities" as a major reason for the poor interest of welfare beneficiaries in local planning. (p. 84). He also notes that efforts to improve tax collection by the local bodies have not been very successful; however, beneficiary contributions have been satisfactory (p. 87).

15. This of course has been noted as a positive feature of village panchayats in Kerala by many researchers, for example, Sharma (2009); Narayana (2005). Sharma (2009) writes: "Arguably, since the GP is far more accessible for direct interaction than centralized government, people are also able to influence it far more through direct interaction with decision-makers." (p. 137)

16. The report of the Oommen Committee (Go K 2009) on decentralization remarked that there was some truth in the frustration expressed in "several quarters against the plethora of guidelines and directives issued from above spelling out the elaborate details of the steps to be followed in overall sectoral and special component plans ... [these] are top-down exercises that can sap initiative and autonomy." (pp 61–2). It notes that the guidelines go into such minute detail that it would be difficult for the "ordinary panchayat president to carry them out" within the stipulated time-frame even with good technical support. However, they did feel that the necessity for guidance

from above still remained and so a pragmatic balance has to be achieved through 'consultative process" . (p. 61).

17. The above arguments are confirmed in Sharma's work (2009) which showed that women and SC/ST members were rarely chairpersons of Standing Committees. She also remarks that they could not "easily be leaders within the Grama Panchayat. In GPs where SC/ST or women representatives were panchayat presidents, some other panchayat representative was often reported to be more influential. In three out of 6 such GPs, the panchayat president admitted to relying a great deal on some other male representative of the general category." But she does say that this is not the case, however, in GPs headed by women from the General Category. (p. 116). As evident in our fieldwork, such women put up greater resistance, often on the strength of 'knowledge of the rules'.

18. Another study by George (2006) noted that women members are still denied meaningful roles in the panchayat even though they are better educated and quite confident of their abilities; they are also much less mobile and forced to bear double- or triple-burdens of work. Importantly her observations about women's acceptability seem to indicate that women need to conform with new elite norms of femininity in order to be acceptable. Women are accepted as having "less sectarian political outlook", because they apparently "display more integrity", and are 'more accessible and transparent." (p. 187). Women are observed to spend more time in social work while "men said they spend more time to perform their administrative role along with their political role." Women, however, are now more confident about handling administration. (p. 187) See also, Chathukulam and John (2000).

19. Here, there seems to be a clear difference between women in the upper-most tier and the lower tiers. Women leaders in the district panchayat are often far more experienced in politics, or are selected for a combination of high education, managerial skills, and cultural and social capital. Hence this tier is often a sure entry-point for women into high politics, especially the state legislature. However, the women leaders at the lower levels are clearly disadvantaged. The district panchayat president also enjoys symbols of power such as a car for herself and protocol

advantages, which are not available to women leaders of lower levels.

20. Researchers have also pointed out that the panchayats are often called upon to minimize the negative effects of processes over which they have no control. Harilal (2005) calls for better top-down regulation in issues that are beyond the control of local bodies. Sharma (2009) notes that "though the more fundamental problems such as the closure of industry and alienation of tribal land could not be addressed at the Grama Panchayat level, the Grama Panchayats were expected to address the manifestations of these problems, i.e., unemployment and poverty." (p. 161)

21. The Chairperson of the State Women's Commission complained that the Jagratha Samitis set up in 2007 in many panchayats in Kerala were largely defunct, and called for their revival. *The Hindu,* 27 September 2010, Thiruvanathapuram edition. [http://www.hindu.com/2010/09/27/stories/2010092750280200.htm]. Accessed, 22 November 2010.

22. Researchers have noted that in Kerala, "Overall, the poor contacted public authorities [i.e. here, the panchayat] mainly for personal matters and the rest of the population for civic functions." Personal matters, here, included "assistance for daughter's marriage and resolving personal disputes." Narayana 2005: 29.

4

Dilemmas and Opportunities: Dalit Women

Dilemmas of Dalit Women

It is often remarked about the 33 per cent reservations that it allowed space for non-elite women in local governance. As mentioned earlier, these women were marginal to the political domain in Kerala, albeit in different ways. Dalit women were confined to the margins of political mobilizations and tribal women remained generally far away from modern politics until recent times. The reservations in local governance have certainly opened up for them a number of opportunities denied hitherto. Indeed, the interviews with women leaders from these groups reveal considerable confidence, optimism, and joy in being able to interact on equal terms with members of powerful communities. "I come from an area where the landlords were very powerful till recently," said one of these interviewees, who had been a tailor before she entered local governance. "But times have changed. I feel embarrassed these days when I see these upper-caste people who used to be so high and mighty once, stand up respectfully with their *mundus* down to their ankles [a gesture displaying respect] when they see me pass. These men are much older too!" Another woman leader who argued that caste was not a major issue anymore (an exception in this group) in Kerala, indirectly admitted otherwise when she spoke of how she had been invited to a major function of the Syrian Catholic Church in her area, where she shared the dais with major dignitaries, only because she was the panchayat president: "…There was a time when the low castes were ignored; not any more. It was great happiness for me when I sat there … I wouldn't have been allowed anywhere close had I not been the president!" However, participant observation in panchayats did reveal the heavy presence of casteist hubris both among officials and local politicians. In one particularly telling case, a Dalit woman president had agreed to meet us at her office at a certain hour in the morning. Since she was late, we asked the Secretary of the panchayat whether she would be delayed, referring to her as 'Madam'. He appeared puzzled: "Madam? Who's that?" When we clarified that we were asking about the president, he said, "Oh, that. She is no Madam, she is an SC." There were many other incidents, especially of the denial of the panchayat vehicle to the SC woman president.

It is interesting that the Dalit women favoured by all parties including the left parties seem to have been chosen for the formal education they have acquired[1] and less for their awareness of issues regarding their respective communities.[2] Indeed, though the trade unions of Kerala, especially on the left, have traditionally included large numbers of Dalit women workers, who are articulate (if one goes by research such as that conducted by Lindberg (2001) on cashew workers), well-aware of the modalities of political struggle, and committed to the party, they are largely outside the leadership of local governance. The unstated selection process is partly dictated by the need to handle bureaucratic workloads in the panchayat, and in the case of cadre parties, partly by the need to find candidates who are capable of following 'party discipline'. The differences between the two generations are significant, particularly the fact that older women do have considerable prior experience in militant political action, while the younger ones are less exposed to it. This is probably the reason why a young Dalit woman leader of local governance described her participation in a mass agitation as if it were a social event: "It was such a lovely experience … we were so many, and we cooked on the roadside and … such fun it was. We all sat down in the middle of the road and drank our rice gruel. We had only gruel and *chammandi*, but how tasty it was. That was probably because all of us were there together..."

The design of decentralized governance structures is such that group interests are acknowledged in welfare distribution, but leadership positions, such as that of the panchayat president, are supposed to be 'neutral', representing the 'general' interest. But as has been noticed elsewhere in India too, women in local governance have to negotiate not just gender, but also class and caste identities (Vyasulu and Vyasulu 1999). Since the claims and interests of different social groups are acknowledged in the norms of welfare distribution fixed from above, 'neutrality' means the proper adherence to these norms. However, as many of our interviewees, both Dalit and non-Dalit, pointed out, the norms are often too rigid and following them too strictly would cause losses to the deserving poor. Thus Dalit women presidents have to adhere to the neutrality mentioned earlier but also try their best to ensure that their communities benefit most by bending (not breaking) the rules as far as possible. This means two kinds of dilemmas. First, Dalit women have to both protect the interests of their communities *and* represent the panchayat generally. Secondly, the norms of welfare distribution have to be respected—indeed defended as absolutely necessary—but stretched to the utmost so that the poorer communities are served the maximum.

All the Dalit women presidents across party lines who we interviewed (some less 'successful' than others), with two interesting exceptions, openly stated that their primary commitment was to securing the funds assigned for SC/ST people and that they were in local governance to protect the interests of SC/ST people.[3] One of the exceptions revealed the consequences of the first sort of dilemma. This was a senior woman leader—no novice in local governance— who stated vociferously that though she belonged to a Dalit community, she was determined to be "fair and equally inclined to all communities". She thus defended her decision (which has been challenged) to implement 'fair distribution' in the wake of tensions over the distribution of the Special Component Plan (SPC) fund to Scheduled Caste beneficiaries for the renovation of houses by dipping into the funds of the panchayat to distribute similar benefits to other castes. Dalit presidents who openly declared their primary allegiance to the SC/ST groups also reported that they did experience such a dilemma. To quote from one such account:

> This was early in my term, I was only getting used to local governance. There was a scheme for smokeless ovens for SC groups, which I quickly accessed. Honestly, I didn't think, at that time, that it was good because my people will primarily benefit. I just thought that this was a generous scheme; it will be good for the panchayat. But when it was implemented, it aroused such discontent—so many complained, 'she's barely in, and look, she has started distributing goodies to her folk!' I was shocked, and ever since, I have been careful in accessing special schemes for SC people. I bring only schemes that benefit all.... My people, however, benefit because I occupy this position. I make it easier for them to access the benefits, without bureaucratic hassle.

The second dilemma is more pervasive. All interviewees agreed that very often, welfare distribution did require them to bend the rules especially when it came to spending funds earmarked for Scheduled Castes and Tribes. Here, however, there was frequent conflict between the president and the officials. "They don't want to do it for us," continued the president quoted above, "they think we are ignorant and so can't play the game. So we get all the excuses—they can't do it because the rules are fixed and if they get caught, they will lose their pension, their emoluments and so on." She also pointed out that despite personal risks, officials were only too ready to bend the rules for those politicians they considered powerful, and for new elite women presidents. "We are not considered powerful enough." This president, a longtime CPM activist and trade unionist, said that she had not experienced much caste difference, and was president of a

non-reserved panchayat. However, she pointed out that caste
discrimination did make a sporadic appearance even there:
"when we appear to be a little bit behind, there will be the
immediate reaction that says she is ignorant, which has a
casteist prick to it. She's of that caste, isn't she? No wonder
she is ignorant!" In such circumstances, the Dalit woman
president may have to even jeopardize cordial relations with
the panchayat officials in ways that may be harmful to her.
In the case of a young Dalit woman president, a very assertive
person, her office staff complained bitterly about how she
had harassed them because they had refused to bend the rules
for her regarding the distribution of funds to Dalit families
for toilets. "She locked the ladies' toilet and walked away,"
one of the female staff said. "When we asked her for the
keys, she refused to give them and said, why don't you try the
bushes outside? You'd then know more about the condition
of people who don't have toilets! Is she a woman at all?"
The speaker of these words obviously did not see the point
that the president was trying to make; all she saw was the
lack of gender in the president, who was presented to us as a
"rapacious, power-hungry, mannish woman".[4]

Caste and 'Gentle Power'

The second dilemma outlined above makes the exercise of
'gentle power' very difficult for Dalit women. A very interesting insight from our interview with Dalit women presidents
was from the deeply ambiguous way in which they endorsed
'gentle power' as an instrument of governing. Almost without
exception, they pointed out that it had to be used, but it was
neither 'feminine' nor empowering. Rather, it was simply a
strategic position one had to assume when the odds were
stacked against you heavily. And even as a strategy it could
not last long, for many reasons.

Securing the cooperation of officials is vital for any president, and our Dalit women- interviewees agreed that 'gentle
power' was needed often to make sure that it was secured.

Echoing the words of most interviewees in this group, a working-class woman president from north Kerala remarked about her experiences with panchayat officials that "... one can't assert any authority, has to speak gently, look sympathetic, otherwise they don't cooperate." However, as mentioned earlier, the rules have to be bent at times, and when officials were loath to take such risks, 'gentle power' was sure to break down. As this woman leader remarked: "there's no way but to assert that everything can't be run purely according to rules. I tell them, if you're going to create problems, I won't be here with you, I will be over there, with the people on strike!"

Secondly, many of our interviewees revealed that they had to often openly state that welfare entitlements and reservations for the SC/ST groups were no favour done to them by the rest of the society but an entitlement guaranteed by the state.[5] In other words, they could hardly depend on love, sentiment, or affective techniques to secure these entitlements—they had to quote the rule straight. A young district panchayat president mentioned this when she elaborated on how she had herself suffered a great deal of indirect casteist insult in her life, but tided over through pointing to the Indian Constitution. "Many SC women members and presidents have told me how awfully demeaning it is; I have always told them to answer these insults directly: never let them forget that this [reservation] is our right, say it in so many words. We don't need a favour from them." These women hardly evoke 'femininity' though they do talk of socialized feminine behaviour. In fact, they evoke more frequently, their education. The district panchayat president quoted above asserted this firmly: "The ability to rule is related to education. If you study, you overcome." Another young Dalit president, of the Congress, told us about how her education gave her the confidence to take on even senior leaders. She related to us an anecdote on how she had to confront the Vice-President of her panchayat. An ambitious woman, she is very active in the Mahila Congress, and once it happened that she had to entrust the responsibility of chairing a meeting of the panchayat board to the Vice-President because she was unintentionally delayed after a district-level meeting of the Mahila Congress. This angered him, as he, according to her, was less educated than her and was also someone "who can't be bothered to look up the rules and do something systematically." He turned against her. To quote her:

> From that day onwards he started harassing me in all possible ways. I too didn't flinch. Don't try to control me because I am an SC woman, I said. He threatened to remove my whip. Ok, I said, please do. But there's an MA degree that the university has conferred upon me. You can't remove that, however you try! ... Senior leaders know that I'm putting up a constant fight with this man. They of course value me as an educated Dalit woman.

Thirdly, Dalit women do need to summon the power of the state more frequently than new elite women to protect themselves against casteist harassment.[6]

Here we were struck by a sharp contrast between the distinctly different responses of two village panchayat women leaders to casteist insult, which also revealed the pitfalls that 'gentle power' holds for Dalit women. One was a very successful president from central Kerala, in her second term, of a CPM 'party family' and sharing the general faith dominant within the CPM that caste issues should be subordinated to class issues. In the interview, she presented herself as welfare distributor par excellence and stressed the importance of gentleness, patience, forgiveness, kindness and other 'feminine virtues' in achieving success in the panchayat. Yet her words clearly revealed that not only was 'gentle power' of little use in a crisis situation, it could also block casteism from view. It thus effectively prevented a critical understanding of caste power and action against it:

> In our panchayat we [members] have been doing for our people what is permitted, and indeed, even what is not ... sometimes it brings great joy, sometimes great sadness. This time during the monsoon when the water level in the river rose dangerously and

we had destructive floods ... no, actually the flood happened because the bund burst. The bund burst because people had weakened it bit by bit, for building their houses and so on -so it was really their fault... This time, the water didn't recede for weeks. We took really good care of the families that suffered from the flood. We collected money, obtained all possible funds, used all the influence we had ... the panchayat doesn't have any big source to meet such exigencies. There are clear norms on how much panchayat funds can be used. But when something like this happens, if the panchayat is inactive, people will ask, what else is the job of the panchayat, but serving the people? ... We were running around to meet their needs, but the people in the camp would come up with fresh sets of needs everyday! I can't hand over bounty like that, there are rules. But here I am not an elected representative, but like an *Aechi* [older sister] and so I can't really refuse them anything ....

She then told us how, in this terrible situation, an impatient man had insulted her in public "very rudely" for a very minor failing, despite the fact that she and other members had done their utmost to help him. All those who heard him abuse her were shocked and advised her to file a complaint with the police right then. She, however, refrained from doing so:

But I didn't react to him there, then. If I did respond, what would people think? The matter will reach the office of my party, and my party colleagues would surely pull him up for what he said, and it will be a mess, police case, and everything ... So I kept quiet ... But it was awful, really ... I thought, however, maybe it was the pressure of the moment that made him do so .... But later he came to my house and apologized. And then I thought: how good that I didn't make a complaint! It made him realize his mistake and admit it himself!

She did not really reveal what the exact nature of the insult was and firmly believes that it was her exercise of 'gentle power'—her mild response, refusal to lodge a police complaint—that effected a change. She also believes that the man apologized because he was repentant. It is striking indeed that she never even considers the possibility that the fear that she may lodge a formal complaint against caste insult might have brought him to apologize.

In sharp contrast to the above is the experience of another young Dalit woman president from north Kerala who had to suffer blatant caste insult for having tried to intervene against the workings of illegal sand-miners. In this case, the woman resisted pressures from her own party colleagues and alliance partners against filing a police complaint:

> We had gone to investigate a case of illegal sand-mining ... they wanted revenge; they blocked our vehicle and it even appeared that the panchayat secretary would be assaulted. I intervened and was met with a barrage of casteist insult! Then a senior gentleman who was living nearby intervened and took me to his house and I had to lock myself from inside. I went ahead and filed a complaint. Not for my sake, I told all my party colleagues who rushed up to pacify me. This is for other Dalit women like me. Other women should not have to suffer casteist insult like this. Would they have dared to use such names had it been an upper-caste woman occupying this seat? And saddest, these fellows are all my neighbors—boys who have grown up around me, who I have raised. That hurt a lot.

Fourthly, Dalit women also have to directly confront those who may try to harass them; they often do not have powerful supporters in the party who may try to mediate and resolve issues. This, as one Dalit woman president put it, makes them "not nice all the time." Many of them related anecdotes of open confrontation with senior members and officials. Two are worth quoting, below. Both reveal that Dalit women can hardly afford to stay civil all the time. The first was told to us by a young woman, the daughter of an agricultural labourer and a cashew-factory worker. Being young, she was put under the charge of the more experienced male vice-president, a new elite leader who knew her from childhood. Initially she put up with being infantilized, but later began to rebel:

> When he crossed the limits, I came out in the open with my protest. That was itself a problem. But then something worse happened. There's a member here—he too is a General member.

One day he came to the office and began to shout at the staff quite badly. I went over there and asked what the matter was. This person also knows me from childhood. That, I suppose, made him jump at me! When I asked him to stop, he retorted: 'Keep quiet, girl! I know that you come from a miserable hovel!' That made me lose my cool, and I hit back, alright, you know, so what—this is the panchayat, I am the president here. You can't create a racket here. It blew into a huge quarrel. I went to the party office and reported. It became a big issue there too. Then we were called to the party office for talks. After that he's been somewhat milder. I carry on with all my tasks caring nothing for such people. I'm really proud that I could complete all the projects I took up.

Another anecdote, related to us by a young and rather inexperienced Dalit woman president, who was certainly not an entirely 'successful' one, also ended with the woman reminding the oppressor that she is indeed the president. If new elite women can afford to muffle the power conferred upon them as the head of the panchayat, it appears that Dalit women can scarcely do so, as the quote below reveals:

There was a Secretary here, a very vulgar man. He knew that I was inexperienced, my husband was not powerful in the party, we are poor, and I had become president only by chance. So he thought he could [sexually] harass me as much as he pleased. I had felt uneasy right from the beginning—his behaviour was quite sickening. He would try to touch me, poke me here and there. Initially I tried to keep quiet; it was such a disgusting thing to reveal! But one day he came in as if to give me a piece of paper—and crossed the limit. He tried to grab my hand, even as people were watching. That REALLY was the limit. I became president for the first time! I slapped him hard on his cheek. The man was stunned. He fell into the chair for a second, holding his cheek. 'Tcchii! How dare you sit down without my permission, you scoundrel!' I shouted. 'I am the president in this panchayat! Get up right now!' The man jumped up and left. He went on leave immediately and got himself a transfer. After that the members have been quite respectful, and some old sharks who had their eyes on me became quite disciplined.

'Success' Harder-won

As may be already evident from the above, 'success' for Dalit women is much harder-fought. The most successful Dalit women in our sample shared a common feature: they were the sole Dalit woman elected in a panchayat in which the president's position was reserved for an SC woman, or in their party in such a panchayat. This gave them considerable negotiating power in the panchayat and with their own party colleagues. Besides, most 'successful' Dalit women presidents have a clear view of the equally entrenched nature of casteism in all political parties and hence display a pragmatic ability to smoothly work with the other party if necessary. This is amply evident from the experiences of the most 'successful' women in this group, who all became presidents not because their party won but because the side which won did not have an SC woman member. Yet they successfully built connections with the other, dominant party members. To quote one of these women:

> I contested as a Congress candidate, but it is not as if I am blind to caste discrimination in that party. I was also a candidate in the 1995 election. Kicking down an SC candidate is a common feature of both LDF and UDF. At that time, my rival was a powerful woman, and my own party colleagues in the Congress betrayed me. I lost for less than 10 votes! ... Now my experience of working with the LDF here has been smooth and we have achieved much together. I'm quite confident of contesting again; a section of the UDF is with me and the LDF supporters say that they will vote for me even though I am a UDF candidate...I am in this seat because I think it will help SC women to walk in with confidence. I openly say this in meetings: 'if you do not receive resources when an SC woman is in power, what is the use of my sitting here?, ... My greatest strength is that I am not in the shade of any party!

Another of the most 'successful' among Dalit interviewees related her experience of resisting attempts to control. She noted that her age (she was 62) and the fact that she was a much-respected school teacher did help ("...the vice-president was my daughter's age and I had taught him in school"). However, it was her status as the sole Dalit woman elected that became the decisive factor:

> I was totally inexperienced when I entered, and there was such little cooperation from others! There was certainly the undercurrent of caste hostility beneath it. When they refused to cooperate, I began to take my own decisions and began to be criticized for that. I went to the party and convinced them; the affair cooled down. But then it heated up every now and then, and I was quite sick of it and finally threatened to resign. That was serious—because I was the only SC woman elected. So they began to behave better.

The younger Dalit women presidents who did not enjoy such an advantage, however, reported that they often faced more of control and surveillance. Some of our interviewees did stress that even though they wished to improve the lot of their own communities, it was the party that gave them the strength to do so and therefore submission to party diktat was everything. However, it appeared quite clearly to us that setting aside the community's interest could actually be hugely disempowering. One particularly telling instance was a contrast we found between two young tribal women activists, both of whom had been active in a major environmental agitation, and who had both contested the elections as rivals. Of these, the woman who won and became the panchayat president obviously had to carry a huge load of expectations, failed miserably to fulfil them, trapped as she was by decisions of the party elite. Further, she was also subjected to violence by her husband as a way of disciplining her within the 'party line'. In contrast, her rival, who lost, continued in the movement and has now grown to be the major spokeswoman of her community, appearing in several public forums on their behalf. But we also came across a tribal woman ex-president from north Kerala (of the second term), who had actually built up her own base in the panchayat through representing the 'general interests' of her local community. To quote her:

> I became the president on the strength of my education. The former president was an ST man, with no education and the panchayat was controlled by the vice-president, a non-ST. The same man was in power when I became president. He was used to controlling everything; the earlier president had been totally passive. And there was a huge age gap between him and me. Things changed, however, when we heard there were plans to dam up the river. Now, this was something that threatened the whole panchayat. I took a firm stand, and when all the people rallied around me, I shook him off ... But I didn't contest again, I now work as the chairperson of the Kudumbashree self-help groups. My leadership was welcomed when there was a crisis and a fighting mood. Wasn't sure whether I'd be accepted when that dimmed ...

It is important to note that in the second case, the community included both tribal and non-tribal people, while in the first, it was mostly tribal people. In the first case, the tribal woman president was forced to publicly relinquish her position in favour of the community to toe the party line, which eroded her base completely. In the second, the issue was vital to both tribal and non-tribal groups, and therefore a conflict of interest between tribal and non-tribal was not involved. Yet in the second case, the woman leader's perception was that such support was not durable, and therefore her decision not to contest again. Tribal women leaders in contemporary Kerala face such dilemmas. This was quite evident in our interviews with tribal women presidents with a background in the CPM-sponsored tribal organization, the Adivasi Kshema Samiti, (AKS). They emphasized the role of the party in defending tribal interests and asserted that while they wished to protect tribal interests, they distributed welfare benefits strictly according to norms to all the deserving poor in the BPL list. That is, they were keen to convince us that they did not bend rules for tribal people. And the contrast between the influence enjoyed by prominent tribal women activists of the CPM—located in high politics—and the heavy controls under which the tribal women presidents of the same party seemed to function was quite evident. The CPM's interest in mobilizing tribals seems to have opened up a window to many young educated tribal women, some of whom have rapidly risen in the internal hierarchy of the AIDWA. One such person, who joined the AIDWA in 1995 rose rapidly to the State and National Committees of the AIDWA. She is currently a ward member and is apparently more powerful than the president of her panchayat:

> Being in this position in the AIDWA means that I have direct contact with leaders, ministers, and so on, and at the state and national levels. How else would a person like me gain such contacts? Since I sit in the National Committee, I know many big leaders—Sujata, Sathyechi, so many others, they are all with me in the State Committee. So if I want to solve an issue I can do so through them... For example, the PHC here had no doctor; a lot of Adivasis have been using it. Then I went to Thiruvananthapuram and met Sreemathiyechi [the present Minister for Health in the state government, P K Sreemathy]. The problem was resolved very soon; in two weeks ... it is the party connection that helps me to work like this.

A further hurdle in the way of Dalit women aiming for popularity is their greater vulnerability to sexual slander, as they tend to be younger. And here, the oppressors may equally be from one's own party. A particularly harrowing instance was shared by a successful woman president who told us about how another Dalit woman-member in her panchayat, who was a good-looking woman, was slandered by all parties for having had an affair, which came to an unhappy end:

> SC women are under great threat. Now there are a large number of young SC women seeking to enter the public, and plenty of men ready to misguide, slander, and spoil their lives. One such case ended badly here ... She was a mild girl ... I remember, when she became a candidate—she was of the rival party— some of our men looked at her photo and said, hey this is a *charakku* [sex-pot]. I reacted sharply—how dare you say such

a thing, would you dare to say that if this girl wasn't a poor SC woman?

A contrast is certainly visible, at least in the abilities of Dalit and non-Dalit women to resist sexual slander and domestic violence. The instances of such resistance we found among new elite women leaders were interesting precisely because these women appeared to be capable of resistance on the strength of self-confidence about their 'flawless reputations', education and 'refinement', and elite family backgrounds. A senior woman panchayat president from central Kerala, who was being abused by her husband over her alleged 'unfaithfulness', pointed out that she resisted him, since she was fully confident of her 'good reputation' not only in the family but also in the panchayat. Indeed, this woman enjoys considerable popularity in the panchayat, belonging to a reputed, politically powerful family, and being a very popular figure. "My children know me well, so do my neighbours, and all the students I have taught, of many generations," she said, confident about her status as a 'family woman' and a respectable teacher. Such strategy may simply be unavailable to the young Dalit woman. We did come across one instance in which a young Dalit ex-panchayat president in northern Kerala had to pay a huge cost: she too faced the same situation at home, but her husband left her, marrying again, and leaving her with no foothold either at home or in the party. Some of our interviewees revealed their domestic troubles: here, cutting across party lines, both women accused their own party men of feeding the fire. One woman, whose husband suspected her of infidelity ("we don't have children, so he is always afraid, I will walk out with another man") tried to talk with party leaders about her problem: "They didn't help, but they did worse—they told my husband that his wife was going all over town slandering him; and they told everybody else about our issues!" Interestingly, unlike these women, very few new elite women were willing to admit such troubles in a formally-recorded interview—most of such admissions came much later, after closer interaction. Age too, is a major axis of social power in contemporary Malayalee society, and therefore the fact that women members and presidents of Dalit and Adivasi communities are younger than their elite counterparts may be a significant factor limiting them. In Kerala, there is much greater expectation on younger women to heed such hierarchies and defer to elders– not surprising given that their accepted location is within the family and community.

Dalit women leaders however spoke of strategies through which they tried to minimize the chances of sexual slander. One woman chose to get herself a two-wheeler to move around the panchayat on her own, to avoid too much close contact with male members and officials; another stressed the fact that she projected herself as a committed housewife: "I leave for work only after finishing all the housework and sending my son to school ... the neighbours do see how much work I do and how committed I am to the family. So slander doesn't work too fast." Others cited this risk as a reason why they were careful to keep the local party men in good spirits. Another stressed self-control ("The office of the panchayat president is a respectable one. One must retain its dignity through one's disciplined behaviour"). All these are of course instances of patriarchal bargaining, and this is a common feature that interviews with this group share with the interviews with new elite women. But as seen before, new elite women are often more successful in such bargaining.

What Empowers? A Job or Politics?

Almost all the interviewees in this group argued that entering local governance can be exhilarating, but their long-term plans were around gaining a steady and well-paying job. This perception came from their experience of even getting into debt—after a term. The constraints seem much more for presidents than for members, and all the more for working-class

Dalit women presidents, as a working-class woman leader revealed:

> Working-class women are rare in local governance because they lose both their work and their income. Male workers are confident of surviving some way or other. But women can't afford to let go of their steady sources of income... they fear debt ... if we discontinue we stand to lose many welfare benefits and bonuses...

Another woman leader, again, a working-class president of the CPM, with considerable experience in the party and trade unionism at the local level, stressed the same point:

> .... I am still primarily a worker in the estate, but presently on leave. Working-class women survive through their labour; they can't do without it. They are not highly educated—this is not really a problem (I myself am a worker who is respected much more than the earlier president, a woman with an MA) but they don't receive any serious party education which would have made up for lack of schooling. The family situation may not be favourable ...so how do they come?

The similarity between these voices and the voices of working-class women explaining their inability to participate in militant trade unionism documented in Anna Lindberg's study of caste, class, and gender among the cashew workers of Kerala (2001) is striking indeed. Lindberg traces the 'effeminization' of the female worker through which she came to be identified very closely with the domestic, and the burden of domestic provision became effectively hers, even though the male-breadwinner norm continued to prevail in wage-fixing arrangements by the State.

Just how crucial an independent source of income is to a young Dalit woman was stressed by the woman leader who told us the shocking tale of sexual slander and harassment of a Dalit woman member of the rival party:

> A steady job is what a Dalit woman needs most. I used to say that frequently to xxx [the woman who was slandered]—get a steady job soon and leave this business, and you will be able to walk

on the streets with your head up. Now you are a 'public person', right, and though we are paid a pittance, they can always say, we are taking public money. When you have a job, you're not rendering public service; you are being paid for your labour!

This president, widely respected in the public, did not want to continue only in politics: "... I am going to try for a good job, and if I get one, I will certainly take it up fulltime. To be in politics, one needs to resist all kinds of temptations and pitfalls. One needs a job for that, a steady income."

The need for income is also important for a host of other reasons. Being younger in general, Dalit women presidents do have higher childcare responsibilities, and unlike a large number of new elite women presidents with similar responsibilities, lack the presence of the extended family to substitute for the mother's presence. Besides, the job of the panchayat president, as a senior Dalit woman president remarked, "... is an expensive one. People expect you to contribute to everything, from personal affairs to public functions. They need you to be everywhere. The honorarium we get is so low!" Unless such expenses are met in some way, the member cannot function effectively, and those who lack resources are therefore more vulnerable to corruption. One of our interviewees, a young woman with little children, pointed out that the wages of organized domestic workers in south Kerala were higher than the honoraria received by the panchayat president! "That makes me suspect," she said, "along with the fact that few of us climb up much further— that we are actually a new bunch of voluntary workers being tom-tommed as 'leaders'!" Indeed, the sole member of this group who reported that she was a fulltime political worker and intended to stay so, when recently contacted, had taken up a fulltime job as a school-teacher.

Conclusion

The experience of Dalit women leaders clearly reveals the new elite moorings of 'gentle power'. In the case of Dalit women, it appears that 'knowledge of the rules' is even more fiercely clung to as a means of self-defense. Nevertheless, some women have indeed gained a great deal of space for negotiation. These are women who are the only SC women members to be elected in the panchayat, and hence are treated with greater respect by both their own party and the rivals in the panchayats.

But in general, success is gained with much greater effort. First, party control brings in a serious dilemma. On the one hand, dalit women need to build a strong base among their own community in order to create an enduring place for themselves. On the other, they do need strong support of political parties, which may demand that they sacrifice community loyalties. Negotiating this dilemma continues to be a difficult task, particularly at the level of local governance, where party strategy often dictates that the non-SC/ST population should be placated. The point is reinforced when we notice some tribal women activists' ability to represent their community at the level of high politics within the CPM. While in high politics, tribal identity is being accommodated for strategic reasons through the AKS, the situation seems to be much weaker for tribal women leaders in local governance, where norms have to be followed, non-tribals have considerable power, and militant rhetoric supporting the demand of the AKS for land seems less forcefully articulated. Besides, even regarding the challenges that Dalit women seem to be sharing with new elite women, such as the risk of sexual slander, domestic and childcare responsibilities, and limited access to financial resources, the former are left with fewer resources to cope with compared with the latter. No wonder then, that individualized strategies of empowerment—steady and gainful employment—and not public presence, appear more empowering to Dalit women.[7] And it may also be important to remember that the articulation of collective demands on behalf of Dalit and Adivasi women are still largely unsuccessful, if increasingly visible, in both high politics and the oppositional civil society in Kerala. Their struggles, then, may appear to them as individual battles which have limited social and political reverberations.

Notes

1. Anwar Jafri and Vikas Singh (2006) note in their work on panchayats in Madhya Pradesh that Dalit and tribal women presidents and members may be enjoying some overall advantages over upper-caste and OBC women because they "have a better chance of being selected as members of panchayat or a sarpanch for their personal characteristics" in contrast to upper-caste and OBC women, for whom the position and political influence of husbands is more important (footnote 29 p. 353). In our sample, however, as observed in Chapter 3, Dalit women presidents seem to be as much from 'party families' as non-Dalits. But while Dalit women presidents in our sample were chosen for their education, they certainly were less educated than new elite women presidents. It appears that while educated Dalit women potentially (though not often actually) enjoy greater bargaining power—being generally few in number compared to the educated new elite women—they are equally subject to the advantages/disadvantages of being members of 'party families'.

2. There may be other considerations as well, especially in the choice of candidates from tribal groups. Suresh (2009) notes in his research on the Mananthawady panchayat in Wayanad, that the tribal woman president there was not identified primarily as representing tribals, but as a "party figure", a person active in, and primarily loyal to, the CPM. (p. 207)

3. Even two interviewees who displayed greater deference to the official line of their party about caste issues—that they should be subordinated to class contradictions—openly stated that caste power was real. They felt that while it was not always apparent, it surfaced whenever the Dalit person had committed a mistake and had to be criticized. The criticism would often contain a casteist barb, of lower caste people being less able or some such. The pervasiveness of such a perception about Dalit members is noted by recent research on panchayati raj in Kerala, for example Sharma 2009.

4. It is clear from our interviews, however, that the efforts of Dalit women presidents do not challenge the general pattern of welfare distribution directed towards Dalits and Adivasis fostered by the state. Go K (2009) comments from a study that covered 11 village panchayats and one municipality in 3 districts that Dalits have received considerable help from village and block panchayats "in building houses, maintenance of houses, construction of wells, latrines, and the like with very little help in improving skills, providing self-employment or regular wage-employment." (p. 115) It notes that the utilization of funds has improved in these panchayats, but "the diversity one would expect from local specificities is missing." (p. 124). Moreover, "The services related to welfare measures for the poor and the SC/ST are ridden with lack of transparency" and this causes their excessive dependence on the whims of the councillor (p. 146). The report also mentions the serious lack of follow-up—which results in the same beneficiaries receiving benefits every year and multiplies bogus claims (p. 147).

5. That such a situation which necessitates the defense of SC/ST entitlements as constitutionally mandated does exist in panchayats is confirmed even by scholars closely linked to the dominant left. (See, for instance, Harilal 2005.) Very recent fieldwork in the Wayanad and Palakkad districts of Kerala also reveals the extent to which such entitlements are being refused—a large number of SC/ST people simply remain outside the BPL list and have no access to the National Rural Employment Guarantee Scheme (Williams et al. 2010). Also see, Suresh 2009.

6. Chathukulam and John (2000) present a case study of a Dalit woman president of a village panchayat who had to face non-cooperation from her own party and the Panchayat Secretary because she refused to toe the line drawn by party functionaries (pp. 85–88). Isaac (2005) argues that women members of local bodies in Kerala have faced lower levels of violence than their counterparts elsewhere (p. 389). However, when he presents instances of 'male chauvinism' against them, interestingly, his examples of women being jeered at or roughly interrupted are all of the harassment faced by Dalit women presidents—and the insults are casteist (p. 397–99).

7. Also, the Dalit women members who we interviewed did complain of much higher levels of neglect and harassment by their upper-caste colleagues than the Dalit women presidents. We heard stories of how the upper-caste women of all parties joined together to isolate the Dalit woman member, treat her with condescension, and keep her under moral surveillance. Here the disadvantage of age—that the Dalit woman member tends to be younger—is quite striking.

5

Extending the 'Social': Muslim Women

Echoing Community Reformism

When asked about the notion of *shaakteekaranam* (empowerment) and its usefulness to Muslim women in Kerala,[1] a very active and dynamic Muslim woman president of the Muslim League, from northern Kerala, responded with a "story":

> One day, a rocket and an airplane met in the skies high above. The plane was impressed by the rocket's fantastic speed, and told her, "how fast you fly! What is your secret?" The rocket threw her a glance and said, "Didn't you notice, my tail is on fire! You too would fly like me if your tail were on fire!" And then she continued, "Well, I'm flying very fast, but I have no clue where I am going and whether I will come back home safe! You are flying slow, yes, but aren't you relieved that you know where you are going, and will get home in time, too?" Well, I think 'empowerment' is what the rocket is experiencing!

Clearly, this amusing yet perfectly lucid characterization of 'empowerment' encapsulates the unmistakable wariness with which many of our Muslim interviewees, especially Muslim League women from north Kerala, approached the question of women's access to public-political power. Ironically enough, the fear seems to be that their agency will be sacrificed as women are propelled by a host of forces over which they have no control, into an unfamiliar realm. The "story" astutely points to the dangers of judging the process from the speed of change alone.

This, we feel, may be read along the almost universal endorsement, at a superficial level, of the social, rather than the political, as the appropriate realm for women, in our interviews with Muslim women leaders at the local level. Unlike the new elite women among whom a clear division is perceptible between women in the lower tiers (village and block) who largely endorsed the social (and hence 'gentle power'), as appropriate for women, and women leaders of the district tier, who were more seasoned politicians preferring the political, Muslim women leaders of all tiers claimed that they were more interested in the social than in the political. Further, most of these leaders reiterated women's submission to Islam and its ideals of feminine humility as indispensable for their entry into the public.

The single most striking feature of these interviews was the apparent reincarnation of early 20th century Malayalee community reformist ideals in and through the present ideals of womanhood, now freshly reinterpreted through the lenses of globalized Islam, very popular in present-day Malabar. Among the key features of community reformist discourse that reverberates in these interviews, the most prominent one is the affirmation of the 'order of gender' (Devika 2007)— the vision of the world as demarcated into clearly gendered public and domestic domains, into which men and women are respectively inserted by Nature and Divine Will. Men and women are also considered to be endowed with specific capacities and dispositions appropriate to each domain. Our interviewees defended this vision of the world drawing upon specific interpretations of Islam that both value femininity and assign it to the specific space of the social. Many of them were keen to argue that women are endowed with capacities that pre-dispose them towards the social; however, they also argued passionately that the social ought to be extended considerably, indeed right into the political.

This clearly echoes early 20th century arguments by first generation feminists in Kerala. As mentioned in the Introduction, the first-generation feminists in Kerala had sought to extend/recast the notion of the 'order of gender' by arguing that many capacities deemed 'natural' to women were of relevance not just to the domestic, but to a great many institutions beyond—which together constituted the 'social'. Our interviewees seemed to be drawn by precisely the concern that animated the first-generation Malayalee feminists: the deployment of putatively 'feminine' capacities for the regulation of the space of the 'social'. Women with ostensibly well-developed 'feminine' capacities were therefore equally or even more qualified to occupy specific areas of public life than men. They must, however, occupy these spaces confirming to a certain Islamic ethics of the self. Vanita League leaders claimed repeatedly that the woman who practised (the appropriately-gendered) Islamic ethics of the self would be self-controlled and truly endowed with 'feminine' qualities, and she would rise above all efforts at sexual slander on the strength of these– citing their personal experience as evidence. Clearly, the leaders of the Vanita League perceive themselves as Reformer-Women who possess the ability to reform other Muslim women not as well-endowed—and thereby justify this non-reciprocal relation of power between themselves and other, 'ordinary' women.

Secondly, many of our interviewees, especially of the Muslim League, seemed to be reiterating the unique relationship of power legitimized in and through early 20th century community reformism in Kerala: that between the Reformer-Man, who had gained access to modern knowledges and institutions earlier and women, the objects of reforming. Such a position of pre-eminence was also claimed by Reformer-Women, who had proven themselves to Reformer-Men that they possessed well-developed 'feminine capacities' and enough familiarity with modern knowledges and institutions. Women-leaders of the Muslim League's women's organization, the Vanita League, claimed the status of Reformer-Women. As one of them remarked, "The Vanita League seeks to empower women within their limits. However eagerly women may come forward, they are still backward in many respects simply out of their lack of experience. Therefore they inevitably need the support and advice of men who have gone ahead earlier." Other studies, too, note the role of men with reformist convictions in ushering women into local governance (for example, Suresh 2009). Our interviewees, quite like many first-generation feminists, added that men's role as guides, strictly understood, was a temporary one, of merely ushering women into the public. When women attained the status of full-fledged, individuated, members of the Muslim community, this guiding role would cease.

Thirdly, early 20th century community reformism's stress on building internalities of individuals and thereby endowing them with specific gendered capacities including the capacity for self-control is very visibly present in many of these interviews. This self-realization is to be attained by closer adherence to the ethics of building the ideal Muslim Self. Late-modern 'westernized' life in Kerala with the abundance of consumption opportunities and the overarching presence of mass media and advanced communication and information technologies is frequently blamed for having crippled the processes by which ideal Islamic internalities are shaped. Our interviewees echoed the early-20th century idea that the capacity to shape subjectivities and cultivate internalities was specifically 'feminine'—and claimed it for themselves as a justification for their presence in public life. The 'code of conduct' that the Muslim League is said to have set up for its female elected representatives was justified: this is only an informal bit of advice, they said. More importantly, however, they argued that this was a tool meant to help women guard themselves against 'westernized life' that erodes internalities. Women, they agreed, are doing much more these days, but there are many women who "misuse their freedom", as a dynamic young leader of the Vanita League claimed. "We have no need for that," she continued, "we don't need western culture, we need to stay in Indian culture." According to a senior woman leader of the Vanita League, herself a leader of a district panchayat, the most pressing problem in Kerala today is a social one: high rates of divorce, which is attributed to our aping the "west".

It is of vital importance to note that the 'Islam' that emerges in these narratives is often characterized as 'Indian Islam' or 'part of Indian culture'. Through this move, many of the practices and ideals sanctioned by early 20th century community reformism (for which the hidden reference point was often a secularized and modernized Hinduism) are reconciled with Islam. For example, many of these women do point out that marriage is a contract in Islam and that remarriage and divorce are not stigmatized.[2] Yet they continue to argue in favour of 'Indian culture' that emphasizes the sanctity and permanence of the marital relationship and disapproves of divorce—and perceive no contradiction between the two positions. Indeed, it may even appear that concerns of early 20th century reformist patriarchy outweigh the concern with Islamic ethics of the self, at least in some crucial issues central to the question of women's rights.

For example, the emphasis on respectable dressing is also strongly reminiscent of early 20th century community reformisms. Most of our interviewees especially of the Muslim League explained their adoption of an Islamic dresscode—usually the saree with long-sleeved, loose long-blouses and the headscarf—the *mafta*—in these terms. Historically, covering the female body has been central to the project of community reform; the covered female body has, since then, signified refinement and civilization (Devika 2007). Given the present context in north Kerala, especially the Muslim-majority Malappuram district, where the heavy migration to the Gulf has opened up the region to globalized Islam—a closer identification within an imagined Muslim heartland in the Gulf—and where wealth is fuelling ambitions of cultural upward mobility, 'decent dress' for the Muslim woman increasingly involves veiling in the Arab style (Osella and Osella 2008; De Jong 2004).

A Muslim activist of the CPM, presently a Branch Secretary, who lost the panchayat election by a very narrow margin, mentioned her refusal to wear the veil as the reason why she lost. The veil, it seems, is now the very symbol of the Muslim woman's membership in the community:

> My opponents had unleashed a vicious campaign, that I didn't cover my head. The people I approached for votes told me that they knew about all the work I was doing in the town area, that they approved of it, but that I didn't cover my head was a great minus-point. Then I told them, you have been seeing me like this since my childhood. If I just alter my appearance for the sake of this election, won't it be betraying you?

Her arguments did not work, and she lost the election. This does highlight the extent to which adherence to dress-codes projected as desirable for Muslim women in the present context in Malabar is necessary for their entry into local governance. However, such a firm demand does not seem to be placed upon men. The fact that men are exempted from strict adherence to the Muslim dress-code gives us reason to think that the female dress-code is understood as not so much an instrument of Islamic self-transformation (if it had been so, there would have been strict insistence on a male dress-code as well), as a marker of sexually-self-controlled femininity, as in community reformist discourse.

A Docile Agent?

Perhaps the statements of our Muslim interviewees must be read in the context of the changing dynamics of the Muslim community in Malabar in the late 20th century and after. The migration of a large number of Muslim men[3] from north Kerala to the Gulf since 1970s has brought considerable wealth to sections of the north Kerala Muslim community which were previously not of the Muslim elite of the region. As has been pointed out elsewhere, the flow towards the Gulf explains the low enrolment of Muslim men in higher education (Miller 1992). In contrast, more women are staying in school and indeed outnumber Muslim men in graduate and postgraduate courses (Mohammed 2007: 89; De Jong 2004: 32–33). Women's education, however, had been actively discussed among the Muslims of Kerala since the late 19th century, and has been a prominent aspect of community reformisms among them since then (Mohammed 2007; Hussain 2009). It was actively promoted in Malabar (which had been a part of British India and hence lagged behind the southern princely states in education) by the Muslim Education Society founded in 1964. Other reformist organizations such as the Mujahid movement and the Jama'at-e-Islami Hind have also been at the forefront of propagating women's education (De Jong 2004: 14; Sikand 2006: 38–41) and in facilitating women's greater access to mosques (De Jong 2004: 15–17).

However, a similar shift is not visible in employment[4] and De Jong notes: "The ambiguity of female employment lies exactly in the fact that gender roles are no longer essentially complementary. Now that women enter the market of employment, men and women are competitive individuals and their relationship is no longer based on mutual dependency." (p. 48). Indeed, she argues that social work, however, remains very highly acceptable and female education is justified as a preparation for unpaid social work: "... the importance of female education can be explained as a preparation to well-perform exclusively female tasks, the upbringing of children and the household duties. Further, unpaid social work does enlarge women's role in society without questioning men's responsibilities as wage earners. Female employment, however, threatens the exclusivity of men's capability to provide economic security for the family." (p. 48). The majority of north Kerala Muslim men who De Jong interviewed for her study disapproved of paid employment for women and argued that it increased the chances of divorce (p. 48). But she notes that a large number of Muslim women students she interviewed did desire paid employment even though they did not discuss it with their prospective husbands and tended to follow the husband's wish after marriage (p. 49).[5]

It appears that the reservation of 33 per cent seats in the local bodies did not clash with the unfolding discourse of gendered community reformism. The projection of the panchayat as apolitical civil space gave the educated women in the Muslim community an opening to extend the terms of the social into the political, a space to which they could legitimately lay claim within the community. In other words, educated Muslim women did have the ideological armour with which they could easily move into these new institutional spaces.[6] Examining the profiles of our interviewees, it is apparent that a great deal of caution has been exercised to ensure that the women leaders of the panchayats are protected from the many threats and risks faced by women who enter the public, especially from conservative elements in their own community and outside. Muslim women in our sample were between the ages of 36–55, a group that is relatively safer from sexual slander. Also, all our interviewees felt that women who were younger were not really suited for local governance precisely because it involved close interaction with many male strangers. They were also very well-supported (except one) by their in-laws, parents, husbands and older children, and hence domestic burdens were not a serious issue. Also, that these women are largely from the Muslim middle-class is reflected in the fact that the large majority of them are married to men in 'respectable' employment or occupation. Other cautionary moves are similar to those adopted by the AIDWA women: they include claiming distance from 'feminists' who supposedly accuse men of being the chief source of all of women's ills, and stressing the centrality of monogamous marriage to healthy social life. But compared with the total sample, fewer Muslim women had attained higher education or were employed.

Women leaders of the Vanita League were keen to stress that unlike other parties, they did not fight for their rightful share of seats—a very 'unwomanly' thing to do. Submission, humility, and patience, they claimed, work better, possibly to persuade the leadership and male members who may feel threatened:

> The Muslim League is a very disciplined party. We don't complain that women haven't been granted enough representation. Many people were displeased that the Vanita League was formed in the first place. But Panakkad Tangal [the undisputed spiritual leader of the Muslim League] is a very forward-thinking person. It was he who insisted that it should come into being. It was formed, and we came into certain positions—not because we demanded. The ordinary women in the party do ask us, and we do, whenever we get a chance, we ask male politicians [in the party], shouldn't more women be inducted? But we don't make a fuss.

And several women leaders of the panchayat who had been inducted into the public through the Vanita League swore that this strategy worked, with instances from their own lives. To quote one such account:

> In the beginning there was much talk that women should not be in the public at all and we all had to suffer many accusations. It changed after some two and a half years or so. I was very careful in my ways, moved with a lot of caution. When on the street, I would walk with my umbrella open so that I didn't brush against anybody ... Then slowly people began to say, very good, she behaves in a very disciplined way. Then when I became a member of the panchayat some patriarchs didn't like it at all. My family, my father, and my husband were fine and so I decided I won't bother too much. And now things have changed so much that they say, look at her, women ought to be like her! She works so properly, she's so much in the public but never caused anybody to speak ill of her, this is what they all say ...

It is worth noting that though many of our interviewees claimed to be guided by an ethics of Islamic self-transformation, their notion of agency was not really similar to that described by Saba Mahmood (2004), which may not be always understood as resistance to patriarchy or a bid for autonomy. In many ways, these agentival acts involve not just acts of resistance, but creating "multiple ways in which one *inhabits* norms" (Mahmood 2004: 23), and these may be quite disinterested in state or juridical forms of power. However, this does not appear to be the case as far as our interviewees were concerned.[7] All our interviewees from north Kerala were deeply aware of the recent changes in Muslim women's lives and spoke of the shifts taken by young women in their own families towards individual autonomy. They told us of daughters who refuse to marry until they gained paid employment, of those who insisted on marrying only men who approved of their paid employment, of young women gaining greater mobility through learning to drive vehicles and so.[8] As a senior Vanita League leader argued:

> Women of today are totally different from women twenty years ago. We have come much ahead ...Women drive vehicles—one in every three drivers is a woman. Also coming home late is so common these days –women may be out till eight or ten at night. And then the mobile phone ...

They were hardly trying to move beyond liberal autonomy, the progressivist narrative, or the liberal political public, and this was evident in the really interesting manoeuvring of the members of Vanita League, the women's wing of the Muslim League. The Muslim League has traditionally been quite apathetic towards the question of women's entry into the political public. The Vanita League was created in response to the reservation of seats for women in local governance. Thus the women leaders of the Vanita League who had indeed gained entry earlier into high politics initially through social work, have been active in shaping the Vanita League as a vehicle facilitating Muslim women's entry into local governance. However, many interviews with both its leaders and activists who are presently leaders of panchayats reveal a determination to avoid confinement in local governance. In fact, both the 'bargain with culture' and the aspiration for entry into local governance appear to be conceived quite unambiguously as instrumental to women's entry into, and obtaining greater space for manoeuvre, in the high politics of the Muslim League, at least by those interviewees who were involved more closely with the Vanita League.

For instance, the Vanita League leader quoted above qualified her observation about women's progress with a quick appeal to stay within "Indian culture". Misuse of the new communications technology came from "western culture", according to her. Nevertheless, in the very next statement, she stressed agency and argued that we do have a choice. "There is much in western culture that is eminently imitable. However, we don't chose to imitate those aspects." And she immediately pointed out that men were twenty years back in time and still unable to come to terms with the huge shifts that had happened. "There's no point blaming globalization", she concluded. Such a double-move is also evident in the manner in which these women differentiate themselves from what they perceive to be the 'feminist' ideal of women's liberation—understood as based on laying the blame for women's oppression upon men. Said one them, distancing herself from the 'feminists': "Woman's womanliness must be respected. The status of the mother must be regarded as an honour. Do not revile men. Don't walk ahead or behind men, walk by their side." However, very soon, she launched a comparison between men and women, stating that "women are capable of taking stern decisions, and far better ones, than men. But too many women like to stay in the comfort zone and allow themselves to be converted into rubber stamps."

Once they have established themselves publicly as 'disciplined' women-members of the Muslim community and the local public (and to them, local governance provides precisely such a public), women leaders of the Vanita League may lay a moral claim to full presence in the Muslim League, a privilege presently denied to them. Senior leaders of the Vanita League were keen to emphasize this:

> Vanita League is not strong enough compared with other such organizations. There are too many restrictions which we are trying to overcome. For example we are not included in the committees, only men. We would have liked to be there even if

only as observers without voting rights. It is not a matter of a few acceptable women leaders being admitted. I mean we need a policy decision by which women will be admitted to committees at all levels ... our work in the Vanita League aims primarily at overcoming such restrictions. It will take time, but will be ultimately successful.

Another woman leader pointed out that these restrictions will have to be removed in the near future as women leaders are proving to be "efficient, loyal, articulate, and indeed far more morally disciplined than even senior male leaders. Now, accusations of moral depravity affect a woman most and so she is always careful. And now women in the party are not the ones affected; it is the men ....(laughs)" Here she was obviously alluding to a certain powerful leader of the Muslim League who was embroiled in accusations of sexual violence. Clearly, there is the hint of a competition between women and men, here, and submission, humility, modesty, diligence, self-control, and other such virtues are precisely the instruments through which these women intended to get ahead in the race.

Extension, Subversion, and Other Means

And besides the endorsement of submission, humility, and modesty, women leaders of the Vanita League use a number of pragmatic arguments to justify women's presence in the political public. These may (a) extend the terms of sexual complementarity so that women gain greater access to public space, (b) utilize the ideal sexual complementarity in subversive ways or (c) go beyond its terms. The frequent citation of the gains made in women's educational capabilities and the fact that they are less engaged in gainful employment as reasons for why they ought to be approached for public work is an example of the first sort of pragmatic argument. As mentioned earlier, this does not disturb the ideal of sexual complementarity, but extends women's roles and spaces within its framework. A good illustration of the second type of argument was the suggestion made by some women leaders that women amass 'social capital' through social work of some sort as a way of gaining greater space for manoeuvre before entering parties. They were emphatic that since women could not take advantage of the opportunity for party work to expand their public presence, 'social work' was inevitable. "I have been able to do a lot for my local community through the Inner Wheel and Jaycees ... women who already possess such contacts are valued more by political parties." She pointed out that women who were active in literacy work, in the ICDS, or the anganwadi are much preferred, and this is not because they were more 'feminine', but because "they have a wide range of contacts that will serve the party well."

Here sexual complementarity is deployed subversively, with women's greater access to the 'social' advanced as crucial to the chances of their entry into the political:

> My experience is that we women must engage in some form of social work and create our own base among the people. Only then will political parties be ready to accept us [on our terms]. Otherwise it is going to be limited to some women getting promoted just for the sake of the reserved seats.

A common instance of the last type of argument is the claim that that with the considerable migration of men from Muslim majority areas like Malappuram to the Gulf, the voters are more frequently women. And "very soon," said one of them, "there will be the need for more women in political work, since men tend to leave for work." Another instance was the argument made by a prominent Vanita League leader who argued that while sexual complementarity was the accepted norm within the Muslim League, the party had to be prepared to deal with a world that did not limit itself to this norm. She pointed to the way in which the visual media continually approached women leaders of the Vanita League as representatives and even spokespersons of the party position on a variety of issues, especially those pertaining to personal law. Here she raised the very important point that the question of the domestic—especially personal law and marriage—has hardly been a 'private' issue as far as the Muslim community has been concerned and it has always been under the scrutiny of the State and the public sphere. Muslim women leaders, who are generally more closely associated with such 'social' aspects, are hardly left to remain silent when such issues come up in the public. In such debates, women leaders of the Muslim League are contacted by the media as representatives of the party. She mentioned one such incident:

> ... We are not on party forums and so we don't have much knowledge of the discussions there. We don't really get to know anything very clearly. So we are forced to ask for information and get along with whatever we can gather ...(laughs) ... You may remember, there was a controversy about marriage registration some time back and I had to give many statements to the media. No women knew clearly what the party's position was on this. I went, on my own interest, to some senior [male] leaders to find out and read up the Kerala Legal Gazette soonest. And so I was able to speak properly about the party's position on this issue.

All three uses of the ideal of sexual complementarity mentioned above indicate that the self-identification of these women with a project involving submission and modesty does not mean that they are disinterested in the political public. And as will be seen below, when Vanita League leaders relate their experience of functioning in local bodies, they do set aside submission and docility. Indeed, the emphasis on agency—in the sense of the ability of actors to choose the levels to which they may be 'enrolled' in the projects of others (Arce and Long 2000)—is quite obvious.

For example, several women panchayat presidents said that though they accepted the suggestion made by the Muslim League leadership that women members should retire to their homes by six o'clock, this cannot be always followed strictly. Here again, women chose to stay back or go, respecting the norm but keeping it entirely flexible: one president revealed to us that she never attended a meeting or even an emergency after eight; it was the vice-president who attended to all such late-evening affairs. Others said that they do, but get their husbands to accompany them. Still others said that they can well attend such emergencies because they were by now accepted to be moral and responsible women. Others cited practical problems but asserted that they had no reluctance to stay out late. One of them, who runs a tailoring shop, described her routine:

> I am up by 5 in the morning. I finish housework by 8: 30 and go to the tailoring shop. I finish up the most urgent work there and reach the panchayat office by 10: 30. I leave the office at different hours. Sometimes I can leave by 3, but sometimes, I have to stay till 7. Our panchayat has no Jeep and so I'm constrained to avoid late outings.

Another woman leader remarked:

> In the League women are told to finish up their work by six in the evening as much as possible. I take my husband along in case of an emergency and do try to avoid going if I can. But there is nothing that stops me from stepping out late in case of an emergency.

And many of these women do wield political power but without being committed to it exclusively, since they continue to grant greater importance to their place in the social. For most of the time, Muslim women leaders identify the 'social' with a realm of charity and altruistic giving, far away from the worlds of power and contestation. However, when they speak of their work, often, the difference between the 'social' and the 'political' is vague. For example, the 'social' seems to also include acts that challenge the abuse of political power in the words of a senior leader of the Vanita League (who firmly located herself in the 'social' centred on "care and service") describing her own participation in local governance as an elected member:

> As part of the Opposition, I was able to raise many more issues than any of my male colleagues. If you ask me why, I'll tell you that this is because there was a forum available for me to raise my

voice. Democracy works only when there is a forum. I raised a number of key issues—about construction works, an exhibition, abuse of position for personal gain, financial misconduct ... all these were seriously debated and I have managed to make the ruling party change its stand.

Strikingly, she did not mention a role in welfare distribution at all here—though she had elaborated on it when she was arguing that local governance was indeed the space of the social which she was making productive through her ideal femininity. Another woman member of the Muslim League, also a Vanita League worker, argued that there ought to be more women in politics even without reservation. "We should have more women like Indira Gandhi or Susheela Gopalan," she said. "They didn't come through reservations. Why leave it all to men?" Nor are they shy of confronting their own male colleagues in specific situations. Relating how she was forced to confront the members of her own party in a dispute about a by-lane, she concluded; "My experience of public work has only made me bolder. I have become bold enough to state exactly what I think is right clearly, openly, and truthfully before anyone. Senior people don't like it when we behave that way. But I do speak my mind and never flinch from staking a claim for what is rightfully ours." Many of these women are adept at asserting themselves politically before the members of other parties even as they endorse sexual complementarity and women's place in the social. A telling instance was reported by a woman leader, a young woman active in the Vanita League:

I have had no problems from the Standing Committee Chairmen but the vice-president is a trouble-maker. He is of the Congress and is a senior leader in this area. But you see, I am the president here. He tends to forget that fact at times. He had the habit of monopolizing Board meetings, not allowing me even a word. I had to finally remind him in public, I am the president, not you. That led to some negative feelings. But I don't care about those.

Even about their party colleagues, Muslim League women were unanimous in their view that their initiatives to induct women into the public were hugely limited by the concern about maintaining patriarchal power in the party. Interviewee after interviewee insisted that it was the reservations alone that had prompted the male leadership to take an interest in women. In every interview, the evocation of sexual complementarity broke down decisively at this point, giving way to the articulation of a perspective that took full critical view of the superiority granted to Reformer-Men in relation to women bidding to be Reformer-Women. That women leaders' marginality to the party need not mean blindness to patriarchy is evident from the following response of a woman leader in her second term, to a question about her experiences as a woman activist in the League:

> I cannot really respond authoritatively to the question about what I felt as a woman active in a political party. Because I do not connect with the party as an activist, but rather as a candidate for a certain elected post in local governance. My relationship with the Muslim League is the limited one between a candidate and a political party. I attend party meetings only if invited. And those are mostly meetings of the Vanita League. But the Vanita League's stand has been changing quite visibly lately. That's clearly because of the reservations. All political parties are forced to bring capable women into the public. That this is not because of their sincerity towards the women's cause is a fact that both they—the political parties—and we women know too well.

Marginality, on the contrary, may offer the possibility of critical positions vis-à-vis the demand for agency in projects of 'empowerment' designed from above—from the state or the male elite in the party or the community. Some statements made by women leaders about their perceptions of their present role as 'anti-Islamic' make sense when viewed in this light. These are women who were wary of politics as overwhelmingly male space and would have preferred to remain outside it. However, they had to contest under huge pressure from their husbands. These statements contain a clear note of protest against Reformer-Men and the non-reciprocal relationship of power they bind the woman subjected to reform. Passivity, here, becomes a means of protest:

> I and my husband, we have no politics. We haven't been in anything... And then I was asked and I said I will contest if my husband agreed. Then he was called ... he agreed under pressure. This is a coastal area ... there was no one willing to contest in the reserved seat for women. So I was put up ...

> I was not interested; it was because of the pressure my husband exerted ...I have got some education in Islam ... according to that there is much in this that is un-Islamic. For example climbing on a stage and sitting next to male strangers ... also constantly interacting with such men ... going to the office ... It bothers me ...

This is a woman with relatively young children; her husband worked abroad. It is obvious that her workload was already heavy and she did not wish to increase it further. She had insisted, right from the beginning, that she would not be available after dark. However, the fact that these statements could well be a protest is apparent from that this woman concluded the interview by stating that she enjoyed public life and that she would try to enter local governance again once her children were older: "I have got used to going out every day. Nowadays when it is a holiday and there is no office, I find it strange and depressing to stay at home." Also, perhaps the diffidence obvious in the responses of many of our Muslim interviewees to our question whether they would contest again indicates not their inability to take a decision, but a refusal to be easily inducted into projects not of their making but largely shaped from above.

Nevertheless, there is perceptible difference between women leaders active in the Vanita League and those with no such experience, who entered the field under pressure from husbands or family. While Vanita League women often seek to preserve their right to independent decision-making, the latter are more open to letting male party colleagues make decisions. Many of the latter stated openly that though the party did not interfere in the day-to-day activities of the panchayat, they awarded contracts to whoever the party recommended. This is in sharp contrast to others, often Vanita League women leaders, who have contested such decisions, demanded information and a share of decision-making.

A contrast is also evident between the former and Muslim women leaders of the CPM at the local level. Recent efforts by the CPM to form a mass base in the Muslim majority areas in north Kerala have also included the effort to promote Muslim women leaders—women activists of 'party families' have been directly promoted in high politics, often into the state legislature or the district panchayat, which is most often a launching pad into high politics, and to high positions in the AIDWA. In contrast to the narratives of the Vanita League members, there is hardly a sense of internal struggle in their narratives. Most often they are narratives structured by an opposition between a 'backward' community in which women are oppressed and the progressive CPM, which appears as a haven, a refuge, for such women. Thus one of our interviewees, a Muslim woman politician of the CPM, formerly a panchayat president, remarked about how being a party activist eased the pain of being confined to the home in a conservative community and how becoming a leader improved her sense of self-esteem. These achievements, it may be noted, are mostly presented as attained not through struggle within the party, but through struggle against the community in almost all cases. These leaders acknowledge gratefully the effort of the party to promote them despite their relative lack of seniority; the paternal protection afforded by the party, too, is remembered with gratitude.

These narratives share many features of the interviews with AIDWA women. The seamless sense of belonging, the sense of complete immersion, the reiteration of family support, all expressed by many AIDWA women (discussed in Chapter 1) reverberate in these interviews as well:

My husband is the CPM branch secretary here as his father was before him. So we have been taking party work forward with everything else. I am also a party member and the president of AIDWA in this panchayat. But I don't work a lot. Just attend all the public meetings. That's about all ...

Another CPM woman leader spoke thus about her party connections:

My husband has devoted his life to the party, that's why I was chosen. If any of the functions are late in the evening, my husband comes along. I have had no bad experiences at all, have been much protected ...party members have taken good interest in my well-being; my husband's influence was crucial there too. I attended all the parliamentary party meetings and so was properly guided in the panchayat. Whenever trouble-makers— corrupt officials—were posted, I have got the party to get them transferred out ...

This is so even for Muslim women who have reached the upper echelons of the party. One of them remarked about her career in the CPM:

My husband brought me into the party; he was an active CPM worker. He was a great source of support until his death. I fought the Assembly elections after his death and the community was very hostile. It was the support of the party that saw me through...It's true that I have been active in the party only for a relatively short while. I can't say I have worked more than many men. Maybe capable women are relatively few; perhaps that it why many of us have come up so fast. Anyway, it is the party that nurtures us step by step.

The struggle of the CPM Muslim women was usually against what they perceived as the 'backwardness' of the community and the threats from elements which read their allegiances to the CPM as anti-Muslim, but with interesting exceptions.[9] Many of the CPM women in this group have braved considerable hostility—even death threats—to establish themselves in the public; as evident earlier, they acknowledge the paternal presence of the CPM as vital to their public existence. Yet many of them choose to symbolically reiterate their allegiance to Islam, naming it as a condition for entry into the public through local governance, which ensures the community's acceptance. Some declared that communism was closer to the egalitarian ideals of Islam and hence there was no clash in their being communist and believing Muslims at the same time; one pointed out that she was protected from scandal because the large majority of the member of the panchayat council were Muslim. Many choose to wear the *mafta* as a way of proclaiming their submission to Islamic gender norms as they seek to enter the public.

Muslim women in the CPM thus struggle to achieve a delicate balance between the party's secularism and membership in the community of believers. They locate themselves in the secular-political but seek to reach out and establish a foothold in the religious-community/social space. Women of the Vanita League seek the reverse. They locate themselves within the community of believers and in the social but nevertheless seek for themselves a foothold in the secular-political. Both are equally strategies aimed at political upward mobility.

Conclusion

The palpable presence of the discourse of community-reformist gender and women's enthusiastic assent to the dichotomous view of the world it entails are striking features of our interviews with Muslim women leaders, especially of the Muslim League. The commonplace understanding of these features, especially of the putative 'code of conduct' that elected women representatives of the Muslim League are expected to conform to, claims that these are efforts to bolster entrenched patriarchy within the community, which would minimize the empowering effects of reservations for women (for example Basheer 2001). In this reckoning, Muslim women leaders' endorsement of community-reformist gender norms and ideals would indicate nothing but their passive status.

However, our interviews do indicate the need for more nuanced analysis of what may appear superficially to be true. First, it needs to be recognized that the Muslim women in the CPM and the Congress do declare their allegiance to Islam, and not just women of the Muslim League. A panchayat president of the Congress in central Kerala was equally approving of the time-limits on women's presence in the public. "The Congress does not insist that women should take part in programmes and committees that go on till late," she said, citing the practice approvingly. "We can speak first, receive a response, and leave early—and we are apprised of the decisions later. So it lets us achieve a balance between work and home." Community-reformist ideals of gender do confine women to the social; however, it is important to realize that such distinctions as the 'social' and 'political', 'private' and 'public', are not ontologically fixed; they have no permanent anthropological reference. The dominant construction of the panchayat as apolitical civil space closer to the social than to the political offers a window of opportunity to Muslim women who identify with the 'social' as differentiated from the 'political'. In that sense, the discursive position they occupy within late 20th century globalized Islam-inflected community-reformism is not necessarily disempowering.

The narratives of Muslim League women revealed that a great deal of stretching, subversion, and setting aside of the resurgent norm of sexual complementarity is indeed happening. Their adherence to community-reformist gender ideals cannot be read as evidence for either passivity or a form of agency that does not desire entry into the liberal public. Their marginality to the party, too, does not automatically mean blindness to male domination. Not only is the perception of political stakes strikingly lucid in many interviews, it also appears that the performance of passivity could be a form of resistance to projects of empowerment imposed from above. Nevertheless, the narratives examined in this chapter do reveal the extent to which Muslim League women leaders regard the present juncture as full of opportunities to enter the public. Local governance, then, seems to indeed hold certain possibilities, especially for women who have historically been not only excluded from politics, but also confined to the very margins of the 'social' until very recently.

Notes

1. Muslims in Kerala constitute nearly one-fourth of the total population. They constitute the majority of the population— 68.6 per cent—in Malappuram district in north Kerala. They are the second largest group in 6 other districts. Malappuram which accounts for 32 per cent of Kerala's Muslim population, ranks lowest in terms of the Human Development Index in Kerala (Kabir 2010: 88). However, according to the Census 2001, in literacy rates, Muslim women (85.5 per cent) are not very far from Hindu women (86.7 per cent). Muslim women also enjoy a favourable sex ratio of 1082 women to 1000 men quite close to that of other major communities (*The Hindu* 23 September 2004 http: //www.hindu.com/2004/09/23/ stories/2004092306010500.htm, accessed, 10 Nov 2010). The infant mortality rate among Muslims too was close to that of the Christians and better than that of the Hindus (Kabir 2010: 92). Yet, as Kabir mentions, post-neonatal death rates seem decidedly higher among the Muslims than others (2010: 92).

2. It has been pointed out that Anglo-Islamic personal law in India was highly respectful of the rights of women; marriage was regarded as a civil contract and bride price was an essential ingredient of the contract, apparently meant to balance the husband's power of arbitrary oral divorce. Agnes (2000) notes that the bias of the English jurists in India against women and their property rights and its convergence with the patriarchal interests of the Indian, Hindu and Muslim systems is apparent in the legal history of the colonial period. (p. 124)

3. According to the Kerala Migration Survey 2007 conducted by the Centre for Development Studies, 48.2 per cent of the total number of migrants from Kerala were Muslim (Zachariah and Rajan 2010: 90). The authors also note that the proportion

of women among the migrants in 2007 was not high—14.4 per cent in all, and a mere 8 per cent of Muslim migrants (p. 94). Kabir (2010) notes that Muslims constitute the largest proportion of households that receive remittances, the average monthly remittance per household being Rs. 6,709.

4. According to Aravindan 2006, Muslim women's work partici-pation rates are the lowest. According to this survey, 60.7 per cent of Muslim women were reported to be 'housewives' compared with 35.5 per cent of Hindu and 32.4 per cent of Christian women. Only 31.8 per cent of Muslim women were job-seekers, compared with 40.5 per cent among Hindu and 41 per cent among Christian women (p. 120).

5. While marriage is obviously prized, dowry rates have been soaring, according to many reports. Basheer (2004) claims that for a 15-year-old bride, a Muslim family in Malappuram will have to provide at least Rs. 50,000 and 50 sovereigns of gold; this amount would double if she was 18 (p. 160).

6. There is some work that indicates that women's representation in the local bodies in Kannur in all districts in north Kerala where there is a substantial Muslim population is not satisfactory (Siddique 2005). The scene is better in Malappuram, where nearly 70 per cent of all elected women in the second term were Muslim. He mentions four key reasons for this: greater sense of security that Muslim women enjoy in Malappuram, greater awareness of their backward status, greater pressure from political parties, and the migration of a large number of men to the Gulf (p. 284).

7. In fact, this does not seem to be the case even in non-political organizations like the Jamaat-e-Islami, which contested the panchayat elections, and indeed fielded female candidates. See *Aaramam* 2010.

8. Some have argued that the Gulf migration is leading to a fall in the age of marriage of Muslim women in Malappuram, with grievous consequences (Basheer 2004). However, earlier research on Muslim women in other areas indicated otherwise. Leela Gulati, for instance, noted in her fieldwork in coastal areas of Thiruvananthapuram district on poor families from which men have migrated, (where Muslims do lag behind other communities in social development indicators) that "since the majority of those who leave are young married men, the wives

they leave behind are young women ... much younger ... since men tend to marry women five to six years younger than them." (p. 20). She notes that of her sample, almost half the men had married women who were below the legal age of marriage (p. 166). Ten out of these 16 women were Muslim, of which seven were married at 14. Nevertheless, she did not find the kind of dreary scene that Basheer (2004) depicts. Rather, she found women developing "their own networks of transmission of information" and the "ability to stand on their own two feet" (pp. 20–21). But reading Basheer's essay against the ongoing transformation of women's lives in Malappuram, it appears that that the distress he sketches is probably a result of the clash between women's greater individuation and heightened ambitions through their heightened chances of better education in recent times, with the compulsion to be married soon for reasons of respectability and economy in dowry payment.

9. For instance, a Muslim woman leader of the SFI from north Kerala remarked that the common notion that "Muslim women had to be coaxed into politics" irritated her. "It is simply untrue," she said. "Now that there is a chance, Muslim women are eagerly taking it, and in all the parties. Just consider Malappuram—how many of us are there in the leadership of the CPM mass organizations? Who dare say that Muslim women are 'backward' in politics? They should take a look at us! In fact, it is the Christian women who are 'backward' in politics, not us!"

6
Women Leaders in Urban Governance

Urbanization and Urban Governance in Kerala

Political decentralization in Kerala coincided with a period of spurt in urbanization in the state. Researchers have remarked that urbanization in Kerala over the 20th century has been a relatively slow, if consistent, process. The degree of urbanization rose from 7.11 per cent in 1901 to 18.78 per cent in 1981; the pace was one of the slowest in India (Sreekumar 1993: 27). There was the striking absence of metropolitan cities in Kerala and more than industrial activity, it was agricultural and trading activities that dominated the urban economic environment (Sreekumar 1993: 58). This meant that urban areas in Kerala were better dispersed spatially, leading to a 'rurban' pattern of settlement: that is, "...the development of urbanized fringes or commuter villages which could not be meaningfully regarded as either urban or rural in a spatial sense." (Sreekumar 1993: 73–4).

However, this pattern seemed to be changing quite significantly in the 1990s and after. Heightened urbanization is linked to the inflow of remittances from the Gulf which fuelled consumption, leading to service-sector-led growth (Sooryamoorthy 1997; CDS 2005: 44). The boom in the house-construction sector since the 1980s is hiking the demand for real estate, and this has contributed to the urbanization of hitherto 'rurban areas' (Gopikkuttan 1990). Added to these was the emerging post-liberalization national context, which generated intense thrust towards reshaping city-spaces throughout the country, in which the prospective arrival of globalized capital and emergence of neoliberal policy frameworks of urban management were key influences. These crucially informed the shape of emergent decentralized urban governance in the mid-1990s (Kundu and Kundu 2004) and this applies to Kerala as well, which spelt out an urban policy in 2002 (Go K 2002).

Scholars have pointed out that some unique steps towards democratizing urban governance were evident in Kerala. For example, parastatals were dismantled to make space for democratically-elected local bodies (Kundu and Kundu 2004: 140); unlike in many other states, ward committees were set up, which were supposed to promote deliberation and consultation from below; it is also one of the states that has passed legislation to set up metropolitan planning committees. However, the gains from these are either ambiguous or outright dubious when viewed from a perspective critical of the new public management framework, which, as has been widely observed in the literature on neoliberal urbanization in other parts of the world (Harvey 1989; Lovering 1995a; Werna 1995), tends to overlook the political dimension of social justice entirely and reduces the welfare and redistribution of resources in urban spaces to a technical issue dealing with mainly physical aspects of life, like social services, infrastructure, and housing (Mahadevia 2005). Policy documents in Kerala display an unmistakable neoliberal perspective. The document 'Urban Policy and Action Plan for Kerala' (Go K 2002) drafted by the government of Kerala notes that urban bodies have been given the authority to formulate spatial plans and therefore Urban Development Authorities have lost their significance—thus, abolished in five towns. However, this does not mean a divergence from the neoliberal thrust of urban policy in India. It seeks to replace Urban Development Authorities with the Urban Regulatory Authority, which is to be "entrusted with the responsibility to ensure private sector participation in municipal services, avoid creation of monopolies in municipal services, maintain quality of services, make sure that the cost of services to the public is reasonable ... [and] function as a forum for receiving complaints/suggestions on all urban services. This authority will be given statutory powers to enforce these objectives..." (Go K 2002). The formation of Master Plans by urban bodies through consultation does not necessarily indicate a shift since land markets are largely in private hands (Kundu and Kundu 2004: 142). As confirmed by all our interviewees unanimously, the most daunting task in heavily urbanizing contexts is the enforcement of building regulations, which they admitted are largely honoured in the breach. There is also research that shows that ward committees in municipalities and the city corporation of Kochi does not add up to democratic participation—in fact the involvement of ward committee members in developmental decisions and activities seems to be poor. A published study based on fieldwork in two city corporations and two municipalities in Kerala (Thomas 2006) notes that the selection of ward committee members was heavily influenced by the preferences of local politicians (p. 167; 181). Moreover, the contractor-raj seems rampant in wards, where in the early phase of the PPC, funds were made directly available to ward committees which formed beneficiary committees to execute works (p. 170). Women's participation is low, despite the fact that women are often present on the strength of the positions they hold (such as that of the local Kudumbashree functionary) (p. 161). Importantly, ward committee members reported that they were rarely consulted by the municipal/corporation authorities regarding the use of public land in their wards (p. 178). They complained that there was no mechanism to solve conflicting interests in wards or to ensure equitable distribution of resources. Those with political clout usually avail of the benefits (p. 184).

The rapidly changing urban scenario does have important implications for gendering governance in Kerala. In our interviews, we observed that besides the different histories mediated by caste and community, the spatial location of women leaders in local governance was crucial in shaping their agency. The political spaces emerging in and through the contemporary urban scenario in Kerala do not conform to certain features of 'local governance' that we mentioned in the Introduction, and this has important implications for women's attempts to assume leadership roles. Indeed, as Mary John (2007) remarks, the study of women leaders in urban governance may perhaps yield better insight into questions about women's entry into politics and access to political power.

Neither High Politics nor Local Governance

The political spaces which have opened up in and through the municipal councils and city corporations in contemporary Kerala are of an ambiguous nature, partaking features of both 'high politics' and 'local governance'. First, it is clear that the ideal of the hyper-moralized 'local community' cannot be easily projected on to these spaces. As elsewhere in the world (Stren and White 1989; Mattingly 1995), urban spaces in Kerala too are being fragmented economically, politically, and socially (that this seems to be a feature, increasingly, of rural areas as well is important and has crucial implications for local governance and gendering local governance) and thus mutually-incompatible multiple interests throng here—big and small business interests, realtors, local middle-class residents, migrant workers, and working-class poor jostle for space in urban wards. However, 'community' often refers to exclusively middle-class interests and so do civil social organizations like Residents' Associations (CSES-CRM-CAPDECK 2003). That is, the evocation of 'community' in urban contexts seems less related to democratizing local governance so that that the urban poor participate, and more to what has been referred to as the 'rhetoric of enablement', which helps mobilize resources (Mc Carney et al 1996). More dangerously, residents' associations are often the preferred 'community-based organizations' in the city to be counted as collaborators in current urban development projects.[1]

However, urban local bodies too function under a number of 'guardian' and 'watchdog' institutions like the Department of Urban Affairs, the Ombudsman, and also have to take into consideration the decisions of bodies set up for various development projects, such as the Kerala State Urban Development Project Empowering Committee and the Kerala Road Fund Board.

Secondly, unlike rural spaces, cities and towns in Kerala are increasingly perceived as spaces meant for corporate and non-corporate capital (these are frequently in conflict) and their 'development' is often treated as synonymous with the new urban management [2] which has the dual aim of setting up infrastructure for global capital and managing poverty among the urban poor. Urban bodies, therefore, cannot focus exclusively on welfare but have to accord priority to the creation of urban infrastructure. Also, urban policy explicitly encourages private sector participation and this gives the notion of 'governance' advanced in urban contexts a rather different spin when compared with its connotations in panchayats.

This means that many issues that are perceived as more relevant to 'high politics' than to 'local governance' are of key significance in urban governance. Thus, in contemporary urban governance in Kerala, we typically find a mix of bureaucratic control along with intense power struggles characteristic of 'high politics', which, however, increasingly rejects urban 'political society', even those elements of political society integrated closely with mass organizations of the dominant left parties.[3] Thus, we see on the one hand a full-fledged democratic set-up of urban governance, but on the other, a huge amount of business in urban areas being transacted through informal channels. Residents' Associations, for example, have been given a prominent place in urban governance; however, it has been observed that "they are actually quite strong lobbies for the interests of their members, who are mostly the middle- and upper-middle class. Though they have more access to local governments than any other organization, usually they do not follow the formal democratic channels (grama sabha, ward assemblies etc.) but have access through informal channels to secure favourable decisions." (CSES-CRM-CAPDECK 2003: 39). There has also been much discussion in the press about how building rules are being systematically flouted by the real estate players who have access to powerful figures in 'high politics' and higher bureaucracy.[4] Given the high degree of political fragmentation, it is not surprising that municipal councils have been far more unstable politically, rocked very often by no-confidence motions and heated politicking especially when the ruling party had only a thin majority (Muraleedharan 2010). And there is some reason from available research, to think that welfare distribution in the urban local bodies serves to bolster political patronage.[5]

The Councils' powers are also limited through multiplication/duplication of authorities in the wake of large urban development projects such as the Asian Development Bank-funded Kerala State Urban Development Project.[6] The loan incited a fiery public debate in Kerala—not only its critics (Raman 2010), but even relatively more sympathetic commentators were critical of the conditionalities that it imposed. For instance, M A Oommen who disagreed with arguments by left intellectuals that domestic resources ought to be tapped better, did also feel that in many clauses, "the ADB's financial plan, while desirable, lacks respect for the robustness of local democracy. ... Given the economic potential of the urban local bodies, the language of and the compulsions following from these clauses need modification." (Oommen 2007: 737). Further, as elsewhere, urban bodies in Kerala are overloaded with work from new responsibilities and are grievously understaffed;[7] they also lack the technical support for projects[8] which often need to be produced in complicated formats required by central government agencies (Go K 2009: 30). Nor is there much clarity on town planning, which, "often results in subjective interpretations and delays." (Go K 2009: 145). Implementing building rules, thus, becomes exceptionally difficult. Besides, "... ad hoc decisions are made whenever slum improvement projects are proposed by the Urban Local Bodies. In the absence of a prescribed 'definition' of slum, even a cluster of 3 or 4 units is treated as a slum area and funds earmarked for slum improvement are spent on them" (p. 146). In short, urban governance in Kerala seems to offer plenty of loopholes and opportunities for patronage and corruption.

From the above discussion, it is evident that the urban scenario is an extremely challenging terrain for women, especially those who have no experience at all in 'high politics'. Neither 'gentle power' nor 'knowledge of the rules' seems to be of much use, at least by themselves, in urban governance. Rather, the ability to negotiate with local politicians and build alliances, increase influence and connections with powerful groups, and seize emergent opportunities seems all-important for enduring success—or perhaps even for sheer survival.

This chapter is based on our interviews with 9 women leaders in urban governance from the past term. These were not all 'successful'; they range from leaders regarded as 'highly successful' to those considered 'utter failures'. Eight were chairpersons of Municipal Councils (out of 18 such posts reserved for women in the last term) and one, the Mayor of a major city corporation (out of the two reserved posts). The most striking feature of this group was the high educational achievements of its members. A good number were lawyers and professors; almost all, even the less educated ones (with the exception of Dalit women) were from middle-class or affluent backgrounds. This is perhaps not surprising given the present identification of urban development with urban management. Age-wise, all of them were above thirty and below 60; those who had young children were heavily supported by other female members of their families. Spouses (with one exception, a widow who came from less-well off circumstances) were well-educated and well-placed, and/or with considerable influence in 'high politics'. Though many reported to be not interested in re-election due to fatigue, some who reported thus did contest the 2010 elections to local bodies. The urban areas in which they held their terms were also diverse, ranging from towns that retain many rural features, to fully-urbanized municipalities.

Neither 'Gentle Power' nor 'Knowledge of the Rules'

A majority of the women leaders of urban bodies we interviewed were conscious of their middle-class moorings. While many of them came from families that had explicit political sympathies, they themselves had remained largely apolitical or at the fringes of mass organizations, mainly pursuing professional careers. But they regarded their middle-class status not as an anomaly but as a feature that political parties recognized as valuable in the context of changing notions of urban governance. An urban leader from one of the municipalities in the Kochi metropolitan area pointed to a political change that she felt had occurred over the past forty years. In the 1970s, the left trade unions were an invincible force in Kochi; they could "hold the place to ransom, if they wanted." But things have changed now. The clout of the unions has decreased considerably. "And somehow, city governance is identified with a middle-class issue. That is why women like me, with more contacts in the middle-class, were chosen." The decline of political society (in Partha Chatterjee's (2003) sense) which had been integrated into the mass organizations of the CPM seems to coincide with the rise of the notion of urban governance as urban management, with all its elite and civil connotations. Highly educated women with minimal links with politics thus appear to be fit to be the new urban managers.

However, almost without exception, all our interviewees from highly urbanized areas were agreed that higher education was of extremely limited value when confronted with the actually existing reality of Kerala's urban scene (an exception was a chairperson of a relatively new municipality which is still largely rural). The more one's education prepared one for public life, the better, they said. Thus, lawyers felt that their experience in law practice not only prepared them better to deal with the politics of the urban scene, it also made them appear less vulnerable than others whose education seemed to place them far away from politics. A woman urban leader with considerable experience of legal practice observed that this was a clear advantage:

> When I entered municipal governance, I was already a practising lawyer of many years' experience and held superior degrees in law. But the truth was that I knew little about governance. I had to ask my junior-most staff about what the Kudumbashree was, I had no clue about the abbreviations that were commonly used to refer to officers and various committees ... But nobody dared to climb on my head or call me ignorant. Somehow, they never noticed that I was so ignorant—and that, I feel, was because I was an experienced professional in law.

This was indeed in sharp contrast with the experience of another woman leader of a rapidly-urbanizing municipality, who had been a school teacher. She had worked in administration too, and so she knew the basics of office management. Yet she was considered, in the early days, to be 'inexperienced' and hence, had to face more interference from both local politicians and officials.

Clearly, the narratives of women leaders in urban governance do reveal that 'gentle power' is of limited value. One important reason for this is the fact that the urban poor are far more fragmented than the rural poor. As mentioned earlier (footnote 5, above), BPL lists in urban areas are often the means for the local councillor's political patronage, and seem to be more unclear and vulnerable to arbitrary change. Insisting on transparency in the lists, many of our interviewees indicated, is near-impossible, for it would alienate councillors, whose support, they felt, was vital for mere survival in urban governance. Though some of our interviewees did attempt to exercise 'gentle power', they had no doubt that it had, largely, a strategic value and this was indeed strikingly different from the views of many 'successful' women leaders of panchayats, who associated it with the 'feminine', 'natural to women'. Urban governance requires full cooperation from the officials of municipalities, observed these interviewees, and it is necessary to placate them. But some interviewees did attribute the stability they enjoyed in their term to a shrewd mix of 'gentle power' and 'knowledge of the rules' strategically deployed. To quote one of them:

> One has to be both gentle and give the message that one knows the rules well. The officials, well, they are pretty sharp and quite wily as well. The Secretary is immensely powerful and one should be careful not to antagonize powerful officials. So you need to be 'soft', tactful [*mayatthil nilkkanam*]. But you should also be able to give the message that if necessary you will be tough, and that you know the norms and procedures ... The vice-chairman is usually a powerful local politician and much senior to you. Again, don't make enemies of him. But never be totally dependent—yet you should give the impression that you are taking his views on everything.

They attributed the disutility of 'gentle power' to the highly fragmented political context in urban areas. All of our interviewees felt that ward members in municipalities were not bothered at all about the general development of the municipality as a whole and only about their own wards. Besides, unlike in the panchayats, the opposition often refused to cooperate, completely stalling decisions crucial to development. One exception, however, argued quite strongly that 'gentle power' was of use here. She said:

> I had contested as an independent supported by a political front, and I felt, early on, that it was necessary to preserve my neutral image. It worked quite well. I also gave a lot of respect to the leader of the opposition who is a very experienced councillor and that served me very well too, even though my own party colleagues were sometimes uncomfortable. But one has to carry with oneself a large number of councilors, so their discomfort was not something I could pay too much attention to! ... I have also been very respectful to senior politicians within our party ... They treat me like a sister ... and the MLA here, he's from the other front, he too has been extremely well-disposed towards

me. He has helped us with many things ... and I am almost like a daughter to him.

This interviewee claimed that another woman urban leader who has been judged to be an 'utter failure', failed because she could not exercise 'gentle power' well. "She was always too stern, too openly confident of her ability to be manage the urban body ... she never would even bother to smile at officials or show respect to party leaders... That made her very unpopular!"

However, she did admit that male leaders did not have to project themselves thus, and this was because "our society is still unprepared to accept a woman leader." But in a later interview, she admitted that her views were proved wrong. The relatively weak utility of 'gentle power' in the urban context was revealed to us when this very interviewee spoke to us later about her experience of losing when she contested the 2010 elections to the same municipality (quite unlike the panchayats, where women who exercise 'gentle power' do get re-elected frequently). This was a shock, she said, and here she felt that she had been let down by her own party. She had been too successful in her deployment of 'gentle power'— "they felt I had established myself without their help... so they allotted me a ward where I had a slimmer chance of winning. They set up things so carefully that I didn't even have a slight doubt until four days before polling. And they succeeded." She pointed out that her party had lost power in her municipality by a very narrow margin of seats and felt that there were elements in the local party who wanted her out of the council, "even at the cost of the party losing power—since I would have cooperated with whoever won to ensure that all the projects that I had initiated be successfully completed." Another woman urban leader who had to face defections and no-confidence motions from rebel members of her own party also felt that she survived these assaults only on the strength of 'gentle power': " I was very mild and so the officials were very protective, and so also my own party."

However she is now completely out of politics, and does not contemplate any kind of public life.

It appears then that for women to survive in urban politics, they have to be able to build alliances on other foundations—quite similar to the situation in 'high politics'. Women in 'high politics' negotiate actively for connections, taking advantage of strategic opportunities. Besides, there are many who rely upon family members powerful in politics. Both these styles are present among women leaders of urban bodies. The first was well-illustrated by the experience of a highly successful woman leader of a municipality who has been elected unopposed from her ward a second time in the 2010 elections—and her party managed to retain power in the face of massive setbacks throughout the State. This leader also stressed the importance of building alliances across political fronts so that the opposition cooperates fully in developmental activities, but she rejected 'gentle power' entirely. 'Knowledge of the rules' was prescribed as the best way of dealing with officials, while building alliances and networks in civil society that cut across political lines was identified as the best way of dealing with local politicians, especially party colleagues. She pointed out that she was relatively junior in the party compared with the chairmen of the Standing Committees. "That doesn't matter if you have strong connections in places where the party does not have any. That makes you indispensable." She said:

> When I first became councillor, I took care to see that my work did not focus exclusively on my ward. I saw to it that my ward was well-provided, but I gradually acquired a lot of experience working on general issues relevant to the municipal area as a whole, which made me indispensable to both fronts. I also gained a large number of contacts with both ordinary people and those in positions of influence. I was already very successful in my profession which involved meeting a lot of people. This gave me a lot of confidence in dealing with my own party as well ... and I have stood as firm as a rock on many issues ... my advice to ladies is—'stay utterly firm when you have taken a decision

about which you are completely convinced'. Don't step back even an inch. Stepping back only makes you look like a *paavam* [docile person].

This leader, who has excellent connections with all sections of people in her municipality, including businessmen, powerful community leaders, and religious organizations, was also insistent that alliances have to be built on 'negotiations' and not on 'gentle power', which she felt "reminds them all the more, this is a woman, a *paavam*". Her first act as the leader of the municipality was to distribute copies of the Municipality Act to all the members. "I told them that I know this Act well, and I expect them to know it well too. We have to work by it, and not by what the officials may say. The Chairman has executive powers—the power to make an official do something he says can't be done."

She was also keen to stress her distance from all possible manifestations of 'gentle power'. She said that she was not 'intimate' to welfare beneficiaries—"I think it is my duty to listen to them very, very carefully. We are public servants and owe them that respect. But I don't listen to their sorrows— that will immediately relegate me to the *paavam* woman's status." Again, she was firm that dealing with opposition members successfully had nothing to do with being gentle: "don't be *paavam*, be fair. Women think that they need to assert themselves only when necessary. That's an illusion. Be firm from the very beginning, but be utterly transparent and fair in all dealings with the opposition. Convince your own members—and stay firm—that being unfair will only make things difficult for us." This seems to have worked for her, judging from her success in the present elections and acceptance as the unquestioned leader of her party in the municipality.

But connections were perceived in other ways as well—as 'family' connections. In this case, women leaders had powerful male kin in political parties, sometimes in positions that enabled them to negotiate with the opposition informally. To quote one of the women leaders who cited such connections:

I am not that well-educated nor am I experienced in politics. Yet I have managed to do things well, and indeed, hold together a terribly quarrelsome group of councillors for five whole years, and actually have been reelected though my party suffered huge loss. My greatest strength was my husband, who had served as councillor in the past two terms and is held in great regard. So right from the moment I came in, I had that respect from others—that I was the wife of a much respected person...

This argument was frequently made by women who led less-urbanized municipalities. The woman leader of the least-urbanized municipality in our sample claimed that she relied entirely on her party to build connections for her; the metaphor of the extended family was frequently used by her to refer to the party. All decisions are taken by the party and so she perceived her role to be a minimal one. Indeed, this leader, who was formerly a leader of the Kudumbashree in the municipality, was keener to talk of welfare distribution and other activities of the Kudumbashree rather than about her work in the municipality. However, such submission is relatively rare among urban leaders compared to panchayat leaders. Even though these women were not 'proxies', it is worth noting that women lacking such family support seemed to be at a clear disadvantage.

The other feature vital to 'success' in urban areas relates to leaders' ability to grasp the changing urban scenario and the increasing stakes in it of the private sector on the one hand, and the middle-classes on the other. Most of the urban leaders we interviewed did not have critical views of the new urban management agenda—and this is not surprising, given their middle-class, relatively apolitical backgrounds. Thus one of them proudly reported that she had got all the roadside hawkers off the road: "I used to be very particular ... would even stop my car, get out, and scold hawkers who plied their carts on the main roads..." None of them felt that the limitation of social justice to the provision of physical amenities and services in urban management, or the pegging of urban infrastructure needs entirely to the race to attract global capital—was problematic. This is quite unlike many of the women leaders of the panchayats who point to consumerism unleashing an intensely depoliticizing logic, which turns constitutionally-mandated political institutions such as panchayats into institutions meant to mitigate the ill-effects of depoliticizing consumption. Indeed, the most 'successful' ones in urban governance swam with the tide. Commenting on the losses to the CPM and the LDF in the 2010 panchayat elections, one of them argued that it was because the party failed to see that people perceived 'development' differently: "People are not interested in welfare anymore. For them, 'development' means roads, large bridges, buildings, modern amenities. We have to work towards that and borrow large sums, if necessary." In contrast, the less successful leaders were quite reluctant to borrow large sums. One of them admitted that she had done a lot in streamlining welfare distribution and making it transparent; however, none of this got noticed: "Welfare, after all, is distributed to individuals. What people count are the more visible things. They felt that we had done nothing—why? Because we didn't build a Town Hall, a Stadium, or large buildings." She remarked that the poor financial condition of her municipality prevented her from hiring consultants and this also meant that they failed to secure central funds for many projects. Welfare distribution was mentioned by some as the activity that gave some women leaders maximum satisfaction, but notably, these were usually of relatively less-urbanized municipalities.

However, it is clear that the goals of urban management cannot be achieved without strong support from political parties, both ruling and opposition. The experience of the Mayor of a major city corporation we interviewed is illustrative of the dilemmas that the woman leader, with relatively less experience in politics, faces. The removal of corruption and improvement of services in the corporation office may be high up on the urban governance agenda, but even this or other tasks cannot be performed without adequate political support. Such failure or 'inefficiency' gets quickly translated into gendered accusations of women's inherent incompetence at dealing with complex situations. She told us:

> The corporation's problems did not spring up one fine morning. The issue of waste disposal, the traffic congestion, the city centre getting overcrowded—all these issues are old.[9] But media and other politicians presented these as new issues before the public, and as my failures, as a woman. But I have tried to intervene effectively in people's issues. In this office, earlier, people could come only via agents. That is not the case today.

This leader's effort was to build for herself a political base through improving administrative efficiency. She claims that she has been able to reduce corruption in the administration, but this does not rescue her from gendered accusations of inefficiency. Remedying corruption in the office, however, may be regarded as a minor gain in the complex immediate circumstances of a rapidly-urbanizing city like Kochi. Her failure to resolve more complex issues—such as that of waste management—was certainly related to her inability to garner enough political support. Her failure was read in gendered terms, she observed, as the 'inadequacy of an inexperienced woman'. The extreme fragmentation of politics in urban areas is such that what were originally deemed as merits of the woman leader, which qualified her for candidature, may end up being perceived as her weaknesses. Thus this leader's highly-educated status came to be perceived as a disadvantage which predisposed her to elitism.[10] And as in the case of the woman leader quoted earlier, whose exercise of 'gentle power' brought her no gains in the political arena, this leader noted: "my middle-class status and connections were now being used against me. Suddenly, I was not a 'people's woman'!"

But it is also important to see that urban governance is not 'high politics': leaders in urban governance are closely supervised by a number of bodies, often constituted by politicians powerful in 'high politics' and senior bureaucrats. A woman leader of a highly urbanized municipality in central Kerala complained vehemently about how urban bodies had to seek 'permission' from, in her words, "innumerable officials, officers, clerks, IAS officers, and who else ..." :

> This was about the solid waste recycling plant project which was approved and about to be tendered. When we approached the KSUDP office, they said that the Empowered Committee had to take a decision on it. This committee ordered that the tender should be routed through the Kochi Corporation. We were not even consulted; we were told after the decision was taken! This was not at all acceptable to us, and I protested quite strongly on a public platform where senior politicians and bureaucrats were present. But they were not willing to re-examine the decision. This caused us such distress—I had to be in and out of the Kochi Corporation, goodness knows how many times, to get it done!

Further, it is important to note that in the present context of intense political fragmentation, it is all the more difficult for political leaders, male or female, to build political bases among city populations.[11] And the middle-class backgrounds of these leaders do not seem to be yielding them any special influence on the middle-classes in cities. Besides, political fragmentation often leads to all sorts of unexpected coalitions which prove to be insurmountable hurdles. The frustrating experience of trying to set up waste-recycling plants in city areas which almost all women leaders from more urbanized municipalities recalled, indicated this. The experience of trying to find land for this purpose was described as truly harrowing. Many interviewees reported that this turned many of their ardent supporters into enemies almost overnight, and when support was not forthcoming from all sections of the municipal council, the project would simply have to be dropped.

In this complex scenario, Dalit women appeared to be disadvantaged. The two Dalit women leaders of urban bodies we interviewed presented two models of disempowerment. One appeared to be completely embedded in her local party, and insisted that all decisions were taken in and through the party, and she had little more to add except her view that the "party is like a family and we meet all our social needs through it." The other seemed quite unable to take advantage of the fact that she became Chairperson because the party which won the majority did not have a successful Dalit woman candidate. During the interview, she was continuously interrupted and corrected by an interfering vice-chairman. She seemed to be disadvantaged by her relatively lower education, lack of connections, and by her working-class status. Indeed, considerable latent violence seems to have been inflicted on this leader by both sides: the ruling side, which wanted to keep her in check, (hence the vice-chairman's overbearing behaviour) and the opposition to which she belonged, which wanted to ensure that she would not change sides. This was indeed in sharp contrast with the experience of many Dalit women in similar situations in the panchayats. However, another Dalit woman leader, V Devayani, the (former) Chairperson of the Palakkad Municipal Council, did survive such a situation quite adeptly. It is worth noting, though, that she may have had greater space for manoeuvre, since the council was deadlocked without a Chairperson for an exceedingly long time and Devayani was sworn in following a directive of the Kerala High Court to fill the post reserved for SC candidates. She apparently remarked that from being completely ignorant of urban governance, she vaulted into high levels of self-confidence "the day I realised how important my signature was." (*Mathrubhumi*, 28 July 2010: 4). Indeed, she left the Congress during the negotiations around candidature in the 2010 panchayat elections, protesting that the Congress had denied her an SC reservation ward, and joined the BJP (*The Hindu*, 1 October 2010, Thiruvananthapuram edition).

Conclusion

As Mary John has noted elsewhere, the relative neglect of women in urban governance by scholars studying decentralized governance is a serious flaw, precisely because it is the urban scene "that includes many more dimensions of the political arena." (2007: 3992) Contemporary urban governance in Kerala, we find, shares many key features of 'high politics', while remaining bound by the limits of 'local governance'. This produces significant challenges for women leaders of urban bodies. Unwillingness to engage with local-level politics appeared to us to be the surest recipe of failure in the urban scene. A woman leader of a municipality who had grappled hard with corruption and the bureaucracy complained thus:

'I have no talent for politicking and these days, unblemished conduct in politics seems to be of least value. I tried my best— was very conciliatory to the opposition and insistent that I will not support corruption. But it was quite useless. Overcoming unwarranted interference took up all my time and getting the bureaucracy to get something done ... that was another torture. I still remember how we were made to run from one government office to another to get a project approved, and my pleas were useless. Finally I got our vice-chairman and some male members to come and they dealt with the issue in a language only politicians can speak. Only then did the department officials clear the hurdles without delay. I can't speak that language, and so this isn't my field.

'Success' also requires that women leaders support the understandings of 'development' entrenched in 'high politics' rather than in 'local governance' though they have to continuously negotiate the structural limitations imposed on local governance. Interestingly, we found these skills to be increasingly of more use to women in panchayats which have undergone significant urbanization (many of which have been recently integrated into urban bodies). Here, powerful processes of political fragmentation are often at work which create heavy instability which women leaders are forced to negotiate. Diligence in welfare distribution pales into insignificance as a strategy; rather, a set of very different skills emerge as vital for not just success, but survival itself. These include the skill to negotiate with all players in the political field, to summon support from a range of diverse political sources other than one's own party, to draw upon diverse forms of social capital (in Bourdieu's sense), and to put together the technical expertise to access funding for infrastructure projects.

But it perhaps important to note that access to powerful politicians in high politics and the ability to negotiate across parties is also vitally necessary even in the panchayats, when the panchayat leader, male or female, seeks to intervene seriously in local development priorities. Rashmi Sharma notes this of the three male presidents in panchayats which appeared to possess a more dynamic agenda of local development based on local needs and resources, and well-beyond efficient welfare disbursement (2009: 123). In village panchayats, women are less likely to possess these skills. However, wherever 'development' continues to be perceived largely as 'welfare distribution', women who exercise 'gentle power' and 'knowledge of the rules' continue to be 'successful' (in the sense of being popular, with strong chances of re-election). But in Kerala's rapidly-changing context, more and more women will have to face the challenge of governing urbanizing spaces and thus may have to necessarily acquire political experience.

This is, no doubt, an extremely daunting task, especially given the context in which the chances of these women building their own political bases among the urban population look exceedingly slim. Nevertheless, it appears that women leaders do not always fail, at least in the continuous process of negotiation with not just the opposition, but with one's own party colleagues. Perhaps it is befitting to end this chapter with a quote from an interview with a highly successful woman leader, who had to not only keep the opposition on her side, but also curb the intrigues of her own party colleagues, without, however, letting the constant internal struggle for power spill into the public:

> Now I do know that I am absolutely necessary for the survival of my party here; so I am hardly challenged directly. But one must always remain alert. I have always been careful to follow

the rules myself and so no one has yet got a chance to attack me personally. Now, recently, I had been abroad for 14 days. I took permission from the government through proper channels but did not hand over charge to the vice-chairman, because I was coming back within 15 days (and there is no rule that I should do this unless I exceeded the 15-day-limit). Now, some of the hostile press caught hold of this and kicked up a fuss—that I had left for a long period without handing over charge to the vice-chairman. They apparently asked him, and he told them that I was away—but he did not bother to tell them that I would be back really soon. Now, that is the kind of hidden missile aimed at a successful woman! It looks minor but can damage our moral authority to take to task the shirkers and rule-breakers in the municipal office! I took it in my stride, though. As soon as I came back I clarified my position, but when asked why the vice-chairman didn't reveal this, I didn't take the bait! They of course wanted to probe whether there is a hidden power struggle in the municipality. But I did want to convey a message to this vice-chairman, someone from my own side, that I did see his game only too well and that I knew how to put him in his place. And so I responded, 'the vice-chairman is on the best terms with me; if your intention is to provoke us, it will not work. He committed a mistake perhaps, and that is probably because he isn't very familiar with rules generally, and the Municipal Act....'

Notes

1. K. Kasturirangan, the Thiruvananthapuram City Corporation's knowledge manager in 2008 for their externally-funded programmes, told *The Hindu* that the community participation fund of the JNNURM would be used to fund projects submitted by community organizations, and that "residents' associations constituted the first choice as community-based organizations in the city". (*The Hindu*, 19 February 2008, Trivandrum edition, p. 3).

2. See, for example, the discussion on the blog *Kochi Now!* [http://www.forum.kochinow.com/] Accessed 15 November 2010.

3. This was certainly not the case a few decades back. The organized working class, into which many political societies had been integrated, were a powerful presence in urban centres

like Kochi, and Kozhikode. There is work that examines the decline of these sections in these cities. See, Noronha 2006.

4. See, Bhaskar 2007 for controversial cases in the last term involving the land mafia which revealed its access to powerful politicians. Also see Bhaskar 2008. In another report on proposed demolition of unauthorized buildings in the rapidly-urbanizing Perumbavoor area near Kochi, the author reported that "the suspension of a tahsildar and four village officers for allegedly conniving with the 'real estate mafia' has attracted the widespread wrath of the Revenue Department Staff ... middle-level officers in the department pointed out that it is almost impossible for a village officer to forestall conversion of paddy fields ...[as this official could not] stand up to the well-organized money power and muscle power of the land sharks." The report further pointed out that "real estate was a multi-million-rupee business and land sharks keep criminal gangs on their rolls to get all obstacles removed. Officials sometimes faced threat to their lives..." (Basheer 2006 : 5)

5. See Thomas (2006); Go K (2009). Go K 2009 notes that in urban bodies, the chances of beneficiary lists being transparent look slimmer: Unlike in the panchayats where beneficiary lists may be prepared in a more transparent manner, in urban bodies, "[in] the absence of city/town level data bank, ad hoc lists are prepared in several cases for every scheme often in a partisan manner favouring those who line up behind the ward councillor/member or those who are with the ruling party." (p. 146). According to the figures presented in Go K (2009), the service sector spending of the municipalities and city corporations continued to rise or registered only a marginal fall between 2006–07 and 2007– 08 compared with panchayats, which all reduced service sector spending, even though only minimally (p. 32).

6. This refers to the approximately $1000 million loan from the Asian Development Bank routed through the Government of India, with a repayment period of 25 years, aimed at three kinds of reforms: modernizing government programmes and fiscal reform, power sector reforms, and the Kerala Sustainable Urban Development, Environmental Improvement and Poverty Reduction Programme (Raman 2010: 140). As Raman points out, there is little difference now in the approaches of the Left

and the Congress governments regarding the neoliberalization of urban policy. The Left derided the UDF government for its hasty acceptance of the loan but accepted the structural adjustment which was part of the loan when it came back to power in 2006. (p. 141).

7. Go K (2009) noted that "The workload of the urban local bodies has increased manifold, without corresponding increase in staff strength and staff capability. Tax administration and revenue raising are major tasks and the whole work related to building permits, prevention of unauthorized buildings, unlicensed trades, managing sand-mining, and revenue thereof, monthly preparation of revenue and expenditure presumably come under tax administration ... Besides there are the workloads relating to various committee meetings, prevention of epidemics, waste management, plastic control, and work relating to the RTI Act. One can go on adding to the list." (p. 83)

8. Kundu and Kundu (2004) note for the national scene that very few urban local bodies in India have the financial standing to recruit technical and professional personnel to strengthen planning. "No attempt has been made to create an institutional network at the central or state level that can provide technical guidance to urban local bodies on industrial or infrastructural projects in the context of the ecological and socio-economic conditions of the region ... Preparing projects in formal or informal consultation with interested companies or 'stakeholders' with the intermediaries of financial institutions, is an easy way out. However, many of the local bodies have neither the technical competence nor the information base to take decisions with regard to, say a proposal for locating an industrial unit, or about its technical and production linkages." (pp. 142–43) This seems to be the situation in Kerala as well. Go K 2009: 75; 145–46.

9. For example, the issue of inefficient waste disposal in the Kochi Corporation assumed gigantic proportions during the last term, and was compounded by the Corporation's attempts to dump the waste at Brahmapuram which was stiffly resisted. In the end the state government decided to entrust the disposal of waste in Kochi to the District Collector, A P M Mohammed Hanish. See, Suchitra and Venugopal 2009). However, this issue was by no means new. The former Mayor, C M Dinesh

Mani, had been severely reprimanded by the Ombudsman for inefficient waste disposal in Kochi. *The Hindu*, 'Corporation Officials Non-Committal about the Next Move', 13 February 2004, Kochi Edition.

10. It may be interesting to compare the political biography of Mercy William, the Mayor of Kochi in the last term, with that of her counterpart in Thiruvananthapuram, C Jayan Babu. Williams was the Head of the Department of Sociology at St Theresa's College, Ernakulam, and head of the Board of Post-Graduate Studies, Mahatma Gandhi University and was active in professional bodies and in the Church. Her husband is a businessman and her parents were government employees. She did not have prior experience in politics. In contrast, Jayan Babu is a fulltime politician with local roots, and is presently located in the upper tiers of the party hierarchy within the CPM. He first contested and served as a councillor in 1988 and was the Mayor during 1988–89 and became the Chairman of the Trivandrum Development Authority in 2000. The lags in road construction as part of the KSUDP did generate accusations of inefficiency against Jayan Babu, but the discourse was strikingly non-gendered.

11. In fact, the present scene is in sharp contrast with that described by one of the important women politicians of the CPM, T Devi, who spoke to us about her work as the only woman member in the Kozhikode urban body in 1979 (out of a total of fifty members). She spoke of how she organized the urban poor who were deprived of basic services, led militant protests for water and other amenities, and organized squatting on government land. The party intervened and the district secretary tried to dissuade her, but she defied him, citing party decisions at the national, state, and district levels. Indeed, through her political work, T Devi built for herself a strong base among the poor, especially poor women, in Kozhikode city. Such a possibility is rare now, partly because of the increasing complexity of the urban scenario and partly because there is considerable shift in the political priorities of almost all political parties, away from the issues of the urban poor.

Conclusion

In the 'Theatre of Uncontrollable Adventure'

What is most striking about the preceding chapters is perhaps the amazing diversity of the experiences and agential strategies of women who have assumed leadership positions in local governance in Kerala. 'Gentle power' and 'Knowledge of the Rules' bring gains to new elite women, which are real, but incapable of dismantling dominant new elite patriarchy. It, however, rarely works for the Dalit woman leader of the panchayat; it works differently for the Muslim woman leader. Space emerges as a crucial factor that shapes agency. The upper-caste new elite woman-president's 'gentle power' is summoned up by the hegemonic projection of the 'panchayat' as the hypermoralized and intimate 'local community'. However, new imaginings of city-spaces render both 'gentle power' and 'knowledge of the rules' less efficacious for women leaders of urban governance. Further, age appears as an important factor that heightens advantage or exacerbates disadvantage across different groups. And at least one "macro-myth" (Banerjee 1998), the perception that women leaders at the local level may end as 'proxies' completely controlled by family members and local politicians, seems to have been rendered largely invalid, at least for Kerala—it seems that researchers may safely leave this debate behind them. The challenge, rather, lies in analysing the different kinds of agency opened up for women and the implications of these for a politics focused on gender justice. Nevertheless, the research does reveal that the chances of women entering high politics through local governance are low. This is a serious weakness.

A second serious weakness perceived is the fact that reformist relationships characteristic of early 20th century new elite patriarchy seem to be reproduced in and through the women leaders. Wherever women leaders of panchayats have tried to forge relations with women, a largely supervisory relationship aiming at the 'uplift' of poor women seems to have taken shape. It was noted in Chapter 3 that women leaders in local governance tend to be bound to the BPL women in the Kudumbashree self-help-group network through relations of 'giving', quite closely informed by new elite values and hence tended to perpetuate reformist power (much of which is secularized upper caste power) through the former. This appears to be a serious snag in the way of the hope that the greater presence of women in local governance will help to reconstruct the notion of 'women's interests' in more complex ways sensitive to the local context. It seems to indicate that the existing divides between women may be deepened. Thirdly, it appears that much of what is understood as positive gains by those who examine local governance through the lens of development may not be actually empowering for women leaders themselves. For example, researchers studying women in local governance in India have noted that women tend to focus more on basic needs and services and more efficient distribution of subsidies etc. (Jain 1996; Banerjee 1998; Purushottaman et.al 2000; Chattopadhyay and Duflo 2004; Kazi 2010). But as was noted in Chapter 3, while women leaders' approachability and gentle behaviour may make them more accessible to welfare beneficiaries, especially women, this may not translate into greater acceptance of women leaders' rightful place in the political public, but rather, reproduce forms of power typically exercised on women in the domestic realm. Again, the 'peaceful' atmosphere that they seem to precipitate in the panchayat may look like a positive gain, but given the vagueness of the term 'peaceful', it may also help to entrench the idea that women are non-political, and thus help perpetuate their confinement in the private. The collapsing of the question of women's full presence in the public-political realm with that of their agency in development is yet another instance of hidden gendered structures of power setting the terms of public discourse on women's rights (Menon 2000) which needs to be unmasked.

This is of course not to argue that efficient welfare distribution is unimportant—it is certainly all-important in regions where the poor are disempowered through lack of modern education and information or support of political parties. While there are indeed social groups which are grievously disempowered in Kerala, a substantial section of welfare beneficiaries do have better access to information and political connections. But even where the poor are largely disempowered, it is important to ensure that welfare distribution should not be 'feminized' in such a way that women leaders are confined to it. In our fieldwork, we did find this happening. Our cautionary argument is similar to the criticism made by Anne-Marie Goetz (2004) against conceiving women as 'political cleaners', agents of anti-corruption, which she points out, could well nourish right-wing positions on women's social roles. Besides, in our fieldwork in Kerala, we did not find that the presence of women leaders was particularly helpful in extending welfare to the poorest who lack education and political clout.

Reflecting on how these weaknesses may be approached as political problems, the necessity of insisting upon women's greater access to the political public must be stressed once again. Women's assertion of their right to enter the public realm, to participate in politics as equals with equal claims to leadership, is in itself a step towards gender justice. Drawing from the political thought of Hannah Arendt, one could say that the space of 'local governance' (and even urban governance) in Kerala into which women have been welcomed is, roughly speaking, closer to what she conceives as the 'world of labour' and incorporates some parts of her 'world of work' too. 'High politics', despite all its flaws, is closer to the space in which what she refers to as 'action' is possible. For Arendt, the world of 'action' is most political, because it relates to interaction and communication with other human beings (Arendt 1958), and thus it is where women could potentially be the 'speakers of words and doers of deeds'.[1] This is why those interested in gender justice cannot be content with reservations in local governance, however extended and fine-tuned; indeed why they cannot be content even with reservations in legislatures at the state or central levels *alone*. Women leaders at *all levels of governance* (and not just high politics) must be recognized as political beings fully present in the public political realm (and not just in formal representative bodies). This calls for breaking down the distinction between high politics and local government.[2] And this is perhaps a far more urgent task for those interested in building a new political community around 'women', than that of actualizing reservations for women in the Parliament or State Assemblies. It is of course a fact that the messy world of politics does not match up to Arendt's notion of the public realm. Nevertheless, it is also the case that only the political-public permits, in whatever limited sense, its members to be 'speakers of words and doers of deeds'. And while 'politics' and 'development' remain separated in the governmental machinery, the women's movement has indeed expanded the public-political much beyond formal party politics. It has raised crucial questions about gender injustice in work and labour as irreducibly central to the world of action, the impact of which should be acknowledged.

To this end, reservations are not enough, but the space they open may be built upon. The significance of the reservation of positions for 'women' as a group in local bodies cannot be underestimated; feminists cannot afford to disengage. It has been noticed that the recognition granted to 'women' in the discourse of reservations in India stresses their 'natural' inclination towards the maintenance of life and that it does not recognize 'women' as a political category (Lama-Rewal 2001; Singer 2007). This is true for Kerala as well. Thus the dominant assumption behind the reservations of positions for women in local governance is that they will occupy (the limited) space marked out as largely concerning 'labour' and some aspects of 'work' in the Arendtian sense (and thus 'local governance' is charged with the rather limited task of overseeing the sustenance of life and the material world). But this need not be treated as fixed. Such is the nature of democracy. As Claude Lefort has argued, modern democratic society is one in which "power, law and knowledge are exposed to a radical indetermination, [it is] a society that has become the theatre of an uncontrollable adventure, so that what is instituted never becomes established." (Lefort 1986: 305). According to him, democracy involves the dissolution of "markers of certainty"—the sovereign image of power—which creates a gap between 'people's will' and institutionalized power that can never be fully filled (Lefort 1988: 19). Modern democracy is characterized by "institutionalized conflict" between two imperatives, 'the will of the people', which is social and egalitarian, and the other, the legal apparatus that embodies sovereign institutionalized power (Lefort 1988: 17), each acting as a counterweight to the other such that the gap mentioned above is never completely filled. This generates the radical indeterminacy of democracy that allows new political identities to be articulated and re-articulated in non-essentialist ways. Indeed, this allows us to think that the possibility of re-imagining 'women' outside the confines of the limited space of 'local governance' rests upon our ability to activate this ever-present possibility of advancing or re-articulating political identities in contingent and non-essentialist ways.

One of the crucial learnings we have acquired through this research is that women leaders of local governance, even those who claimed that they were uninterested in politics, do recognize themselves as located within fields of political power, albeit reluctantly and even as they proclaim themselves to be disinterested in political power. They were aware, to varying degrees, that local governance is essentially controlled by players in high politics, that they did not enjoy full access to the latter realm, and that they could speak and do as political actors only in strictly limited ways. Indeed, for some of our interviewees, part of their disaffection with 'politics' was precisely their perception that the public-political realm had deteriorated to the extent to which it was no longer shaped by political communities but by various predatory interests. But many who voiced such views also perceived their entry into local governance as offering a degree of relief from confinement in the private, even as they pointed to its narrow focus and its distance from the public. It is fascinating to note how the hope about the possibility of entering a truly political community continues to glimmer, despite many negative experiences, in many of these narratives. Here are the words of a young woman president of a village panchayat from south Kerala who had managed to gain remarkable assent in her panchayat in a very short while through her efforts to bring in more and more sections of the local population, especially the poorest, into decision-making processes, but who had to step down early because her rising popularity threatened local politicians, who conspired to remove her:

> I learned, the hard way, that rising above narrow considerations, bringing in the ideas of more and more people into the everyday business of governing, is utterly dangerous. But I do not regret what I did, for today, even though not in power, I am treated by the people of the panchayat as a 'public leader' [*pothunetaavu*] though I am not really a powerful politician...

> ... I became aware of politics and of things beyond the panchayat and how the world is changing. This changed the way I think. I began to speak my mind and fearlessly point to things going wrong, though it was not easy at all. But that was the only way I'd value myself. The more fearlessly I speak, the more I value myself.

> .... The most valuable thing that I learned in this is the pleasure of public life. Mummy and others [referring to her mother-in-law and relatives] in this house tell me often, enough of this, give it up, this is wearing you out. I tell her, Mummy, the pleasure of this must be experienced to be known. So many people salute

you with affection when you step out of the house! Truly, it is only when we come out of the narrowness of our homes that we learn to love ourselves. We learn to value ourselves. This can happen only in the public. No matter how much love we receive in our homes, this cannot happen.[3]

This is what makes us feel that these women are potentially the locus of political, not just developmental, change. But as was made evident in Chapter 1, the Kerala AIDWA, which straddles high politics and local governance, seems to be a largely conservative force and with no clear strategy. Perhaps its continuing inability to project itself as a political force relates to its vacillation between the worlds of 'high politics' and 'local governance'. This seems to be reproducing the dominance of the former over the latter rather than destabilizing it. Feminists, however, are perhaps best placed to initiate a new imagination of public-political community. Engagement with women leaders in local bodies ought to become a key focal point of the political work of feminist activists. Quite unlike present-day leaders of the AIDWA in Kerala whose location decrees that they wait for promotion to 'high politics', feminist activists do not wait for permission to enter the public-political realm. They challenge patriarchy directly by seizing space in the public-political realm, as political actors who utilize their presence to stubbornly raise questions of gender injustice in the worlds of not only action, but also labour and work. Put succinctly, feminists are more capable of relating to women leaders of local governance as political beings rather than as agents of development. This may further the feminist project of transforming the public-political world of action through the recognition of gender injustice in labour and work (most often recognized as pertaining to 'development') as fully political; on the other hand, women leaders of local government will not be confined to supervisory roles in the worlds of labour and work and denied access to the world of action.

At least in Kerala, feminist activists (and prominent AIDWA leaders, especially those perceived to be endowed with stocks of intellectual capital) participate in the relegation of women leaders of local bodies into the worlds of labour and some aspects of work, to the extent that they perpetuate an essentially pedagogic and non-reciprocal relationship with the latter. The most common channels of interaction are through NGO work in gender training and knowledge-related gender mainstreaming activities in planning, budgeting, or setting up Jagratha Samitis meant to provide gender-justice at the village-level. In all these ventures, feminist activists and groups supply knowledge and expertise that may indeed be very useful. However, this mode of interaction cannot aid the re-articulation of 'women' as a political category. For it generates a form of power not unlike that which emerged in and through community reformisms in early 20th century Kerala, in which the Reformer and the objects of reform are bound together by an essentially irreversible pedagogic tie.[4] It is also worth noting that feminist activists and groups in Kerala relate quite differently to women politicians in 'high politics'. During the confrontation between feminist groups and political parties in the late 1990s over sexual violence (Devika and Kodoth 2001), women politicians were approached as allies in the struggle for gender justice, but not women leaders in local governance. The former were implicitly considered capable of Arendtian action, while the latter were implicitly relegated to the worlds of labour and work.

Needless to say, the creation of a new political community through the engagement of feminists with women leaders of local governance which regards them as political beings may help to break the unhelpful barrier currently prevalent between 'high politics' and 'local governance'. Besides enabling women leaders in local governance to enter the world of action, this is also vital to generating 'power' in Arendt's sense—as collective strength achieved through collective action, the "... potentiality in being together", that which is produced when human beings act collectively (Arendt 1958: 200–1). A primary condition for a new political community is, no doubt, the renouncement of 'pedagogic power' by feminists and fresh efforts to relate to women leaders of local governance not just through channels of communication set up by the state (in which the pedagogic relation is more likely to be produced), but also through setting up new ones in the political public. In our interviews, we did notice resistance to the 'pedagogic power' of the feminist activist among women leaders of the panchayats. Even when they agreed that what the gender trainers offered did not lack substance, many women leaders felt that they preached too much. Interestingly, most of the women presidents who mentioned this often used the term 'feminist' as interchangeable with 'gender trainer', though they were not sure whether the trainer they had met was actually a feminist—in fact, both terms were attached to a certain kind of pedagogue, who, in their opinion, claimed unquestionable knowledge of the 'truth' of patriarchy![5] However, there were more serious observations about the gender trainers' lack of respect for plurality and their inability to engage in creatively understanding the experiences of others. To quote the response of a village-panchayat president from south Kerala to our question about the usefulness of gender training:

> Yes, yes, it is good and all the points they make are good ... but... well ... it just can't be used. There is much substance in gender budgeting ... but how can the woman member be strengthened so that she can demand it forcefully—that is a question we never get to ask. We need to acknowledge the ground reality and then think of how to tackle it. Now, in theory, a newly-inducted and inexperienced woman member can stand up and tell the male president, who is also likely to be a powerful man in her party, that she disagreed with his views. But not in practice. That would be probably the end of her political life, even her social life! Feminists know a lot, but perhaps they should step into our shoes and give us more practical advice on how to get a grip over patriarchy on the ground ... and so ... I have to say, they don't know what we face...

And reminding us of the fact that the category 'women' does not exist readymade for feminist mobilization, a Muslim woman president said:

> Gender training is informative in some ways—one gets to know a lot about gender budgeting, women's practical and strategic needs ... all that is quite new to most of us. But the truth is that I can't discuss the problems that trouble me most. Now I am very well-accepted both by the people, my community, and my party as an efficient president who can hold her own, but there is a nagging feeling I can't get over—that is about the roles that I am allowed to play as a woman. I can't help feeling that Islam actually requires women to be good mothers—and that I have entered the wrong place, just because I want to please my husband, party colleagues, and my community—for selfish, this-worldly gain. This tension hurts because I am a pious woman. I have been to gender trainings over the past many terms but have never felt confident enough to raise this. I know I will be told to get rid of my outdated ideas.

These quotes do hold some clues on how feminists may be able to carry out the work of rearticulating 'women' as a political category through engagement with women leaders of local governance. Respect for plurality both between feminists and the women leaders, and for plurality within these groups, would be of vital significance here. As indicated above, gender training, for instance, cannot assume its subject to be singular. Here again, Arendt's thoughts towards building a political community respectful of plurality seem to be of use. As Joanne Cutting-Gray (1993) notes, in Arendt, alterity is the historical human condition of being other or different—not something that affects only the marginalized but is integral to human individuality. She points out that 'sympathetic sisterhood' or 'brotherhood' tends to treat the difference of others as a problem to be resolved through incorporating the other in the self and hence does not make space for the 'unique, distinct person' who neither relinquishes the political demand for respect of her/his difference, nor allows her/his self to be assimilated into the mainstream for the sake of social assimilation. Cutting-Gray notes that the trouble with sympathetic sisterhood is that "what are ties with similar others are mistaken for the bonds of communicative practice" (p. 45) and is not sufficient for building a political community. Instead, what may be vital is "... seeing the difference of all things through our *alteritas* [which] opens us to a plurality of differences, to other perspectives. This insight into multiplicity sharpens the political edges of our otherness." This would help us to imagine a female political subject who "historically reflects on otherness as a contingent and no longer as a totalitarian, hostile other." (p. 49). Perhaps it is a new political community of this sort that feminists ought to aim for in their engagement with women leaders of local governance:

> First, the politics of alterity radically pluralizes otherness by recognizing that any attempt to banish, control, or socially engineer difference implicitly bars us from knowing ourselves and others. Second, it opens the public space to these differences even among feminisms by encouraging disagreement and the responsibility to understand and respect what we reject. That means understanding and bearing the burden of events, neither denying their existence nor submitting to their brutality. Third, a genuine feminist politics of alterity, because it cannot be limited to feminism, implicitly responds to all who have shared the historical condition of otherness. That is, it recognizes female alterity not as belonging exclusively to one special group or human being marked by history but as a political and therefore locally situated "fact" that temporally outweighs other questions of who we are. It suggests a philosophy, that is, a hypothetical structure of the political, suited for a world in which respect for rights keeps open innumerable places for the meeting of theory and practice... (Cutting-Gray 1993: 49)

One of the striking features of women in political power we noted in the chapter on the history of women's presence in the Malayalee political realm in the 20th century is the intense masculinism of women politicians. Women who have made it into high-politics, we argued, have to either be content with a subordinate role, reliant usually on powerful male politicians, or, if they do escape this role, conform to patriarchal models of leadership. As noted in Chapter 2, the opening up of such opportunities to occupy masculinist spaces of power seemed to require precisely the suppression of any politicized allegiance to 'women' as a distinct group. In striking contrast, Arendt's notion of political community, as a model of politics pivoted on the recognition of alterity, offers a powerful critique of the dominant models of citizenship, both of the liberal and civic-republican variety (Moynagh 1997). In such a political community, women leaders' interventions in local development, for instance, would be centred not on masculinist self-display and the power over the other, but on a struggle for individuation which respects plurality. In other words, it would mean "the emergence of a distinct self ... a self possessed of not fame per se, but of individuality, a self that is never exhausted by the (sociological, psychological, and juridical) categories that seek to define and fix it." (Honig 1995: 159). Another point to be considered is whether such a politics of plurality, and the specific non-essentializing 'collective power' it may release, will not challenge gender inequalities in the postcolonial societies of the South more effectively, where women's citizenship is shaped by the relationship between the state and (the male elite of) particular communities (Mukhopadhyay and Singh 2007).

In short, to reflect on the title of the book, the lesson learned seems to be that we should neither trust the efficacy of the 'old lamp' blindly nor unequivocally declare the 'new lamp' useless. Neither the old nor the new brings benefits that are entirely unproblematic. The point, it appears, is to believe in our agency as public–political beings. This would require that we both desist from embracing the old as if it promised untold merit, and work with the new so that we may, indeed, conjure up from it a new political community based on plurality and respect for otherness.

Notes

1. The present feminist reappropriation of Arendt questions earlier feminist denunciations of her work as irretrievably masculinist (for example, Rich 1979; for a more sympathetic critique, see Benhabib 1995). Bonnie Honig, for example, points out that the distinctions that she makes between the private and public should not read as rigid and immutable. She suggests that we read Arendt's notion of the public realm as "not as a specific topos, like the ancient Greek agon, but as a metaphor for a variety of (agonistic) spaces, both topographical and conceptual, that may occasion action..." (Honig 1995: 146). This would be to argue that "nothing is ontologically protected from politicization" and that in this amended account of Arendt's public realm, the "distinction between the public and private is seen as the performative product of political struggle, hard-won and always temporary ..." and that "the division between the political and the non-political... articulated as a concern for the preservation of the political but is itself an antipolitical instance." (p. 147). See also Dietz 1991.For an argument that defends Arendt's agonism against the charges of masculinism, see Honig's (1995) critique of Benhabib 1995.

2. All the more because even women in 'high politics' are rarely accorded full presence. Notice the tendency to identify even women legislators and ministers with 'feminine' concerns, which are reproduced in the research on them too. For instance, see Singh and Pundir 2002.

3. Recently, we learned that this leader contested the 2010 panchayat elections from her panchayat and won with a decisive majority—as an independent candidate.

4. This applies also to the efforts at networking elected women representatives in many states. Such efforts have most often focused on governance and developmental issues and training for these, and indeed, failed to connect with the feminist movement in India. For this reason, these networks place the women representatives all the more within the apolitical civil social world. It has been noted that though feminist NGOs do try to "weave feminist concerns into the work of the networks" (Behar and Aiyar 2003: 4939), it is difficult to expect change given that these efforts do not challenge the fundamental

confinement of women in local governance to the worlds of labour and work.

5. Gender training in Kerala is now not carried out exclusively by feminist activists. While firm figures are not available, it is safe to say that a whole range of people who claim expertise of various kinds—graduates in sociology and social work, minor KSSP activists, officially designated resource-persons, lawyers, doctors, trainers from the Kerala Institute of Local Administration and other government training institutions—offer gender training in the panchayats. However, the perception of our interviewees that they are all 'feminists' does say something about both the persistent defaming of feminists (discussed in Chapter 1) and the inability of feminists to build a different kind of relationship to women in local governance.

Bibliography

Articles

'A Cochin Lady'. 1925. 'Cochin Legislative Council', *Malayala Manorama* 28 March.

Agnes, Flavia. 2000. 'Women, Marriage, and the Subordination of Rights', in P Chatterjee and P Jegnathan (eds), *Subaltern Studies XI: Community, Gender, and Violence*, New Delhi: Permanent Black, 106–137.

Amma, A Bhageeraty. 1944. 'Women's Position', *Vanitamitram* 1, 4, 208.

Amma, V K Chinnammalu. (1924/2005), 'Samudaayathil Streekalude Sthaanam', in J Devika (ed and trans) *Herself: Early Writings on Gender by Malayalee Women*, Kolkata: Stree/Samya, 75–82.

Amma, T N Kalyanikutty. 1944. 'Patrakkurippukal', *Vanitamitram* 1, 3, 102–4.

Amma, E Narayanikkutty. 1930 /2005. 'Streekalum Khadarum', in J Devika (ed and trans) *Herself: Early Writings on Gender by Malayalee Women*, Kolkata: Stree/Samya, 130–34.

Anandi T K 2001. 'Swarnakumari Menon: An Interview', *Samyukta* 1, 1, 45–50.

Arce, A and N Long. 2000 'Reconfiguring Modernity and Development from an Anthropological Perspective', in A Arce and N Long (eds) *Anthropology, Development and Modernities*, London: Routledge, 1–31.

Arun, Shobha. 2008. 'Managing Assets and Vulnerability Contexts: Vistas of Gendered Livelihoods of Adivasi Women in South India', Working Paper no. 32, Brooks World Poverty Institute, University of Manchester.

Arunima, G 2005. 'Friends and Lovers': Towards a History of Emotions in 19th and 20th Century Kerala, in Bharati Ray (ed), *Women of India: Colonial and Post-Colonial Periods*,

ICPR Series on Indian Science, Philosophy and Culture, New Delhi: Sage, 139–58.

Babu, Abhilash. 2009. 'Governmentality, Active Citizenship, and Marginalization: The Case of Rural Drinking Water Supply in Kerala, India', *Asian Social Science* 5, 11, 89–98.

Bandyopadhyay, D, Saila K Ghosh and Buddhadeb Ghosh. 2003. 'Dependency vs. Autonomy: Identity Crisis of India's Panchayats', *Economic and Political Weekly* 38, 38, 3984–91.

Banerjee, Mukta. 1998. 'Women in Local Governance: Macro Myths, Micro Realities, ' *Social Change* 28, 1, 87–1000.

Basheer, K P M. 2004. 'The Gulf Wife Syndrome', in Mohan Rao (ed), *The Unheard Scream: Reproductive Health and Women's Lives in India*, New Delhi: Zubaan, 148–67.

———— 2006. 'Land Revenue Department to Demolish Illegal Buildings', *The Hindu* 20 January, Kochi Edition, 5.

Baviskar, B S. 2003. 'Impact of Women's Participation in Local Governance in Rural India', Paper presented at the Rural Network Conference, Inverness, June.

Benhabib, S. 1995. 'The Pariah and Her Shadow: Hannah *Arendt's* Biography of Rahel *Varnhagen'*, *Political Theory* 23, 5–24.

Beevi, Haleema. 1938/2005. 'Swagathaprasangam', J Devika (ed and trans) *Herself: Early Writings on Gender by Malayalee Women*, Kolkata: Stree/Samya, 168– 73.

Behar, A and Y Aiyar. 2003. 'Networks of Panchayat Women: Civil Society Space for Political Action', *Economic and Political Weekly*, 38, 47, 4936–40.

Bhaskar, B R P. 2007. 'Land Racketeers thrive under political and official patronage', 10 September [http://keralaletter. blogspot. com/2007/09/land-racketeers-thrive-under-political.   html] Accessed, 15 November 2010.

———— 2008. 'New Land Scandal Generates Feeling of Déjà vu', [http://keralaletter.   blogspot.com/2008/01/new-land-scandal-generates-feeling-of. html] Accessed, 15 November 2010.

———— 2008a. 'Changing Grammar of Protest Stumps Political Establishment', 14 April. http://keralaletter. blogspot.com/ 2008/04/changing-grammar-of-protest-stumps. html [accessed, 2 October 2010]

Biju, B L. 2007. 'Public Sphere and Participatory Development: A Critical Space for the Left in Kerala', *Mainstream* XLV, 25.

[Accessed, 6 November, 2007]. [http://www.mainstreamweekly. net/article163. html]

Bijoy C R and K R Raman. 2003. 'Muthanga: The Real Story', *Economic and Political Weekly*, 38, 2, 1975–82.

Bhaskar, Manu. 1997. 'Women Panchayat Members in Kerala: A Profile' *Economic and Political Weekly*, 32, 17, WS 13–21.

Bhattacharya, Dwaipayan. 2006. 'Writers' Building and the Reality of Decentralized Rural Power: Some Paradoxes and Reversals', in N Gopal-Jayal, A Prakash, and P K Sharma (eds), *Local Governance in India: Decentralization and Beyond*, New Delhi: Oxford University Press, 91–124.

CPM [Communist Party of India (Marxist)]. 2005. http://cpim.org/ documents/2005_dec_women.pdf [accessed, 2 October 2010]

——— 2008. Nineteenth Party Congress Political and Organizational Report http://cpim.org/documents/2008–19cong-pol-orgreport.pdf [accessed, 24 September 2010]

Chacko, Mrs I C 1927/2005. 'Nammude Streekal', in J Devika (ed and trans), *Herself: Early Writings on Gender by Malayalee Women*, Kolkata: Stree/Samya, 96–105.

Chandy, Anna. 1935. 'Oru Niyamavaikalyam', *Shreemati*, Special Issue, 23–4.

——— 1935a. 'Daurbalyabodham', *Malayala Manorama* Annual Number, 14–5.

Chathukulam, Jos and M S John. 2000. 'Empowerment of Women Panchayat Members: Lessons from Kerala', *Asian Journal of Women's Studies*, 6, 4, 66–101.

——— 2002. 'Five Years of Participatory Planning in Kerala: Rhetoric and Reality', *Economic and Political Review* 37, 49, 4917–26.

Chatterjee. Partha. 2003. 'On Civil and Political Societies in Post-Colonial Democracies', in Sudipta Kaviraj and Sunil Khilnani (eds), *Civil Society: History and Possibilities*, New Delhi: Foundation Books, 165–78.

——— 2008. 'Democracy and Economic Transformation in India', *Economic and Political Weekly* 43, 16, 53–62.

Chaturvedi, Ruchi. 2008. 'Violence, Justice, and a 'People's Democracy' in Kerala, South India', Paper presented at the Association for Asian Studies Annual Meeting, Atlanta.

Chattopadhyay, R and E Duflo. 2004. 'Women as Policy Makers: Evidence from a Randomized Policy Experiment in India', *Econometrica* 72, 5, 1409–1443.

Childs, Sara. 2004. 'A Feminized Style of Politics? Women MPs in the House of Commons', *British Journal of Politics and International Relations* 6, 1, 3–19.

Chiriyankandath, James. 1993. 'Communities at the Polls': Electoral Politics and the Mobilization of Communal Groups in Travancore', *Modern Asian Studies,* 27, 3, 643–65.

Craig, D and D Porter. 2005. 'The Third Way and the Third World: Poverty Reduction and Social Inclusion Strategies in the Rise of 'Inclusive' Liberalism', *Review of International Political Economy* 12, 2, 226–63.

Crenshaw, K 1994. 'Mapping the Margins: Intersectionality, Identity Politics, and Violence Against Women of Colour', in M A Fineman and R Myukitiuk (eds), *The Public Nature of Private Violence*, New York: Routledge, 93–118.

Cutting-Gray, Joanne. 1993. 'Hannah Arendt, Feminism, and the Politics of Alterity: "What Will We Lose if We Win", *Hypatia* 8, 1, 35–54.

Dahlerup, D. 1988. 'From a Small to a Large Minority: Women in Scandinavian Politics', *Scandinavian Political Studies* 11, 275–98.

———— 1998. 'Using Quotas to Increase Women's Political Participation', in A Karam (ed.), *Women in Parliament: beyond Numbers*, Stockholm: IDEA, 91–106.

Das, M K. 2000. 'Kerala's Decentralised Planning: Floundering Experiment', *Economic and Political Weekly* 35, 49, 4300–03.

Deshpande, Rajeshwari. 2004. 'How Gendered Was Women's Participation in Election 2004?', *Economic and Political Weekly* 39, 51, 5431–36.

Devika, J. 2006. 'Housewife, Sex Worker and the Reformer: Controversies over Women Writing their Lives in Kerala', *Economic and Political Weekly.* 21, 17, 1675–83.

———— 2007a. 'Fears of Contagion? Depoliticisation and Recent Debates Over Politics in Kerala', *Economic and Political Weekly*, 25, 42, 2007, 2465–78.

———— 2008. 'Modernity with Democracy? Gender and Governance in the People's Planning Campaign, Kerala', in Smita

Mishra-Panda (ed), *Engendering Governance Institutions: State, Market and Civil Society*, New Delhi: Sage Publications, 57–80.

—— 2008a. 'Will the Left's 'Negative Hallucination' End in Kerala', 22 August http://kafila.org/2008/08/22/will-the-leftsnegative-hallucination-end-in-kerala/ [accessed, 4 October 2010]

—— 2009. 'Vaikom Viswan and Little Bo-Peep', 19 May http://kafila.org/2009/05/19/vaikom-viswan-and-little-bo-peep/ [accessed, 4 October 2010]

—— 2010. 'Inaugurated: The Malabar Moral Police', 13 January, http://kafila.org/2010/01/13/inaugurated-the-malabar-moral-police/ [[accessed, 4 October 2010]

Devika, J and Avanti Mukherjee. 2007. 'Re-forming Women in Malayalee Modernity: A Historical Overview', in Swapna Mukhopadhyay (ed) *The Enigma of the Kerala Woman: A Failed Promise of Literacy*, New Delhi: Social Science Press, 102–130.

Devika, J and Praveena Kodoth. 2001. 'Sexual Violence and the Predicament of Feminist Politics in Kerala', *Economic and Political Weekly*, 36, 33, 3170–77.

Devika, J and Binitha V Thampi. 2010. 'Mobility towards Work and Politics for Women in Kerala State, India: A View from the Histories of Gender and Space', *Modern Asian Studies*.

Dietz, Mary G. 1992. 'Context is All: Feminism and Theories of Citizenship', in C. Mouffe (ed), *Dimensions of Radical Democracy*, London: Verso, 63–88.

—— 1991. 'Hannah Arendt and Feminist Politics', in Mary Lyndon Shanley and Carole Pateman (eds), Feminist Interpretations and Political Theory, University Park: Pennsylvania State University Press, 232–52.

Duflo, Esther. 2005. 'Why Political Reservations?', *Journal of the European Economics Association* 3, 2/3, 668–78.

EPW [Economic and Political Weekly]. 1990. 'Kerala Economy at the Crossroads', Special Issues on Kerala. 25(35–36) and 25(37).

Elman, Amy. 2003. 'Refuge in Reconfigured States', in L A Banaszak, K Beckwith, and D Rucht (eds), *Women's Movements Facing the Reconfigured State*, Cambridge: Cambridge University Press, 94–113.

Fraser, Nancy. 2005. 'From Redistribution to Recognition? Gender Equity and the Welfare State', *Political Theory* 22, 4, 591–618.

Gallo, Ester. 2004. 'Unorthodox Sisters: Gender Relations and Generational Change in Malayalee Transnational Marriages', Paper presented at the Kerala Council for Historical Research Colloquium, Thiruvananthapuram, November 7.

George, Mariamma Sanu. 2006. 'Towards Participation and Inclusion: Mainstreaming Gender in Decentralization', in R Mohanty and R Tandon (eds) *Participatory Citizenship: Identity, Exclusion, Inclusion*, New Delhi: Sage Publications, 179–99.

Goetz, Anne-Marie. 2004. 'Political Cleaners: How Women are the New Anti-Corruption Force. Does the Evidence Wash?', [http://www.u4. no/document/showdoc. cfm?id=124], Accessed, 26 November 2010.

Gomathy, K. 1933. 'Streekalum Nivarttanavum' [Women and the Abstention Movement], *Malayala Manorama* 20April, p. 3.

Gopalakrishnan, K G. 1994. *Vimochanasamaram: Oru Padhanam*, Thiruvananthapuram.

Gopikuttan, G. 1990. 'House Construction Boom in Kerala: Impact on Economy and Society', *Economic and Political Weekly* 25, 37, 2083–88.

———— 2002. 'Public Housing Schemes for Rural Poor in Kerala: A Critical Study of their Suitability', Discussion Paper no. 9, Kerala Research Programme on Local-level Development, Thiruvananthapuram: Centre for Development Studies.

Grossberg, L. 2006. 'Does Cultural Studies Have Futures?': Cultural Studies, Contexts and Conjunctures', *Cultural Studies* 20, 1, 1–32.

Hall, Stuart. 2003. 'New Labour's Double Shuffle', *Soundings* 24, 10–24.

Hapke, Holly M. 2001. 'Petty traders, Gender and Development in a South Indian Fishery', *Economic Geography* 77, 3225–49.

Harilal, K N. 2008. 'Redesigning Local Governance in India: Lessons from the Kerala Experiment', in F Saito (ed.), *Foundations for Local Governance: Decentralization in Comparative Perspective*, Heidelberg: Physica-Verlag, 75–92.

Harris, John. 2001. 'Social Capital Construction and the Consolidation of Civil Society in Rural Areas', Working Paper No. 00–16, London: London School of Economics and Political Science.

Hassim, Shireen. 2010. 'Rethinking Feminist Politics in the Era of Quotas: A Comparison of Indian and South African Experiences', Paper presented at workshop 'Women and Quotas' at TUFS, Tokyo, June 6.

Heller, Patrick. 2000. 'Degrees of Democracy: Some Comparative Lessons from India', *World Politics* 52, 4, 484–519.

Heller, Patrick, K N Harilal, Shubham Choudhury. 2007. "Building Local Democracy: Evaluating the Impact of Decentralization in Kerala, India", *World Development* 35, 4, 626–48.

Honig, Bonnie. 1995. "Towards an Agonistic Feminism: Hannah Arendt and the Politics of Identity", in B. Honig (ed), *Feminist Interpretations of Hannah Arendt*, Pennsylvania: Penn State Press, 136–66.

Isaac, Thomas, T M. 2005. 'Women Elected Representatives in Kerala (1995–2000): From Symbolism to Empowerment', in G Mathew and L C Jain (eds), *Decentralization and Local Governance: Essays for George Mathew, Hyderabad*: Orient Blackswan, 366–416.

Jafri, Anwar and Vikas Singh. 2006. 'Mainstreaming Gender in District Plans in Madhya Pradesh', N. Gopal-Jayal, A Prakash, and P K Sharma (eds), *Local Governance in India: Decentralization and Beyond*, New Delhi: Oxford University Press, 324 -54.

John, M E. 2000. 'Alternate Modernities? Reservations and the Women's Movement in the 20th Century', *Economic and Political Weekly*, 35, 43/44, 3822–29.

——— 2007. 'Women in Power? Gender, Caste and the Politics of Local urban Governance', *Economic and Political Weekly*, 42, 69, 3986–95.

Jezerska, Z. 2003. 'Gender Awareness and the National Machineries in the Countries of Central and Eastern Europe', in S M Rai (eds), *Mainstreaming Gender, Democratizing the State? Institutional Mechanisms for the Advancement of Women*, Manchester: Manchester University Press, 167–83.

Kabeer, Naila. 1999. 'Resources, Agency, Achievements: Reflections on the Measurement of Empowerment', *Development and Change* 30, 435–64.

Kabir, M. ????. 'On the Periphery: Muslims and the Kerala Model', in K Ravi Raman (ed), *Development, Democracy, and the State: Critiquing the Kerala Model of Development*, London, New York: Routledge, 87–101.

Kalyani, Vatakkecharuvil P K. 1924/2005. 'Keraleeya Hindu Streekalodu Oru Abhyarthana' (An Appeal to the Hindu Women of Kerala), in J Devika (ed and trans), *Herself: Early Writings on Gender by Malayalee Women*, Kolkata: Stree/Samya, 83–5.

Kandiyoti, Denise. 1988. 'Bargaining with Patriarchy', *Gender and Society* 2, 3, 274–90.

Katrak, Ketu H. 1992. 'Indian Nationalism, Gandhian "Satyagraha', and Representations of Female Sexuality', in Andrew Parker, M Russo, D Sommer and P Yaeger (eds), *Nationalisms and Sexualities*, New York: Routledge, 395–406.

Kazi, Seema. 2010. 'Democratic Governance and Women's Rights in South Asia', Report prepared for International Development Research Centre, Canada and Department for International Development, UK.

Keating, Christine. 2003. 'Developmental Democracy and Its Inclusions: Globalization and the Transformation of Participation', *Signs* 29, 2, 417–37.

Kodoth, Praveena. 2008. 'Gender, Caste, and Match-making in Kerala: A Rationale for Dowry', *Development and Change* 39, 263–83.

Kooiman, Dick. 1995. 'Communalism and the Indian Princely States: A Comparison with British India', *Economic and Political Weekly* 30, 34, 2123–33.

Kranz, Susanne. 2008. 'Feminism and Marxism in the All-India Democratic Women's Association: A Leftist Approach to the Women's Question in Contemporary India', Paper presented at the Annual Conference of the Economic History Society, University of Nottingham.

Krishna, Anirudh. 2006. 'Poverty and Democratic Participation Reconsidered: Evidence from the Local Level in India', *Comparative Politics* 38, 4, 439–458.

Kudva, Neema. 2003. 'The Experience of Women in "Panchayati Raj" in Karnataka, India', *International Journal of Politics, Culture and Society* 16, 3, 445–63.

Kundu, A and D Kundu. 2004. 'Urban Local Government and Private Sector Partnership in Gujarat', in P. Wijnaraja, S. Sirivardana (eds), *Pro-poor Growth and Governance in South Asia: Decentralization and Participatory Development,* New Delhi: Sage Publications, 132–70.

Kurien, John. 2000. 'The Kerala Model: Its Central Tendency and the 'Outlier'", in G Parayil (ed), *Kerala: The Development Experience*, London and New York: Zed Books, 178–97.

Lakshmi Devi. 2001. 'Education, Employment and Job Preferences of Women in Kerala: A Micro Level Study', Discussion Paper No. 42, Thiruvananthapuram: Kerala Research Programme on Local-Level Development, Centre for Development Studies.

Lama-Rewal, Stephanie Tawa. 2001. 'Fluctuating, Ambivalent Legitimacy of Gender as a Political Category', *Economic and Political Weekly* 36, 17, 1435–1440.

Leiten, G K. 1977. 'Education, Ideology, and Politics in Kerala', *Social Scientist* 6, 2, 3–21.

———— 1996. 'Panchayats in Western Uttar Pradesh: 'Namesake Members'", *Economic and Political Weekly* 31, 39, 2700–05.

Lovering, J. 1995. 'Creating Discourses rather Than Jobs: the Crisis in the Cities and the Transition Fantasies of Intellectuals and Policy Makers', in P Healey, S Cameron, S Davoudi, S Graham, & A Madani-Pour (eds), *Managing Cities: the New Urban Context*, Chichester: John Wiley, 109–26.

Mahadevia, Darshini. 2005. 'Sustainable Urban Development in India: An Inclusive Perspective', [http://www.archidev.org/IMG/pdf/Sustainable_Urban_Development_in_India_An_Inclusive_Perspective.pdf], Accessed 15 Nov. 2010.

Muraleedharan K G. 2010. 'Votebankukalil Nikshepakar Kurayunnu', *Mathrubhumi*. 29 July, 4.

Manicom, Linzi. 2001. 'Globalising 'Gender' in –or –as Governance? Questioning the Terms of Local Translations', *Agenda* 48, 6–21.

Mannathukaren, Nissim. 2010. 'The Conjuncture of 'Late Socialism' in Kerala: A Critique of the Narrative of Social Democracy', in K Ravi Raman (ed), *Development, Democracy, and the State:*

Critiquing the Kerala Model of Development, London, New York: Routledge, 157–74.

Mathew, George. 1991. 'Social Background of Kerala District Council Members', *Economic and Political Weekly* 26, 21, 1320–1321.

Mattingly, M. 1995. 'Urban Management in Less Developed Countries', DPU Working Paper No. 72, London: Development Planning Unit/University College, London.

Mazumdar, Sumit and M. Guruswamy. 2006. 'Female Labour Force Participation in Kerala: Problems and Prospects', Paper presented at the Annual Meeting Programme, Population Association of America, Westin Bonaventure, Los Angeles, California, March 30– April 1.

McCarney, P, M Halfani and A Rodriguez. 1995, "Towards an Understanding of Governance: the Emergence of an Idea and its Implications for Urban Research in Developing Countries", in R Stren and J Bell (eds), *Perspectives on the City; Urban Research in the Developing World*, Vol. 4, Toronto: University of Toronto, 91–141.

McMillan, J. 2001. 'Will Scottish Devolution Make a Difference?', *The Political Quarterly* 72, 36–46.

Meera V. 1983. 'Women Workers and Class Struggles in Alleppy', *Social Scientist* 11, 12, 47–58.

Mendus, S. 1992. 'Losing the Faith: Feminism and Democracy', in J Dunn (ed), *Democracy: The Unfinished Journey*, Oxford: Oxford University Press, 207–20.

Menon, Bindu M. 2005. 'Identification, Desire, Otherness: *Susanna* and Its Public', *Deep Focus* January-March, 61–9.

Menon, Kunnathu Janardana. 1955. 'Abhinava Chaturvarnyam' (1934), in *Lekhavati,* Kozhikode: Prakashakaumudi Printing, 105–15.

Mohan Giles and Kristian Stokke. nd. "The Politics of Localization: From Depoliticizing Development to Politicizing Democracy", http://www.keg. lu. se/ngm/html/papers/paper_stokke.pdf [accessed, 4 October 2010]

Mohanty, Bidyut. 1995. 'Panchayati Raj, 73rd Constitutional Amendment and *Women*', *Economic and Political Weekly* 30, 52: 3346–50.

Mondol, Ansuman. 2002. 'The Emblematics of Gender and Sexuality in Indian Nationalist Discourse', *Modern Asian Studies*, 36, 4, 913–36.

Mukherjee, Vanita and T N Seema. 2000. 'Gender, Governance and Decentralized Planning: The Experience and People's Campaign in Kerala', Paper presented at the *International Conference on Democratic Decentralisation*, 20–23 May, Thiruvananthapuram.

Mukhopadhyay, Maitrayee and Navsharan Singh. 2007. *Gender Justice, Citizenship, and Development*, New Delhi: Zubaan, IDRC.

Mukundan, M V and M Bray. 2004. 'The Decentralization of Education in Kerala State, India: Rhetoric and Reality', *International Review of Education* 50, 3/4, 223–43.

Muralidharan, Sarada. 2003. 'Gender and Decentralization: Opportunities and Challenges', *Kerala Calling*, October.

Mohanty, Bidyut. 1999. 'Panchayati Raj Institutions and Women', in B Ray and A Basu (eds), *From Independence Towards Freedom: Indian Women Since 1947*, New Delhi : Oxford University Press, 19–33.

Moynagh, Patricia. 1999. 'Hannah Arendt, Citizenship Responsibility, and Feminism', *Hypatia* 12, 4, 27–53.

Muralikrishnan A P. 2003. Interview with M P Parameshwaran, *Mathrubhumi Weekly*, October 26–November 1, 42–45.

Nair, N D Gopinathan. 2000. 'People's Planning: The Kerala Experience', Discussion Paper No. 16, Kerala Research Programme on Local-level Development, Centre for Development Studies, Thiruvananthapuram.

Nair, N D Gopinathan and P Krishnakumar. 2004. 'Public Participation and sustainability of Community Assets Created under the People's Planning Programme in Kerala: Selected case studies', Discussion Paper No. 60, Kerala Research Programme on Local-level Development, Centre for Development Studies, Thiruvananthapuram.

Nair, K Sivasankaran. 2000. 'Travancore up to AD 1729', in T Madhava Menon (ed) *A Handbook of Kerala* Vol. I, Thiruvananthapuram: International School of Dravidian Linguistics, 142–56.

Namboodiripad, E M S. 1975. 'Perspective of the Women's Movement', *Social Scientist* 4, 4/5, 1–8.

———— 1994. 'Ullu Thuranna Samvaadam Aavashyam', [http://www.keralapadanacongress.in/sites/default/files/EMS%20 SPEECH.pdf], Accessed 13 April 2011.

Narayana, D. 2005. 'Institutional Change and Its Impact on the Poor and the Excluded: The Indian Decentralisation Experience', OECD Development Centre Working Paper No. 242, Geneva.

Narayanan, N C, and S Mohammed Irshad. 2009. 'Governance of Drinking Water in Kerala: Analysis of Recent Institutional Changes', Proceedings of the Kerala Environment Congress. Trivandrum: Centre for Environment and Development, 171–185.

Noronha, Ernesto. 2006. 'Headload Workers of Kerala, India: The Critical Role of 'Detrading'', *Labour and Management in Development Journal*, 7, 2, 1–22.

Norris, P. (1993), 'Conclusions: Comparing Legislative Recruitment', in J Lovenduski, and P Norris (eds) *Gender and Party Politics*, London: Sage Publications, 309–330.

Nussbaum, Martha. 2003. 'Gender and Governance: An Introduction', in M Nussbaum, A Basu, Y Tambiah, and N Gopal-Jayal, *Essays in Global Governance*, New Delhi: United Nations Development Programme, 1–19.

Oommen, M A. 2007. "Kerala: Why the ADB Loan for Urban Development?", *Economic and Political Weekly* 42, 9, 734–39.

———— 2010. 'Freedom, Economic Reform, and the Kerala 'Model', in *Development, Democracy, and the State: Critiquing the Kerala Model of Development*, London, New York: Routledge, 71–86.

Osella Fand C Osella. 2008. '"Iam Gulf": The Production of Cosmopolitanism among the Koyas of Kozhikode', in Edward Simpson, Kai Kresse (eds), *Struggling with History: Islam and Cosmopolitanism in Western Indian Ocean*, New York: Columbia University Press, 323–54.

Patel, Sujata. 2000. 'Construction and Reconstruction of Woman in Gandhi' in A Thorner and Maitreyi Krishnaraj (eds), *Ideals, Images, and Real Lives: Women in Literature and History*, Hyderabad: Orient Longman, 288–322.

Rai, Shirin. 1999. 'Political Representation, Democratic Institutions and Women's Empowerment: The Quota Debate in India', *Democratization*, 6, 3, 84–99.

Raman, K Ravi. 2010. 'Asian Development Bank, Conditionalities, and the Social Democratic Governance: Kerala Model Under Pressure?, in *Development, Democracy, and the State: Critiquing the Kerala Model of Development*, London, New York: Routledge, 135–56.

Ramesh, P Nd. 'Malnutrition among women in Kerala: An Analysis of Trends, Differentials, and Determinants', [http://pdfcast.org/pdf/malnutrition-among-women-in-kerala-an-analysis-of-trends-differentials-and-determinants] Accessed, 10 Nov 2010.

Rammohan K T. 2008. 'Caste and Landlessness in Kerala: Signals from Chengara', *Economic and Political Weekly* 43, 37, 14–16.

Randall, V. 1998. 'Gender and Power: Women Engage the State' in V. Randall and G. Waylen (eds), *Gender, Politics and the State*, London: Routledge, 34–57.

———2006. 'Legislative Gender Quotas and Indian Exceptionalism: The Travails of the Women's Reservation Bill', *Comparative Politics* 39, 1, 63–82.

Rose, Nikolas. 2007. 'Governing the Social', N. Gane, *The Future of Social Theory*, London, New York: Viva-Continuum, 167–85.

Roy, Anupama. 2002. 'The Womanly Vote' and Women Citizens: Debates on Women's Franchise in Late Colonial India', *Contributions to Indian Sociology*, 36, 3, 469–93.

Sahadevan A. 2007. 'Gauri Amma/Jyoti Narayanan', in *Keralam 50 Varsham: Sambhaashanangal*, Kottayam: DC Books, 73–82.

Saito, C and R Kato. 2008. 'Contrasting Experiences of Decentralization in Two States of India', in F. Saito (ed.), *Foundations for Local Governance: Decentralization in Comparative Perspective*, Heidelberg: Physica-Verlag, 93–111.

Samuel, Lina. 2007. 'Women, work and fishing: An examination of the lives of fisherwomen in Kerala', *South Asia Research* 27, 2, 205–227.

Santhakumar C, G Gopikuttan, Praveena Kodoth, T P Sreedharan, V Sasikumar. 2008. 'Procedural Changed Required for Making Local Self-Government's Role Effective in Rural Housing in

Kerala', Research and Policy Note No. 1, Thiruvananthapuram: Centre for Development Studies.

Saraswati, Kumari. 1955. 'Vanita Sanghatana' (Women's Organisation), *Kaumudi Weekly* 6, 10, 13–15.

Sawer, M. 2002. 'The Representation of Women in Australia: Meaning and Make-Believe', *Parliamentary Affairs* 55, 1, 5–18.

Sharma, Rashmi. 2003. 'Kerala's Decentralisation: Idea in Practice', *Economic and Political Weekly* 38, 36, 3832–50.

Siddique, Aboobakker P. 2005. 'Panchayati Raj and Women in Kerala: The Case of Muslims', in Zoya Hasan and Ritu Menon (eds), New Delhi: Oxford University Press, 284–304.

Singh P and J K Pundir. 2002. 'Women Legislators in UP: Background, Emergence and Role', *Economic and Political Weekly* 37, 10: 923–928.

Sreekumar T T. 1993. 'Urban Process in Kerala', Thiruvananthapuram: CDS Occasional Paper Series.

Steur, Luisa. 2010. 'Adivasi Workers' Struggle and the Kerala Model: Interpreting the Past, Confronting the Future', in *Development, Democracy, and the State: Critiquing the Kerala Model of Development*, London, New York: Routledge, 221–37.

Strulik, Stephanie. ?????. 'Engendering Local Democracy Research: Panchayati Raj and Changing Gender Relations in India', in David Gellner and Krishna Hacchethu (eds), *Local Democracy in South Asia: Microprocesses of Democratization in Nepal and Its Neighbors*, New Delhi: Sage Publications, 350–79.

Subramanian, Madhu. 2004. 'Decentralization Without Social Mobilization in Kerala', P Wignaraja, Sushil Sirivardana (eds), *Pro-poor Growth and Governance in South Asia : Decentralization and Participatory Development*, New Delhi: Sage Publications, 78–131.

Suchithra, M and P M Venugopal. 2009. 'The Environmental Refugees of Brahmapuram', *India Together*, 20 January [http://www.indiatogether.org/2007/jul/env-bpuram. htm], Accessed, 3 December 2010.

Sundström, Aksel. 2008. 'Leaving the 'Proxy Woman or Politician' Dichotomy: A Qualitative Study of the Possibilities and Obstacles for Elected Women's Participation in Indian Local Governance', Minor field study paper, University of Gothenburg. [http://

www.quotaproject.org/other/Aksel_Sundstroem_Thesis.pdf],. Accessed, 26 November 2010.

Suresh, T G. 2009. 'Understanding Grassroots Power and Excluded Communities in Kerala', in B. S. Baviskar and George Mathew (eds), *Inclusion and Exclusion in Local Governance: Field Studies from Rural India*, New Delhi: Sage Publications, 199–228.

Thomas, Jacob. 2006. 'Functioning of Ward Committees in Kerala: A Case Study', in K C Sivaramakrishnan (ed), *People's Participation in Urban Governance: A Comparative Study of the Working of Ward Committees in West Bengal, Maharashtra and Kerala*, New Delhi: Concept Publishers, 138–200.

Tornquist, Olle. 2000. 'The New Popular Politics of Development: Kerala's Experience' in Govindan Parayil (ed.), *Kerala—the Development Experience: Reflections on Sustainability and Replicability*, London: Zed Books, 116–38. .

———— 2007. 'The Politics of Democratic Decentralisation', in M A Oommen (ed), *A Decade of Decentralisation in Kerala*, New Delhi: Har Anand Publications, 23–40.

Tharamangalam, Joseph. 2010. 'Human Development as Transformative Practice', *Critical Asian Studies* 42, 3, 363–402.

Vanitakusumam. 1927–28/2005. 'Streekal Iniyum Unarukayille?', in J Devika (ed and trans) *Herself: Early Writings on Gender by Malayalee Women*, Kolkata: Stree/Samya, 109–11.

Varkey, Ponkunnam. 1948/1999. 'Ms. Mascrene', in *Toolika-chitrangal*, Kottayam: Sahitya Pravarthaka Sahakarana Sangham, 91–6.

Velayudhan, Meera. 1984. 'Women Workers and Class Struggles in Alappuzha', *Samya Shakti* 1, 2, 8–11.

———— 1999. 'Growth of Political Consciousness among Women in Modern Kerala', in P J Cheriyan (ed), *Perspectives on Kerala History*, Thiruvananthapuram: Kerala State Gazetteers, 486–511.

Vijayan, Aleyamma. 2007. 'A Decade of Gender Mainstreaming in Local Governance in Kerala', in M A Oommen (ed) *A Decade of Decentralisation in Kerala*, New Delhi: Har Anand Publications, 141–74.

Vijayalakshmi, V. 2006. 'Transparency, Accountability, and Governance: Local Government in Kerala and Karnataka', in Gopal-Jayal, A Prakash, and P K Sharma (eds), *Local*

Governance in India: Decentralization and Beyond, New Delhi: Oxford University Press, 385–424.

Vissandjée, Bilkis, Shelly Abdool, Alisha Apale and Sophie Dupéré. 2006. 'Women's Political Participation in Rural India: Discerning Discrepancies through a Gender Lens', *Indian Journal of Gender Studies* 13, 425–50.

Vyasulu, P and V Vyasulu. 1999. 'Women in Panchayati Raj: Grassroots Democracy in Malgudi', *Economic and Political Weekly*, 34, 52: 3677–3686.

Vyasulu V. 2004. Transformation in Governance since 1990s: Some Reflections', *Economic and Political Weekly* 9, 23, 2377–85.

Waylen, G. 1998. 'Gender, Feminism, and the State: An Overview', in V Randall and G Waylen (eds). *Gender, Politics, and the State*, London: Routledge, 1–17.

——— 2009. 'What Can Historical Institutionalism Offer Feminist Institutionalists', *Politics and Gender* 5, 2, 245–52.

Werna, E. 1995, "The Management of Urban Development, or the Development of UrbanManagement? Problems and Premises of an Elusive Concept", *Cities* 12, 5, 353–359.

Williams, Glyn. 2004. 'Evaluating Participatory Development: Tyranny, Power and (Re-)Politicization', *Third World Quarterly* 25, 3, 557–78.

Williams, Glyn, Binitha V Thampi, D Narayana, Sailaja Nandigama, Dwaipayan Bhattacharyya. 2010. 'The Politics of Defining and Alleviating Poverty: state strategies and their impacts in rural Kerala', Paper presented at Centre for Law and Governance, Jawaharlal Nehru University, 23 October.

Yoder, Janice. 1991. 'Rethinking Tokenism: Looking Beyond Numbers', *Gender and Society* 5, 178–92.

Zachariah, K C and S Irudaya Rajan. 2010. 'Stability in Kerala Emigration: Results from the Kerala Migration Survey 2007', in S Irudaya Rajan (ed), *Governance and Labour Migration*, New Delhi: Routledge, 85–112.

Books and Reports

Aaramam 2010. *Swafa: Oru Orma*, Souvenir of the Kerala Women's Conference of the Jamaat-e-Islami, 24 January 2010, Kuttippuram.

Aravindan, K P (ed). 2006. *Kerala Padhanam: Keralam Engane Jeevikkunnu? Keralam Engane Chintikkunnu?* Kozhikode: Kerala Sastra Sahitya Parishat.

Arendt, Hannah. 1958. *The Human Condition,* Chicago: University of Chicago Press.

Ayappan Sahodaran K. 1965. *Saddesheeyam,* Ernakulam.

Banaszak, L A, K Beckwith, and D Rucht (eds). 2003. *Women's Movements Facing the Reconfigured State,* Cambridge: Cambridge University Press.

Basu, Amrita. 1992. *Two Faces of Protest: Contrasting Modes of Women's Activism in India,* Berkeley: University of California Press.

Bhatt, Shanta. 1995. *Women Parliamentarians of India,* Udaipur : Shiva Publishers Distributors.

Bhaskaran. 2004. *Mother Forest: The Unfinished Story of C K Janu,* (trans. N. Ravisankar), New Delhi: Kali for Women.

Centre for Development Studies (CDS). 2005. *Human Development Report: Kerala,* Government of Kerala: Thiruvananthapuram.

———— 2008. 'Gendering Governance or Governing Women? Politics, Patriarchy, and Democratic Decentralization in Kerala State, India', Research report submitted to IDRC, Canada, Mimeo, Thiruvananthapuram: Centre for Development Studies.

Centre for Socio-Economic and Environmental Studies (CSES), Centre for Rural Management (CRM), and CAPDECK. 2003. 'Emerging Issues in Panchayati Raj in Kerala: A Study Report', Kochi, Kottayam, Thiruvananthapuram: CSES, CRM, CAPDECK.

Chandrika, C S. 1998. *Keralathile Streemunnettangalude Charithram,* Thrissur: Current Books.

Cheriyan, Akkamma. 1977. *1114–nte Katha,* Kottayam: DC Books.

Cherukad, Govinda Pisharoty. 1989. *Muthassi,* Thrissur: Kerala Sahitya Akademi.

Datta, Bisakha. 1998. *And Who Will Make the Chapatis? A Study of All-Woman Panchayats in Maharashtra,* Kolkata: Stree.

De Jong, Matthea Agnes. 2004. 'A Moral Dress for Modern Women: Female Muslim Students in Kerala – Interpreting the Veil', Unpublished MA thesis submitted to the University of Amsterdam.

Dean, J. 1996. *Solidarity of Strangers: Feminism after Identity Politics*, Berkeley: University of California Press.

Devayani, K. 1983. *Chorayum Kanneerun Nananja Vazhikal*, Kozhikode: Deshabhimani Publications.

Devika, J. 2007. *En-Gendering Individuals: The Language of Reforming in Early Twentieth Century Keralam*, Hyderabad: Orient Longman.

Dietrich, Gabriel and Nalini Nayak. 2002. *Transition or Transformation? A Study of the Mobilisation, Organisation and the Emergence of Consciousness among the Fishworkers of Kerala, India.* Madurai: Department of Social Analysis, Tamilnadu Theological Seminary.

Eapen, Mridul and Soya Thomas. 2005. 'Gender Analysis of Select Gram (Village) Panchayats Plan-Budgets in Trivandrum District, Kerala', New Delhi: UNDP.

Erwer, Monica. 2003. *Challenging the Gender Paradox: Women's Collective Agency and the Transformation of Kerala Politics*, Goteborg: Department of Peace and Development Research, Goteborg University.

Forbes, Geraldine. 2000. *Women in Modern India*, Cambridge: Cambridge University Press.

George, K K. 1993. *Limits to Kerala Model of Development: An Analysis of Fiscal Crisis and Its Implications*, Thiruvananthapuram. Centre for Development Studies. Monograph Series.

Georgekutty, M V. 2003. 'Rural Democracy and Political Participation: A Case Study of the Role of Women with Special Reference to Kottayam District', Unpublished Doctoral Thesis submitted to Mahatma Gandhi University, Kottayam, Kerala.

Ghosh, Archana, Stephanie Tawa Lama-Rewal. 2005. *Democratization in Progress: Women and Local Politics in Urban India*, New Delhi: Tulika.

Government of Kerala (Go K). 2002. 'Urban Policy and Action Plan for Kerala' [http://www.kerala. gov.in/annualprofile/urban. htm], Accessed 15 November 2010.

———— 2009. *Report of the Committee for Decentralized planning and Development*, Thiruvananthapuram.

Giddens, Anthony. 1994. *Beyond Left and Right*, Cambridge: Polity Press.

Gill B. 1999. *Winning Women: Lessons from Scotland and Wales*, London: Fawcett.

Gulati, Leela. 1993. *In the Absence of their Men: The Impact of Male Migration on Women*, New Delhi: Sage Publications.

Harvey D. 1989. *The Condition of Postmodernity: an Enquiry into the Origin of Cultural Change*, Oxford: Blackwell.

Hust, Evelyn. 2004. *Women's Political Representation and Empowerment in India Now: A Million Indiras Now?*, New Delhi: Manohar Books.

Hussain, Shamshad. 2009. *Nyoonapakshattinum Lingapadavikkumidayil: Keralathile Muslimstreekale Kurichoru Padhanam*, Thiruvananthapuram: Kerala Bhasha Institute.

ISI. 1997. *How and Why Women Entered Panchayat's Election Process*, New Delhi: Indian Social Institute.

Isaac, Thomas. T. M. 1998. *Decentralisation, Democracy and Development*, Thiruvananthapuram: Kerala State Planning Board.

———— 2005. *Janakeeyasootranattinte Rashtreeyam*, Kottayam: DC Books.

Isaac, Thomas, T M and Richard W Franke. 2000. *Local Democracy and Development: People's Campaign for Decentralised Planning in Kerala*, Delhi: Left Word Books.

Isaac, Thomas, T M and K N Harilal. 1991. *Keezhadangalinte Arthasastram*, Kozhikode: Kerala Sastra Sahitya Parishat.

Jain, Devaki. 1996. 'Panchayati Raj: Women Changing Governance', Gender in Development Monograph Series, New York: UNDP

Jeffrey, Robin. 2003. *Politics, Women and Well-Being: How Kerala Became 'A Model'*, Delhi: Oxford University Press.

Jeejeebhoy, S. 1995. *Women's Education, Autonomy and Reproductive Behaviour: Experiences from Developing Countries*, Oxford: Oxford University Press.

Josephine, M C. 2007. *Porattangalile Pen Perumakal*, Thiruvananthapuram: Chintha Publications.

Kaushik, Susheela. 1998. *Participation of Women in Panchayati Raj in India: A Stock Taking*, New Delhi: National Commission for Women.

Krook, Mona Lena. 2009. *Quotas for Women in Politics: Gender and Candidate Selection Reform Worldwide*, New York: Oxford University Press.

Kumar, Girish. 2006. *Local Democracy in India: Interpreting Decentralization*, New Delhi: Sage Publications.

Kumari, Abhilasha and Sabina Kidwai. 1999. *Crossing the Sacred Line: Women's Search for Political Work*, Hyderabad: Orient Longman.

Kumari, Ranjana and Dubey Anju. 1994. *Women Parliamentarians*, New Delhi: Har-Anand Publications.

Lefort, Claude. 1986. *The Political Forms of Modern Society; Bureaucracy, Democracy, Totalitarianism*, Cambridge: Polity Press.

———— 1988. *Democracy and Political Theory*, Cambridge: Polity Press.

Lindberg, A. 2001. *Experience and Identity: A Historical Account of Class, Caste and Gender among the Cashew Workers of Kerala, 1930–2000*, Lund: Department of History, Lund University.

Lister, Ruth. 2003. *Citizenship: Feminist Perspectives*, Basingstoke: Palgrave Macmillan.

Mackay, F. 2001. *Love and Politics: Women Politicians and the Ethics of Care*, London and New York: Continuum.

Mahmood, Saba. 2004. *Politics of Piety: The Islamic Revival and the Feminist Subject*, Princeton: Princeton University Press.

Menon, Chandu, O. 1889/1991. *Indulekha*. Kottayam: DC Books.

Menon, P Shungoony. 1878/1983. *History of Travancore*, Thiruvananthapuram: Government of Kerala.

Menon, P K K. 1972. *The History of the Freedom Movement in Kerala* vol. II., Thiruvananthapuram: Government of Kerala.

Miller, Roland E. 1992. *Mappila Muslims of Kerala: A Study in Islamic Trends*, Hyderabad: Orient Longman.

Minson, Jeffrey. 1986. *Genealogies of Morals: Nietzsche, Foucault, Donezelot and the Eccentricity of Ethics*, London: Macmillan.

Mohammed, U. 2007. *Educational Empowerment of Kerala Muslims: A Socio-Historical Perspective*, Kozhikode: Other Books.

Nair, K. Sivasankaran. 2005. *Venadinte Parinamam*, Thrissur: Current Books.

Nanivadekar, Medha. 1997. *Electoral Process in Corporation Elections; A Gender Study*, Mumbai: Bharatiya Stree Sakhti.

Oommen, T K. 1985. *From Mobilization to Institutionalization: The Dynamics of Agrarian Movement in 20th Century Kerala*, Bombay: Popular Prakashan.

Osella, Filippo and Caroline Osella. 2000. *Social Mobility in Kerala: Modernity and Identity in Conflict,* London: Pluto Press.

Parameswaran, M P. 2004 *Nalam Lokam: Swapnavum Yadharthyavum,* Kottayam: D. C. Books.

―――― 2005. *Empowering People: Insights from a Local Experiment in Participatory Planning,* New Delhi: Daanish Books.

Parpart, J, P Connelly, E Barriteau (eds) 2000. *Theoretical Perspectives on Gender and Development,* Ottawa: IRDC.

Parayil, Govindan (ed). 2000. *Kerala: The Development Experience,* London and New York: Zed Books.

Peterson, V S and A S Runyan. 1999. *Global Gender Issues: Dilemmas in World Politics,* Colorado and Oxford: Westview Press.

Phillips, Anne. 1995. *The Politics of Presence,* Oxford: Oxford University Press.

―――― 1998. *Feminism and Politics.* Oxford: Oxford University Press.

Pillai, C V Raman. 1973. *Prahasanamala.* Kottayam: Sahitya Pravarthaka Sahakarna Sangham.

Pillai, T K Velu. 1940/1996. *The Travancore State Manual* Vol. 1, Thiruvananthapuram: Kerala State Gazetteers.

PRIA (Society for Participatory Research in Asia). 1999. *Women in Leadership in Panchayati Raj Institutions: An Analysis of Six States.* http://www.pria.org/downloadfile/Bwoomi.pdf [accessed 26 August 2007]

Purushothaman, Sangeetha, Padma Anil Kumar and Simone Purohit. 2000. *Engendering Local Governance: The Karnataka Experience,* Bangalore: Best Practices Foundation, The Hunger Project.

Raghavan, Putuppally. 1985. *Kerala Patrapravarttana Charitram.* Thrissur: Kerala Sahitya Akademi.

Rai, Shirin M. 2008. *The Gender Politics of Development,* New Delhi: Zubaan.

Ramazanoglu, C (ed). 1993. *Up Against Foucault: Explorations of Some Tensions Between Foucault and Feminism,* London: Routledge.

Ray, Raka. 1999. *Fields of Protest: Women's Movement in India.* Delhi: Kali for Women.

Rowlands, J. 1997. *Questioning Empowerment: Working with Women in Honduras,* Oxford: Oxfam.

Rich, Adrienne. 1979. *On Lies, Secrets, and Silence: Selected Prose 1966–1978.* New York: W W Norton.

Riley, Denise. 1995. *"Am I that Name?" Feminism and the Category of 'Women' in History,* Minnesota: University of Minnesota Press.

Sandbrook R, M Edelman, P Heller, and J Teichman. 2007. *Social Democracy in the Global Periphery,* Cambridge: Cambridge University Press.

Santha E K. 1999. *Political Participation of Women in Panchayati Raj: Haryana, Kerala and Tamil Nadu,* New Delhi: Institute of Social Sciences.

Saradamoni, K. 1999. *Matriliny Transformed: Family, Law, and Ideology in Twentieth Century Travancore,* New Delhi: Sage Publications.

Sharma, Rashmi. 2009. *Local Government in India: Policy and Practice,* New Delhi: Manohar.

Siim, Birte. 2000. *Gender and Citizenship: Politics and Agency in France, Britain, and Denmark,* Cambridge: Cambridge University Press.

Sikand, Y. 2006. *Muslims in India: Contemporary Social and Political Discourses,* Gurgaon: Hope India Publications.

Singla, Pamela. 2007. *Women's Participation in Panchayati Raj: Nature and Effectiveness,* New Delhi: Rawat Publications.

Sinha, Mrinalini. 1995. *Colonial Masculinity: The 'manly Englishman' and the 'effeminate Bengali' in the late Nineteenth Century,* Manchester: Manchester University Press.

Sinha, A K. 2004. *Panchayati Raj and Empowerment of Women,* New Delhi: Northern Book Centre.

Singer, Wendy. 2007. *'A Constituency Suitable for Ladies' and Other Social Histories of the Indian Elections,* New Delhi: Oxford University Press.

Slater, D (ed). 1985. *New Social Movements and the State in Latin America,* Amsterdam: Centre for Latin American Research and Documentation (CEDLA).

Sooryamoorthy, R. 1997. *Consumption to Consumerism in the Context of Kerala,* New Delhi: Classical Publishers.

Stokes, Wendy. 2005. *Women in Contemporary Politics,* London: Polity Press.

Stren, R and R White (eds), 1989. *African Cities in Crisis: Managing Rapid Urban Growth*, San Francisco : Westview Press.

Sukumar, Mini and Soya Thomas. 2003. 'Experience of Kerala in Local Governance: The Gender Concerns', Mimeograph.

Thampi, Binitha V. 2007. 'Economic Role of Women and It's Impact on Child Health and Care: A Study in Kerala', Ph D Thesis submitted to ISEC, Bangalore.

Thayyil, Anne. 1954. *Ee Kattukal Ninakkullataanu* [These Letters Are For You] Vol. 4, Kottayam.

———— 1990. *Idangazhiyile Kurishu* [Autobiography], Kottayam.

Tornquist, Olle, P K Michael Tharakan. 1995. *The Next Left?: Democratisation and the Attempts to Renew the Radical Political Development Project – The Case of Kerala*. Copenhagen: Nordic Institute of Asian Studies Report Series, No. 24.

Vijayan, Aleyamma and J Sandhya. 2004. *Gender and Decentralized Planning, Kerala, India*. Thiruvananthapuram: SAKHI Women's Resource Centre.

Wrammer, Eva. 2004. 'Fighting Cocolanisation in Plachimada: Water, Soft Drinks, and a Tragedy of the Commons in an Indian Village', Unpublished thesis, Lund University, Lund.

Young, I M. 2000. *Inclusion and Democracy*, Oxford: Oxford University Press.

Zachariah, M and R Sooryamoorthy. 1994. *Science for Social Revolution? Achievements and Dilemmas of a Development Movement – The Kerala Sastra Sahitya Parishad*, London: Zed Books.